Seven Stories of Threatening Speech

Seven Stories of Threatening Speech

WOMEN'S SUFFRAGE
MEETS MACHINE CODE

Ruth A. Miller

THE UNIVERSITY OF MICHIGAN PRESS

Ann Arbor

First paperback edition 2013
Copyright © by the University of Michigan 2012
All rights reserved

Published in the United States of America by
The University of Michigan Press
Printed and bound by CPI Group (UK) Ltd, Croydon, CR0 4YY

2016   2015   2014   2013   5   4   3   2

A CIP catalog record for this book is available from the British Library.

Library of Congress Cataloging-in-Publication Data

Miller, Ruth Austin, 1975–
    Seven stories of threatening speech : women's suffrage meets machine code / Ruth A. Miller.
        p.   cm.
    Includes bibliographical references and index.
    ISBN 978-0-472-11796-3 (cloth : alk. paper) —
    ISBN 978-0-472-02778-1 (ebk.)
    1. Women—Suffrage—United States—History—19th century.
    2. Speeches, addresses, etc., American—History and criticism.
    3. Suffragists—United States—Language.   4. English language—Political aspects—United States.   I. Title.

JK1896.M63   2011
324.6'23097309034—dc22

                                                            2011014839

ISBN 978-0-472-03528-1 (pbk. : alk. paper)

Acknowledgments

I received support and inspiration from a number of directions as I researched and wrote this book. I am grateful to my dean, Donna Kuizenga, and chair, Roberta Wollons, for granting me sabbatical leave and for encouraging me to use it for this perhaps unexpected project. I am similarly grateful for the intellectual atmosphere that they and others have cultivated at UMass-Boston. It was at a UMass-Boston symposium that Matt Brown pointed me toward the writing in science and technology studies that eventually became the framework for this book, and it was over a series of conversations on and off campus that Alex DesForges, Sari Kawana, Terry Kawashima, and Jack Spence showed me the value of expanding my disciplinary interests. In addition, three of my students wrote theses over the past few years that were essential in directing my attention toward some of the major questions underlying this study. I owe enormous thanks to Kate Danckert Hollis for finding and describing new intersections between early feminist writing and late modern revolutionary theory, to James Falzone for his stalwart defense of anachronism, and to Jayme Mills for demonstrating that secularist ideologies are at work in an array of modern texts, most not necessarily having to do with religion. The contributions that each has made to my thinking should be clear to anyone who reads this book.

Away from UMass-Boston, this project also benefited from a number of conferences, symposia, and informal discussions. I can't thank Austin Sarat enough both for suggesting ways in which I might rethink my initial critique of agency and for his constant encouragement as I have repeatedly reformulated the aims of my research. In addition, the insightful comments and questions I received after presenting a later version of this research at the University of British Columbia's Center for Women's and Gender Studies were invaluable to me at a critical moment in the life of the project. Finally, I am grateful to John Parry, as always, for his brilliant and challenging commentary on my writing, to the anonymous reviewers for their thoughtful, careful, and useful suggestions on the manuscript, and to Melody Herr for her extraordinary work as an editor—for taking the time to talk seriously with me about the book, its scope, and its goals.

As a coda, I should also mention my gratitude to Jack Miller, who influenced the development of this book more than I'd like to admit—and who always made it very, very clear when it was time to stop writing.

Contents

Contents

PART ONE : A Framework for Inquiry

In his 1949 *Recent Contributions to the Mathematical Theory of Communication*, the mathematician Warren Weaver introduced the field of information theory via an explanatory metaphor: "An engineering communication theory," he stated,

> is just like a very proper and discreet girl accepting your telegram.
> She pays no attention to the meaning, whether it be sad, or joyous,
> or embarrassing. But she must be prepared to deal with all that
> come to her desk. This idea that a communication system ought to
> try to deal with all possible messages . . . is surely not without
> significance for communication in general. Language must be de-
> signed (or developed) with a view to the totality of things that man
> may wish to say; but not being able to accomplish everything, it too
> should do as well as possible as often as possible.[1]

Weaver's metaphor was a comfortable one by the mid-twentieth century—based on the fact that it was indeed "girls" who operated telegraph
offices. The gendered assumptions behind only "man" wishing to communicate or to transmit what he may wish to say, while the proper and
discreet girl ignored the content or meaning of messages, would likely
not have raised many questions in 1949. Nor would much of Weaver's audience have registered the possibly more disquieting assumption that, in
addition, man's communicative efforts in this passage are measured by
their failure—in the end inexpressible or impossible to accomplish in

their "totality"—whereas the girl's operational activities are measured by their success.

It would in fact be difficult to argue that the gender divide in the midst of this mathematical treatise is a genuine divide at all. "Man" here undoubtedly refers to all humans, regardless of gender, whereas the "girl" is clearly a cipher for a nonhuman and disembodied (even if physical and mechanical) informational phenomenon. By introducing information theory via this metaphor, however, Weaver was nonetheless drawing on a preexisting, familiar, and at least century-old theme—as well as setting a foundation for later discussions of the computational speech or language to which information theory would give rise: men's speech was human speech, and as such, it was beyond physical systems—concerned with communication, with representation, with description, with knowledge, or with subject formation.

The girl's speech, contrarily, was nonhuman speech, and as such, it was material, situated, and part of the physical world. It was material and physically situated, however, not in the sense that it was embodied or embedded in human bodies, but rather in that it operated over mechanical systems or networks—in this case, telegraph systems or networks, and later computational systems or networks. The girl's nonhuman speech, unlike man's human speech, was concerned with sorting, storing, producing, and proliferating information. It had little to do with communication, meaning, or knowledge—and nothing to do with subject formation.

More to the point, men's intellectual and subjective human speech was under a constant, if implicit, threat from the girl's physically situated and systemic nonhuman speech. Men's speech, as Weaver made clear, was indeed always doomed to failure—even as the girl's speech was always effective, efficient, and operational. According to this analysis, that is to say, feminine speech posed a threat, even though it was a limited mechanical or computational activity, whereas masculine speech was always threatened, even in its centrality as the intellectual activity at the heart of human subject formation. It is this threat posed by women's speech as computational speech, as informational speech, or, more precisely, as a variation on machine code,[2] that is the topic of this book.

Stories of threatening feminine speech—and here, stories of the women's suffrage movement in the United States and England—indeed are one set of stories (but not the only set) that lend themselves productively to a retelling from the vantage point of nonhuman,[3] computational linguistic activity. If nothing else, recognizing that the threat posed by women's speech might be identical to the threat posed by machine code opens up new avenues for historical narrative and new arenas for political theory. That feminine, or feminist, speech might, like code, threaten, or execute through, physical systems, mechanical networks, and material environments, rather than, or in addition to, overwhelming human subjectivity, identity, or agency, for instance, means that the work that such speech has done and is capable of doing might be in need of reevaluation.

Moreover, in the case of suffragists' speech, this alternative approach raises the possibility that both nineteenth-century commentaries on, and twenty-first-century histories of, voting have missed a key issue—the nonhuman, computational character of politically threatening speech, of speech that operates but never communicates—that has nonetheless been fundamental to contemporary trends in electoral politics. Although the purpose of retelling the stories of women's suffrage here is primarily that they are one of many examples of the physical work that threatening speech can do, therefore, these retellings also gesture toward an alternative theory of electoral politics, based squarely in speech as a variation on code.

That information, and especially information manifested in cybernetic structures, has frequently been gendered female over the twentieth and twenty-first centuries has certainly not gone unnoticed by feminist scholars. Donna Haraway's influential work in the 1980s and 1990s, for example, explored a number of implications of associating women with cyborgs or, more broadly, with constructs like "nature."[4] More recently, and more relevant to this book, N. Katherine Hayles has written extensively on the gender implications of what she terms digital subjectivity. As the title of her book, My Mother Was a Computer—drawn from Anne Balsamo's statement that her "mother actually did work as a computer," and that in the early twentieth century "it was predominantly women" who "were employed to do calculations" as "computers"[5]—makes clear, Weaver's telegraph girl was by no means a solitary figure as a literal or figurative embodiment of information technology. Women as computers have a long and distinguished history—a history as impressive and complex as the history of women as cyborgs or women as nature.

At the same time, however, what Haraway, Hayles, and others writing in this field have ordinarily emphasized in their discussions of women as technology are the human and bodily implications of this long-standing association. In her *How We Became Posthuman,* for instance, Hayles introduces her argument by asking what "gendered bodies have to do with the erasure of embodiment and the subsequent merging of machine and human intelligence in the figure of the cyborg."[6] How, she asks, is it that cybernetic technologies, which "can no longer be separated from the human subject," both hold out the possibility of a "conjunction" of "enacted and represented bodies," and also deny the "natural inevitability" of such a conjunction?[7]

Hayles, that is to say, elaborates on existing feminist concerns with the *human* implications of women as machines as much as she explores the *computational* implications of this association. Like other scholars in this field, she too describes, convincingly, what happens to women as humans—rather than what happens to women as machines—when these narratives come into play. It is true that unlike many of these other scholars, Hayles does not implicitly or explicitly make the methodologically problematic suggestion that being less human and being more mechanical is an undesirable state of affairs—as doing so would simply reify the human versus nonhuman dichotomy against which she is writing. But her interest in human embodiment, agency, and subjectivity remains the same.[8]

By emphasizing embodiment, agency, and human subjectivity in this way, however, scholarship about women and technology has largely ignored computational *speech,* and, more to the point, it has ignored computational speech as a mechanical, rather than human, phenomenon. To the extent that speech plays a role in many of these arguments—even when it is speech executed by machines—this role is evaluated according to its relevance to human subject formation. Stories of women as machines, speaking like machines, are read as, literally, dehumanizing, and thus in turn more often than not oppressive. Rather than addressing computational speech as a phenomenon in its own right—irrelevant to human embodiment, agency, or subjectivity—this scholarship more often than not evaluates it as simply one further example of the cold, frightening, emotionless, yet erotic "schizoid android" of, for instance, Philip K. Dick novels that, as Hayles points out, is "typically gendered female."[9]

Although the argument underlying this book draws extensively on this existing feminist work on women and information technology or cybernetics, therefore, it also departs from it in significant ways. Without losing sight of the valid warnings of Hayles and others about the perils of ignoring embodiment, agency, and human subjectivity—and addressing these warnings explicitly in later chapters—it nonetheless shifts focus away from bodies and toward language. This is not a book about the blurring of the line between human and nonhuman bodies, or about the challenges that information technology might pose to gender relations, to human subjectivity, to human agency, or for that matter, to nonhuman agency. Its scope is narrower than that. It is about the operation and execution of nonhuman, computational speech, and the threat that this speech poses to physical or environmental systems. It is about speech that *can*, but certainly not *must*, manifest itself in human linguistic activities like those of the suffragists, and about speech that *can*, but certainly not *must*, work through—or threaten—human environments like electoral political structures. More to the point, it is a book that rests on the idea that, although gender relations are *one* set of power relations that might benefit from a retelling via machine code, gender is not the only analytical category that looks quite different from a computational perspective.

The book thus rests on a perhaps provocative methodological claim: that the focus on bodies and subjectivity—and more particularly on agency—has not only drawn attention away from all that computational speech might do, but has actually made a scholarship of computational speech impossible. As a result, the retellings of the stories of suffragists' threatening speech that make up the bulk of this text deliberately ignore agency—or, more precisely, they demonstrate how and why the vocabulary of agency causes this methodological harm. At the heart of the argument presented here is the idea that it might be useful to describe the activities of speech and language without recourse to the vocabulary of agency, and without recourse to discussions of human bodies or human identities.

Making this case via a retelling specifically of suffragists' speech also leads to an implicit historical claim—that the twentieth- and twenty-first-century themes invoked by Weaver and discussed by so many feminist theorists were developed within a long-standing, and well-established, political and historical tradition. Or, put bluntly, suffragists' speech is one example of machine code executing before machines existed to execute it. Moreover, that suffragists' speech might, as code, be threatening more because of its physical, mechanical, or environmental capacities than because of its communicative or representational capacities—because it executes rather than transmitting messages, because it sorts information rather than producing knowledge, or because it alters environments rather than engaging in the epistemic violence of subject formation—in turn leads to a number of political implications.

Emphasizing nonhuman linguistic activity at the expense of human speech acts, for example, is a means of engaging with, and expanding on, the recent work challenging the idea that mapping humans onto physical systems or environments—equating, for instance, humans with nature—is *necessarily* an oppressive act. As Bruno Latour has already demonstrated, once the false dichotomy between politics and nature, or between human and nonhuman, has disintegrated, the violence involved in the act of "dehumanization" loses much of its coherence. As the stories in this book likewise make clear, a case can be made that once the artificial line between human speech and nonhuman speech has blurred,[10] the violence involved in including some within human, political, and ostensibly linguistic realms and consigning others to nonhuman, environmental, and ostensibly nonlinguistic realms weakens considerably.

Similarly, arguing that language can and must be physical or material—enacted by mechanical, computational systems—but that this physicality need not be embodied or biological, avoids what is frequently referred to as the problem of Cartesian subjectivity.[11] Instead of starting, as so much existing literature does, with an opposition between body, materiality (and frequently femininity) on the one hand, and mind, language (and frequently masculinity) on the other—and then either valorizing or condemning this opposition (or, alternatively, attempting to bridge the supposed gap)[12]—this interpretation posits an alternative relationship. Here, language and materiality are paired on the one side against mind and body on the other. Or, more precisely, mind and body together operate here as two of many possible, and *minor*, nodes of a wider physical, mechanical, and material linguistic system. Once again, therefore, the violence involved in both the assumption of disembodied subject positions[13] and the consigning of certain humans (for instance, women) to a nonlinguistic, bodily, and material existence[14] loses much of its momentum.

Or, and perhaps most provocatively, given the interpretation here, it is just as difficult to make the political case that X or Y speech act is oppressive because it is dehumanizing, as it is difficult to make the case that a nonmaterial language does violence by representing physical bodies. If nonhuman linguistic activities take the historical center stage, if nonhuman language is more material and more physical than human bodies, and if speech is irrelevant to representation—as machine code is—then none of these accusatory positions hold. In their place, it becomes possible to develop an alternative, and less accusatory, history of speech at work—operating over nonhuman, human, political, computational, and natural systems and networks. Telling, in other words, what looks like a purely human story of threatening speech—the story of women's suffrage—as a story instead of machine code, or of computational language that executes in the absence of humans and in the absence of human or nonhuman agency, opens up an arena not only for a broad, environmental theory of language, but for an alternative and affirmative history of what speech has done and might do.

This introductory section, therefore, is composed of four chapters that address some of the major scholarly or intellectual traditions that underlie this computational, systemic, and environmental retelling of seven stories of women's suffrage. The first chapter describes in broad strokes the long-standing historical tradition that identifies speech by its threatening characteristics as much as by its empowering characteristics. This is a tradition that more often than not posits speech as a *physically* harmful activity, and indeed, the primary point of this chapter is that identifying the computational or environmental aspects of speech is simply one variation on a preexisting theme. The physical threats posed by speech have long been recognized—and to retell stories of suffragists' threatening speech as a type of machine code is to operate within a well-established intellectual field.

The next three chapters bring together some of the more recent scholarly work on which this alternative narrative of suffrage draws and from which it departs. The first, on machine code, systems, and environments, situates the theory of nonhuman speech developed here within existing writing on language, networks, and the environment. More specifically, it makes the case that describing suffragists' speech as a type of environmentally threatening code is not a completely isolated move—and that, once again, a scholarly literature on the environmental harm that speech can cause already exists and already serves as an effective framework for these seven stories of the suffrage movement. Although the suffrage movement is not ordinarily addressed in writing about science, technology, and the environment—except, perhaps, to the extent that suffragists made (inappropriate) use of Darwinian biological and social models[15]—this chapter makes the case that doing so is not beyond the realm of historical possibility.

The next chapter is more confrontational. Reviewing some of the more influential recent work on agency—be it agency in the liberal, critical, human, posthuman, or distributive traditions—it outlines one of the major themes of the book: that the vocabulary of agency causes methodological harm. It makes the broad argument that regardless of how nuanced a theory of agency might be, recourse to such theories closes the door on multidimensional descriptions of what speech, and particularly what nonhuman speech, can do. Demonstrating some of the theoretical contradictions that underlie discussions of speech that highlight agency, this chapter sets a foundation for the more empirical examples of speech without agency that appear in later parts of the book.

Finally, the last of these introductory chapters links the stories of suffragists' speech presented here to a number of representative works within the extensive field of scholarship about women's suffrage writ large. Although this book is not an effort to influence or alter the historiography of this field—the stories of suffrage as examples of a certain type of speech, rather than commentaries on a particular historical moment—the fact that Anglo-American suffragists' speech *is* the primary example of machine code at work in the world here means that this literature at least deserves consideration. This fourth chapter thus makes the case that the retelling of suffragists' speech is at least tangentially relevant to the history and historiography of women's suffrage—that it can be relevant to discussions of women and the vote.

Indeed, this chapter implicitly underlines a running theme that appears throughout the book: that language becomes fractal as well as physical when it is reconfigured in a computational mode. It should therefore not be surprising that the seven stories of threatening speech presented here can be relevant to the history and historiography of women, voting, and electoral politics. Or, alternatively, it should not be surprising that Warren Weaver's telegraph girl—seemingly isolated in her box and her web of meaningless messages, operating as nothing more than a node on a mechanical and informational network—can be as much a part of the history of suffrage and electoral politics as she is a part of the history of speech.

Chapter One : Threatening Speech

Threatening speech is by no means a new topic of political and historical concern. A bibliography of writing addressing the harm that speech might do—to humans, to environments, to states, to citizens, to the world in general—would be a daunting work, and indeed, it is not the purpose of this chapter to produce a coherent narrative of hundreds of years of speech doing damage. Nor is its purpose to make some claim about the influences or interactions among the sometimes quite disparate theories of threatening speech that would likely constitute this bibliography. Instead, the following pages bring together five impressionistic examples of writing on the more narrowly defined *physical* threats that speech might pose, in order to set a foundation for the seven stories of suffragists' speech that appear in the next section.

Once again, the point of engaging in this literature review is to show that describing the specifically computational characteristics of physically threatening speech is not a completely outlandish move—and that doing so is in fact simply a variation on a well-established scholarly theme. At the same time, this computational trajectory does nonetheless diverge in certain respects from much of the existing writing in this tradition. Most fundamentally, addressing physically threatening speech as a variation on machine code downplays human linguistic activity in a way that even the least liberal and least humanistic writing on harmful speech does not. Although the seven stories of suffragists' speech that make up the bulk of this book do not ignore the fact that humans speak, therefore, they address human speech, if at all, as one operation within a widespread linguistic network—thereby relegating human agency and subjectivity to the sidelines of the historical narrative. As a result, they not only draw on the centuries-old tradition sketched in this chapter, but also take this tradition in a new direction.

With that in mind, a good place to start a review of writing on threatening speech is with Thomas Hobbes's 1651 *Leviathan*. Although Hobbes is often understood to be a philosopher solely of war and self-interest, many commentators have pointed out that he also develops a sophisticated theory of political—and environmental—speech. As Thomas Dumm has noted, for instance, one of the major problems that Hobbes seeks to solve in *Leviathan* is what he sees as the constant clamoring of disconnected and careless voices.[1] Michel Foucault likewise emphasizes that what Hobbes is describing in his work is not so much a theory of war, as a theory of the state of war, made up of linguistic "presentations, manifestations, signs, emphatic expressions, wiles, and deceitful expressions."[2] As a philosopher of sovereignty and power writ large, Hobbes thus has a number of things to say about the political, but also the environmental—and arguably, if implicitly, the proto-computational—problems posed by speaking.

Hobbes repeatedly returns, for example, not just to the role that speech plays in founding political structures, but also to how speech assaults these structures—be they juridical, popular, or executive. Excessive speech, for instance, is, according to Hobbes, a means of complicating and circumventing the law—law being an arena of politics that, precisely because of its linguistic character, is particularly vulnerable to speech.[3] Meanwhile, charismatic speech that might appeal to a mass population is not just a form of rebellion in his analysis, but akin to witchcraft.[4] Even the well-considered speech that rests at the heart of contract, representation, and therefore sovereignty is on the one hand frighteningly strong—simultaneously word and action, a means of transforming right—and on the other hand, weak, meaningless, and easily broken.[5] Speech, in other words, is terrifying not just for the message or meaning that it might convey. It is terrifying because—like war, rebellion, and witchcraft—it also produces purely physical effects on physical as well as political bodies. Speech is terrifying because it *is* both word and action, both symbol and physical effect, a state of being inextricably linked to material as well as social existence.

As a result, both fear of speech and freedom of speech are complicated things in Hobbes's universe. Speech is first and foremost the thing that founds politics: it is the defining characteristic of sovereignty,[6] and to the extent that one talks about speaking freely, one is talking about a sovereign act. Again, though, speech also assaults sovereignty physically, as a form of rebellion or witchcraft. Both worthy of valorization and worthy of fear, defined both by its signifying power and by its physical power, speech cannot be relegated to a single, coherent metaphysical category. Hobbes is thus forced in *Leviathan* to set up a series of unexpected or mismatched oppositions that he then attempts to resolve as he explains what speech might do. There is, for example, always a potential struggle between a sovereign's inappropriate physical or bodily passions and an individual's disloyal linguistic activities—where "good" resides in the former and "evil" in the latter.[7] In addition, he argues that

> when the words *free*, and *liberty*, are applied to anything but *bodies* they are abused; for that which is not subject to motion, is not subject to impediment. . . . [S]o when we *speak freely*, it is not the liberty of voice, or pronunciation, but of the man, whom no law hath obliged to speak otherwise than he did.[8]

These are both unusual takes on the relationship between speech and sovereignty. In the first, Hobbes is describing not a tension between the sovereign's speech and the individual's speech, or between the sovereign's bodily passions and the individual's bodily passions. Instead, he sets up an opposition between sovereign *passion*, on the one hand, and individual *speech*, on the other—an opposition, moreover, in which the sovereign's right to represent the individual manifests itself precisely in the sovereign's bodily and physical triumph over the individual's speech activities.

Freedom of speech, in other words, is defined here as the sovereign's ability to indulge in bodily or physical passion and the individual's inability to say anything about it. The two are fundamentally linked to one another—language properly political only to the extent that it relates to the physicality of the sovereign. Or, as Samantha Frost has argued with regard to Hobbesian thought rather than language,

> Hobbes articulates a distinctive materialism that not only refuses the possibility of the Cartesian incorporeal thinking self but also refuses the very terms under which matter is conceived of as unthinking. Indeed, we can find in Hobbes's philosophy and political theory an account of what it is to conceive of subjects as "thinking-bodies."[9]

It is arguably for this reason that in the second passage Hobbes is so explicit about the bodily nature of freedom and freedom of speech. Speaking freely is an activity that must be mediated through bodies coerced, impeded, or free from coercion. Speaking freely is not about conscience, message, or meaning—it can be understood only when it is situated within the realm of bodies or, more broadly, like witchcraft, within the realm of the physical or natural world. Speech is physical. And freedom of speech is a means of defining, understanding, and controlling physical as well as—or *as*—political environments.

Indeed, as much as Hobbes describes the physical threats posed by speech with primary reference to the effects of *human* speech on *human* or political bodies, he also concerns himself with the threat that nonhuman speech might pose to physical and natural environments. As Latour, for example, notes in his analysis of the famous debate between Hobbes and his contemporary, the empirical scientist Robert Boyle, the key to Hobbes's ostensibly antiempiricism position is his assumption that

> one of the greatest dangers for civil peace comes from the belief in immaterial bodies such as spirits, phantoms or souls, to which people appeal against the judgments of civil power. . . . [I]nert and mechanical matter is as essential to civil peace as a purely symbolic interpretation of the Bible. In both cases, it behooves us to avoid at all costs the possibility that the factions may invoke a higher Entity—Nature or God—which the sovereign does not fully control.[10]

Listening for speech in a dynamic rather than inert nature, in other words, is dangerous for two reasons. First and foremost—and in a relatively familiar reading of Hobbes—it is dangerous in that it places linguistic authority outside of the purview of the sovereign. Above all, Hobbes desires civil peace; civil peace rests on complete sovereign authority; and sovereign authority demands the sovereign's appropriation or incorporation of all conceivable speech, including the speech of nature.

In addition, however, nature's speech also poses a second threat in this analysis—a threat less to civil peace, less to sovereignty, and more to environments and systems. By creating a forum in which inert matter—possessed of nothing more nor less than its physical presence—becomes, at the same time, a dematerialized linguistic force that operates across spaces like laboratories, scientists such as Boyle risk exposing not just political bodies, but physical, metaphysical, and spiritual *spaces*, to linguistic assault. In producing a realm for the play of this nonhuman speech—this speech that brings together physical matter, on the one hand, with nonmaterial spirits, phantoms, or souls, on the other—Boyle calls into question the idea that speech *can* be physical only to the extent that it works on or through bodies.[11] He raises the possibility of a speech that is physical also in its operation through spaces and environments. He raises the possibility, one might in fact argue, of a proto-computational speech—of a speech that operates alongside of, or in competition with, human, sovereign, or political speech, and whose force or threat is situated in its systemic and environmental capacities rather than in its bodily capacities. And this speech, Hobbes implies, is just as damaging to the world as political speech is to sovereignty.

Or, put another way, when empirical scientists (perhaps paradoxically) map the physical world—where language is always, as Hobbes makes clear, situated or bound up in material bodies—onto spiritual worlds, where language is by definition a shifting, nonmaterial phenomenon, they downplay the political and bodily work of speech in favor of its systemic work. As a result, they open up the possibility, at least, that speech might damage spaces, nonspaces, and systems as much as it damages sovereign and subject bodies. Although the primary threat that nonhuman speech poses in Hobbes's writing is that it, like human speech, poses a threat to political authority, therefore, its work through physical systems, spaces, nonspaces, and environments is clearly an issue of almost equal concern.

This multifaceted threat posed by speech—to political systems, to political bodies, to physical bodies, and to physical systems—is not unique to early modern European writing on the topic. The duty of "commanding right and forbidding wrong" in Islamic political theory, for instance—although it may seem far removed from Hobbes's universe of speech as contract and speech as rebellion—rests on similar assumptions. Indeed, the ways in which this duty has been interpreted and put into practice, especially in the early modern period, suggest that it too can serve as a useful entry point into a discussion of physically threatening speech. As Michael Cook has argued in his book on the topic,[12] the duty to speak out against wrongdoing was repeatedly attached in the medieval, early modern, and modern periods to theories of just warfare. Like Hobbes, that is to say, early modern Muslim political philosophers described this form of speech as a military act. As the prophetic tradition that serves as a basis for much of this discussion states, "the finest form of holy war . . . is speaking out . . . in the presence of an unjust ruler . . . and getting killed for it."[13]

Moreover, the relationship between authority—in the Hobbesian sense of those who represent or those who command[14]—and speech was, once again, fundamentally a physical or material one. The verses in the Quran that address commanding right and forbidding wrong, for example, state that it can occur "in 'deed, word, and thought.'"[15] And although, as Cook notes, scholars disagreed about whether it was in fact possible to associate the physical "deed" directly with linguistic "word" and metaphysical "thought,"[16] many did conflate the three. Ali al-Qari, a mystically inclined seventeenth-century writer, even suggested that "performance in the heart may actually mean performance by means of the heart through the mustering of a sort of mental energy . . . which, through divine intervention, may actually bring about the desired result."[17]

This mode of speech, in other words, packed a familiar and distinctly physical punch. Like the speech described by Hobbes, it both reinforced and undermined sovereignty—and it did so in part by confusing linguistic and bodily existence. Both those who were spoken to and those who spoke altered their bodily status in the process. Someone who "fails to forbid wrong," for instance, was described "as a dead man among the living."[18] And yet, as the story with which Cook begins his study—of a "verbal suicide mission," in which the speaker appears "dressed and perfumed for his own funeral"[19]—makes clear, someone who did not fail to forbid wrong was equally dead among the living. Both speaking and failing to do so shifted a body from life to death and from death to life. Or, more precisely, speaking in general, regardless of whether it was manifested in voices raised or voices silenced, was as much a bodily or biological activity with bodily or biological repercussions as it was a political or intellectual activity.

The extent to which these political as bodily, or bodily as political, threats posed by speech became likewise *physical* or *material* threats to environments or systems—as Hobbes, at least, hinted they might—becomes particularly clear, however, in the writing of more recent, twentieth- and twenty-first-century political philosophers. Carl Schmitt, for instance, developed a key aspect of his theory—the apparent opposition between the properly political act that is the sovereign decision and the apolitical activity that is parliamentary discussion or debate[20]—with specific reference to the simultaneity of physical, political, and linguistic bodies, systems, and environments. Indeed, according to Schmitt, the defining characteristic of the decision, or of proper political speech, is its embodied nature—whereas the defining characteristic of apolitical discussion is its attempt to escape embodiment, to turn the "bloody battle" into a "parliamentary debate."[21] Key to proper political speech, in other words, is not what it might mean, but where and how—bodily and biologically—it might be situated.[22]

What must be emphasized, however, is that both decision *and* discussion are physically harmful in Schmitt's universe—the first because it is embodied, and the second, paradoxically, because it is not. Indeed, parliamentary discussion or debate, in its *avoidance* of embodiment, arguably poses the more proto-computational and systemic, rather than human or bodily, threat. Whereas the decision assumes speech to be identical to bloody warfare or to biological life and death[23]—and thereby relentlessly *human*—parliamentary discussion refuses to accept that speech could ever have such bloody, bodily, or human effects.[24] As a result, parliamentary speech, unlike the decision, plays out relentlessly over nonhuman networks, systems, and environments.

Describing it as a "perpetual," "everlasting," never ending, and overwhelming linguistic activity that stalls systems and forever defers action,[25] for instance, Schmitt defines parliamentary debate as, essentially, a viral threat.[26] Saturating these systems and environments with contentless or meaningless information until they cease to function or reduce themselves to feedback loops, parliamentary debate is thus as potentially damaging to physical networks as the bloody, bodily sovereign decision is to human life or existence. Indeed, by shifting focus *away* from humans and their bodies, this mode of speech, at least as Schmitt describes it, poses the greater physical threat—breaking down the environments of which humans form one small part. As such, it, more than the decision, is in many ways a direct descendant of the nonhuman, natural speech against which Hobbes also warned.

More recent writing on physically threatening speech has focused increasingly on its bodily and biological operations. Catharine MacKinnon's work on pornography, for instance, rests squarely on the idea that—in this realm, at least—free speech is identical to brutalized life.[27] Linked as it is to pornography, free speech potentially becomes, according to MacKinnon, not only a means of silencing women, but a form of "terrorism" and "enslavement."[28] Like Hobbes, therefore, MacKinnon argues that speech is never solely a linguistic activity—it is word and action, a physical performance and a mode of physical existence. As she asks in *Feminism Unmodified,* "the idea is that words or pictures can be harmful only if they produce harm in a form that is considered an action. . . . [B]ut which is saying 'kill' to a trained guard dog, a word or an act?"[29] Once again, speech is—like warfare or rebellion—terroristic; its harm lies not in its meaning but in the fact that, contentless, it can be physically mobilized in any direction.

Indeed, MacKinnon argues that interpretations of free speech in the United States have traditionally understood language as something *to* free precisely to the extent that it is effective in doing harm.[30] Moreover, according to this interpretation, it is the abstractness—or, in another echo of Hobbes, the problematic dematerialization—of freedom of speech that has allowed both the concreteness of the bodily harm inflicted by it, and its apparent relevance to United States constitutional theory.[31] The fact that freedom of speech is understood to be one of the most sacred of rights in the United States, she suggests, is not an accident: "what is conveyed is not only that using women is as legitimate as thinking about the Constitution, but also that if you don't support these views about the Constitution, you won't be able to use these women."[32] Like Schmitt, Hobbes, and Ali al-Qari, then, MacKinnon also understands speech to be political or effective only to the extent that it is bodily or physical. It is only in its infliction of bodily harm that it is indeed speech.

Despite the fact that her work joins up so effortlessly with the existing, centuries-old tradition of writing on threatening speech, however, MacKinnon's discussion of the bodily harm that speech can do has nonetheless drawn a great deal of criticism. According to Wendy Brown, for example, when MacKinnon associates the free speech of men with the silence and physical or sexual enslavement of women, she is not only setting up a false dichotomy between emancipatory speaking and enslaving silence, but also—and more so—producing an authoritarian system of embodied gender and sexual identity.[33] Advocating a gender identity that is by definition sexualized and victimized, Brown continues, MacKinnon subjects bodies and identities to invasive, intensive, and hyperbolic legal and political regulation. According to Brown, that is to say, MacKinnon's speech is its *own* act of bodily harm. It constrains, confines, and binds bodies or embodied subjects, even as it attempts to sketch a politically emancipatory alternative to liberal free speech.

Despite starting her critique of MacKinnon—and of theories more generally that link speaking always to empowerment—with the *bodily* threats that speech might pose, however, Brown also sketches a number of *systemic* and *environmental* threats posed by language at play. In a reflection on the affirmative potential of silence, especially in the writing of Primo Levi and Adrienne Rich, for instance, Brown notes that

> Primo Levi makes drowning function as a symbol for a lost linguistic order that itself signifies a lost civil order, for being at sea in words that do not communicate and by which one cannot communicate. In a radically different context, Adrienne Rich also relates drowning to speech: "Your silence today is a pond where drowned things live." . . . [W]hat if the accent marks were placed differently, so that silence becomes a place where drowned things *live*—a place where Levi's drowning inmates survive despite being overwhelmed by the words that fill and consume the air necessary for life? . . . [W]hat if silence is a reprieve from drowning in words that do not communicate or confer recognition, that only bombard or drown?[34]

Once again, the threat posed by speech in this passage is first of all a threat, via the meaninglessness of words and via the absence of messages conveyed or subjects formed, to human existence. Speaking produces a sea [of] words in which human subjects, and indeed human bodies, might easily drown. Speech in turn becomes, as it was in the earlier scholarship, a question of biological, as well as subjective, life or death.

As Brown herself notes, however, an alternative—and arguably not just biological, but broadly environmental and computational—interpretation of these passages is equally possible. If words that "do not communicate or confer recognition"[35] are damaging not just because they undermine human subjectivity, not just because they suffocate human bodies, but because they "fill and consume the air," then the threat that they pose is an environmental threat as much as it is a subjective or bodily one. It is identical to the threat posed by, say, the minutely incremental spread of an oil slick, by the invisible proliferation of polluting waste, or by the infinitely iterated replication of a computational, as much as a biological, virus.

Like Schmitt's parliamentary debate, or like Hobbes's scientific or spiritual discussion, therefore, Brown's speech here causes as much systemic harm as subjective or political harm. Indeed, in a distinct echo of Schmitt, Brown evaluates the political harm that speech can do with specific reference to its capacity physically and spatially to overwhelm systems and environments—"to usurp," as she puts it, "public space with often trivial matters, rendering the political personal in a fashion that leaves injurious social, political, and economic powers unremarked and untouched."[36] Physically threatening speech thus once again quickly expands beyond the realm of human bodies to be evaluated, at least implicitly, according to its capacity to alter, to shift, or to saturate systems, environments, and spaces.

The purpose of this chapter has, once again, not been to compile a complete review of writing on threatening speech. Rather, these five representative approaches to the potential physical harm that speech might cause serve as a jumping off point for rereading stories of nineteenth-century suffragists' speech as stories of machine code. That speaking is physically dangerous—and that speech might be more effective, or harmful, as a *thing* mobilized or executed, without content, meaning, or message, rather than as a *form* for communicating, representing, or recognizing—is clearly part of a long-standing historical and political tradition.

Moreover, as the work in particular of Hobbes, Schmitt, and Brown suggests, the physicality of threatening speech need not be discussed solely with reference to human bodies or human subjectivity. As much as they, like MacKinnon or Ali al-Qari, do start and end with human bodies or human "hearts"—and as much as they concern themselves with what threatening speech does to human interests and human politics—they also set the stage for a nonhuman, environmental, systemic, and at least *proto*-computational interpretation of language at work and play. Although their intention in noting these nonhuman aspects of threatening speech is without question to emphasize the extent to which humans and human politics remain under linguistic threat, therefore, their work nonetheless opens additional, alternative, and promising, methodological doors.

Chapter Two : Machine Code, Systems, and Environments

The fact that writing on threatening speech has historically addressed nonhuman linguistic activities—and the environmental or systemic implications of these activities—only obliquely does not mean that such speech has been altogether ignored in recent scholarship. There has been a growing interest over the past decades both in nonhuman, ecological, or computational language and in the systemic or environmental operations of this language. On the one hand, for instance, scholars like Hayles have convincingly demonstrated that the information theory underlying computational languages—and more narrowly, machine code—has been inextricably bound up with the semiotic theory of twentieth-century writers such as Ferdinand de Saussure and Jacques Derrida.[1] On the other hand, those working in the intellectual field that, for example, Latour has cultivated have described in effective detail how speech operates through, or emerges from, ecologies and natural systems or networks.

Starting at the intersection of the work inspired by Hayles and the work inspired by Latour, this chapter once again makes the case that the seven stories of suffragists' speech in the next section rest comfortably within an existing scholarly tradition. Addressing in particular the systemic and environmental threats that machine code, as one variation on nonhuman speech, has posed, it describes how the methodologies developed by philosophers of science and technology can be profitably applied to histories like the suffrage movement. Indeed, implicit in this chapter is the idea that writing such a history from the vantage point of science and technology studies might help to reduce many of the anthropocentric tendencies that trouble these fields. Whereas the majority of the chapter is devoted to a discussion of how computational speech potentially harms systems, networks, and environments, therefore, the last few paragraphs suggest that doing away with the lingering interest in humans and human speech that exists in writing about these issues might also be a profitable methodological move.

With that in mind, one of the benefits of Latour's focus on fields or systems rather than on actors or subjects is that it allows him to free his writing on speech from the dichotomies—between subject and object, between nature and culture, between science and politics, or between human and nonhuman[2]—that have remained at the heart of much of semiotic theory. Although other writers, such as Derrida and Jean Baudrillard, have effectively destabilized many of these dichotomies and oppositions,[3] Latour goes a step further and shifts linguistic activity not only away from the realm of the individual humanist subject but toward something else—toward fields, ecologies, or nature. Instead of undermining dialectical interpretations of speech because these interpretations are ethically, politically, or aesthetically suspect, that is to say, Latour makes the case that, *empirically*, these interpretations do not stand. He argues that the oppositions between subject and object or human and nonhuman should be dissolved not because such oppositions are somehow philosophically dubious, but because these oppositions do not describe language actually at work.

In his *Politics of Nature*, for instance, Latour states explicitly that speech may "no longer [be] a specifically human property,"[4] and that the distinctions especially between subject and object that underlie so many analyses of speech actually suppress, short-circuit, or hamper linguistic activity.[5] To the extent that Latour is developing a theory of speech, therefore, it is a theory that extends speech beyond the realm of the individual human and that evades not only any opposition, but any distinct line, between what had once been the ontologically stable categories of speaking subject and mute object.[6] The linguistic activity of nonhumans—"galaxies, neurons, cells, viruses, plants, and glaciers"[7]—and the linguistic activity of humans are inextricably linked; they become operational not in and of themselves, but only in relation to one another.

With specific reference to how this linguistic activity plays out in a laboratory, Latour argues that the primary duty of scientists is thus to invent "speech prostheses that allow nonhumans to participate in the discussions of humans, when humans become perplexed about the participation of new activities in collective life."[8] Ideally, when nonhumans speak via these prostheses, "what is at stake"

> is only a simple translation, thanks to which things become, in the laboratory, by means of instruments, relevant to what we say about them. Instead of an absolute distinction, imposed by science, between epistemological questions and social representation, we find in the sciences, on the contrary, a highly intense fusion of two forms of speech that were previously foreign to one another.[9]

The laboratory, that is to say, is an arena in which speech arises precisely out of the interactions among humans, nonhumans, and their intermediaries. Rather than understanding nonhumans as mute or—worse, according to Latour—as indisputable "facts speaking for themselves," nonhumans participate with humans in a mode of speech that reinforces relationships or networks and that sidelines individuals or subjects.[10]

Moreover, scientists set up their laboratories in this way not because everyone and everything has some sort of political or ethical right to make its voice heard, but because there is no such thing as human speech existing in and of itself, or of speech inhering in a single subject or object. Speech here has little to do with human subjectivity or identity; instead it has to do with fields and environments. Indeed, Latour is careful to note that he is not advocating a situation in which "we allow ourselves to merge controversy with discussion and then simply add nonhumans to the debate,"[11] or in which speech becomes "a self-evident phenomenon that properly belongs to humans and that could be offered only metaphorically to nonhumans."[12] He is not saying that nonhumans, like humans, ought to be possessed of a pseudohuman identity or agency and ought to be allowed, somehow, to use speech as a tool in order to persuade others of what is correct or true. And finally, the point here is not that nonhumans might also exist within, and thereby reformulate, discursive structures in order to achieve subjecthood. Rather, Latour is arguing that speech can, and in some cases should, be understood as something relevant to networks or systems in addition to, or instead of, relevant to the identity of speaking subjects.[13]

This network- or system-conscious interpretation of scientific or ecological linguistic activity lends itself well to a comparison with the network- or system-conscious descriptions of machine code that appear in the writing of Hayles and others who have been influenced by her scholarship. Indeed, like the speech enabled by prostheses in the laboratory, machine code is far more relevant to the fields within which it operates than to any human or, for that matter, nonhuman who might be speaking it. It is effective, in other words, precisely to the extent that it is working on systems, and not to the extent that it is conferring recognition or bolstering or undermining subjective existence. As Hayles quoting Alexander R. Galloway puts it, one of the fundamental defining characteristics of computer code is not its relationship to the identity or subjectivity of its speakers, but that it is "a very special kind of language. *Code is the only language that is executable.*"[14]

Hayles has discussed the human implications of this executability in some detail, but two less anthropocentric aspects of her analysis of it are more relevant here. The first of these is how the executability of machine code relies on a distinctive—and arguably peculiar[15]—theory of information that developed over the course of the twentieth century.[16] The second is how this executability has turned machine code into a type of speech that is, once again, distinctively and peculiarly physical.[17] Both the information theory that gave rise to computer language and the alterations to the physical world that executing computer language entails have turned machine code into something that can operate *as* speech *only* insofar as it is shifting systems or environments. Or, put differently, given these two aspects of its executability, computational speech not only can, but *must*, change the world around it.

The indebtedness of cybernetics and computer language to early twentieth-century information theory has been noted not only by Hayles but by many others writing in the fields of science and technology studies.[18] What Hayles emphasizes, however, and what is particularly key to the stories told here is that these theories of information begin by separating, as she states, "information from meaning"[19]—they define "information" as "a mathematical function that depend[s] solely on the distribution of message elements, independent of whether the message ha[s] any meaning for a receiver."[20] As an example of this theory of information in action,[21] Hayles notes, for instance, that if every number in a given transmission "comes as a surprise"—that is to say, if every transmitted number is random, and does not follow a pattern—then "every number conveys new information. By this reasoning, the more random or chaotic a message is, the more information it contains."[22]

As far as mathematical systems are concerned, this means that "chaos" can be reread as "rich in information rather than poor in order," and that "the production of information" might be "good in itself, independent of what it means."[23] More narrowly, as far as machine code and computer language are concerned, communication increasingly relates not to the speaker, the listener, the message content, or even the interaction among speakers, listeners, and messages, but to the system, field, or environment that speakers, listeners, and messages produce. Or, as Weaver wrote in 1949 in reference to Claude Shannon's interpretation of information, "the concept of information applies not to the individual messages (as the concept of meaning would), but rather to the situation as a whole."[24] Computer language, in other words, is not just executable language, but language that has meaning only in relation to its environment—only to the extent that it defines, formulates, or disrupts environmental networks. Not only is it unconcerned with identity—human or otherwise—its existence is predicated on an explicit shift in focus away from identity and toward systems.

More to the point, the physical character of code—its operation as a physical language in and of itself, rather than, or in addition to, its existence as a language with physical secondary effects produced by programmers—has likewise remained a given in much of the mathematical, philosophical, and popular writing of the past century.[25] As Hayles puts it in a comparison with human speech, "whereas in [human or "natural"] performative utterances *saying is doing* because the action performed is symbolic in nature and does not require physical action in the world, at the basic level of computation *doing is saying* because physical actions also have a symbolic dimension that corresponds directly with computation."[26] Unlike the traditional human speech act, the computational speech activity does not derive its physical manifestations from its symbolic ones. Although the intentions or desires of its human operators may come tangentially into play—turning speech into action—the machine running code, or the machine actually in the process of speaking, is essentially, and far more effectively, turning nonhuman action into nonhuman speech.

At the same time, it is perhaps unsurprising that the problematic physicality of code appears first and foremost in writing on its biological work on human bodies. As Eugene Thacker has noted, for example, a theme that appeared repeatedly in the critical rhetoric surrounding the late twentieth-century biotech industry was that there was a recognizable "intersection between genetic and computer 'codes,'"[27] such that "change the code, and you change the body."[28] These critiques of the biotech industry indeed faulted code for ostensibly erasing the line between "bodies and information"—a move that in turn threatened to transform human bodies into *both* nothing more than things, *and also* nothing more than nonthings, dematerialized expressions of genetic information that might be bought, sold, and patented.[29] Code, that is to say, operated in these scenarios—scenarios, incidentally, that Thacker, Hayles, and others critique—not just across virtual networks, but across biological and bodily ones.[30]

More relevant here, however, code likewise operated across environmental, ecological, mechanical, and spatial networks. Indeed, more often than not, the bodily or biological threats posed by code have turned, incrementally, into environmental threats—with human bodies taking up more marginal, and arguably more appropriate, positions as minor parts of greater physical systems.[31] Greg Egan's science fiction novel *Quarantine*, for example, involves, as Hayles writes, "an engineered virus" that produces "all manner of monstrosities, from buildings growing flesh to people sprouting roots that sink into the ground."[32] Or, as Nigel Thrift and Shaun French have noted in a less apocalyptic mode, cities have always been "intertextual," and now with the advent of code, "are quite literally written," with software "the latest expression of this cursive passion."[33]

In other contexts, such as Elaine Graham's analysis of what she calls "post/humanism," the key to "digital technologies" broadly defined is their use "not so much as *tools*—extensions of the body—as total *environments*."[34] She quotes David Holmes's discussion of "virtual domains": these areas "'cannot be viewed as instruments in the service of pre-given bodies and communities, rather they are themselves contexts which bring about new corporealities and new politics.'"[35] On the one hand, therefore, humans, or more specifically, human citizens, remain central to these stories. On the other hand, as Graham also makes clear, these virtual domains not only sideline human subjects and tools in favor of environments and contexts, but also insist on the constant renewal, regeneration, or alteration of these environments.

In this way, Graham's analysis of what is essentially human subjectivity in a new context begins to hint at code's more pervasive, if potential, environmentally threatening characteristics—characteristics that appear even in optimistic work such as Stephen Wolfram's *A New Kind of Science*. Wolfram's claim in this work, as it is summarized by Hayles, is "that computation does not merely *simulate* the behavior of complex systems; computation is envisioned as the process that actually *generates* behavior in everything from biological organisms to human social systems."[36] Regardless of whether Wolfram's claim is accurate,[37] the *threat* at the heart of his discussion is, once more, an environmental one. If computer language can be mapped onto all environmental systems, *and if all environmental systems can be mapped onto computer language*, then the speech of computers not only operates by altering environments, it *is* the environment. Taken to one dystopian logical conclusion, the implication of this analysis is that if the speech of computers ceases, so too does the physical world.

To the extent, therefore, that computer language privileges systems, networks, and fields over content, sender, and receiver, to the extent that these systems, networks, and fields are both virtual and physical, and to the extent that code's executability is not just unique but uniquely environmental, the harm inherent in this language is a harm that simply cannot be evaluated by starting with human subjectivity. It is a harm predicated on the simultaneity of speech and environment, on the operation of speech *as* environmental change, and—in more extreme variations—on the simultaneous cessation of speech and the environment. Code poses an environmental threat in these scenarios because code is the environment. Or, alternatively, code is executable because it is environmental.

It is indeed as a result of these characteristics of computational speech that this book relies on what some may consider an unnecessarily narrow definition of the term "physical environment," and a problematically broad definition of the term "smart environment." Once again, the physical environments that are identical to, brought into being by, and threatened, harmed, or dissolved as a result of this nonhuman speech are emphatically natural and ecological[38] at the same time that they are computational. These are not environments that are rhetorically mediated, politically or socially constructed, or that pack their punch via metaphors. They are environments made up of objects and things rather than of ideas and of representations—and the language that threatens them is likewise a physical rather than social or political phenomenon. The environmental repercussions of computation are such that the spaces associated with code can *only* be physical. If these environments do have political or social repercussions, they are secondary—and they remain secondary throughout the stories told in this book.

Perhaps paradoxically, therefore, the *smart* environments that come into being in these stories as suffragists speak and as suffragists' language operates are defined here *less* narrowly than such spaces ordinarily are. Usually the term "smart environment" is linked, explicitly or implicitly, to human behavior. The term might refer, for instance, to houses, offices, cars, or other, by definition, *inhabited* areas that are pervaded by computation—that have been engineered by humans as distributed systems in which, once again, humans can interact, behave, or communicate with machines or with other humans in a more effective manner.[39] As Thrift and French have noted, however, "too often in the past, [such spaces] have been studied as if human agency is clearly the directive force" in their elaboration[40]—an analytical move that misses what they describe as the "new and complex form of automated spatiality" across which code operates, a move that ignores the "automatic production of space," in which "new landscapes of code . . . make their own emergent ways."[41] Smart environments, in other words, need not be smart solely in their relation to humans and human needs. In addition, these spaces can speak in and of themselves. They can operate linguistically regardless of human desires, choices, agency, or for that matter inhabitation.

Whereas Thrift and French situate this automated spatiality primarily within the (arguably anthropocentric) "city,"[42] the environmental characteristics of code on which this chapter is predicated gesture toward a much wider applicability for the concept of automated space. If "software" or code does signal "a fundamental reorganization of the environment, a vast system of distributed cognition through which the environment increasingly thinks for itself," if "rather than bricks and concrete . . . we have words and strings of words,"[43] and if these words might be as much ecological as they are computational, then these smart environments need not be limited to houses, offices, cars, or other spaces inhabited specifically by humans. In addition, these environments can be extended throughout natural and mechanical space—can be defined not according to who or what may incidentally live in them or through them, but how and to what extent they operate, *themselves*, as simultaneously physical and linguistic systems. Put differently, nature or the wilderness[44] can be just as smart as any wired household or surveilled urban street.

The working definitions of "the environment" that these environmental threats posed by code demand, therefore, are both narrowly focused *and* general or broad. "The environment," such that it appears in the seven stories that follow, is physical, natural, *and* smart. To the extent that code is the environment, and to the extent that it alters the environment as it goes into operation, the environment itself, or, for that matter, nature, will speak in the same way that any machine might speak—going into linguistic operation as a system rather than as a subject, and leaving human activity incidental at best.

There is, in other words, a clear intersection here between Latour's work on speech, science, and nature, and Hayles's work on computational language, information, and machine code. In part, this intersection mirrors other intersections between nature's speech and computational speech. As Kristin Asdal notes, for example, the "actual term 'ecosystem' came into play through the modern use of computers and modeling."[45] Likewise, the chaos theory that Hayles discusses and links to information theory posits a "global environment" in which, for instance, "a seemingly small event . . . can have immediate and large scale effects on an entire coastal area."[46] Finally, there is the influential, if problematic, idea that Hayles challenges—that "in a world despoiled by overdevelopment, overpopulation, and time-release environmental poisons, it is comforting to think that physical forms can recover their pristine purity by being reconstituted as informational patterns in a multidimensional computer space," that "a cyberspace body, like a cyberspace landscape, is immune to blight and corruption."[47]

In addition to these existing points of intersection, however, machine code meets up with nature's speech in a more pointed way—because its operation raises many of the same questions about the work of language that nature's speech raises. Like Latour's speech prosthesis and speaking fact, the operation of code suggests not just that speech is more than a solely human characteristic—it suggests that speech can, in some cases, be wholly irrelevant to humans. Like both the speech prosthesis and the speaking fact, code emphasizes the simultaneity, under certain circumstances, of linguistic activity and the production, alteration, or destruction of fields, systems, or environments. And finally, like both the speech prosthesis and the speaking fact, the operation of machine code makes clear not only that speech *can* be discussed in a vocabulary of systems rather than subjects, but that, perhaps, it *ought* to be discussed in this way.

It will have become clear by now that the theory of speech on which the stories and history in this book rely is deeply indebted to the writing of scholars working in the fields of critical science and technology studies. At the same time, however, this history also diverges from many of the trends in these fields, implicitly and explicitly challenging a number of the methodological assumptions that underlie them. Most fundamentally and most importantly, the stories here raise the question of whether it *is* in fact politically, aesthetically, or ethically suspect—as it is frequently assumed to be by scholars of critical science studies—to ignore humans when developing an alternative narrative of, in this case, speech.[48]

Humans in fact remain key components, and frequently singular components, of much of the scholarly writing on nonhuman speech and behavior—and those three crucial aspects of human subjectivity—identity, agency, and embodiment—likewise remain at the heart of much of the inquiry in the field.[49] This central role that humans play in the scholarship is clear in the titles of books such as Holmes's *Virtual Politics: Identity and Community in Cyberspace*.[50] It is similarly clear when, for instance, Graham starts her study with the statement that "this is a book about what it means to be human," and then describes how she will locate "human identity" within digital discourses.[51] As much as these scholars profitably reformulate, reframe, or resituate human identity, agency, and embodiment within, say, the discourses of cybernetics or biotechnology, that is to say, they by no means take the additional step of questioning the relevance of human subjectivity altogether.

Indeed, many of the scholars working in science and technology studies explicitly warn readers *against* ignoring human subjectivity—citing the many perils involved in dismissing embodiment and agency especially. In both *How We Became Posthuman* and *My Mother Was a Computer*, for instance, Hayles argues that to dismiss the body from discussions of information and computation is to dismiss much of what is valuable about science studies scholarship. In the former, she makes the case that although "cybernetic construction[s] of the posthuman" are often posited as "critiques of the liberal humanist subject," the way in which these theories downplay embodiment—unlike "feminist and post-colonial theories"—in fact reinforces the assumptions underlying liberal humanism.[52] "The erasure of embodiment," she argues, "is a feature common to *both* the liberal humanist subject and the cybernetic posthuman. . . . [T]o the extent that the posthuman constructs embodiment as the instantiation of thought/information, it continues the liberal tradition rather than disrupts it."[53]

Important to science studies scholarship, in her view, is therefore keeping "disembodiment from being rewritten, once again, into prevailing concepts of subjectivity," and putting "back into the picture the flesh that continues to be erased in contemporary discussions about cybernetic subjects."[54] This is an argument that Hayles reiterates in other contexts,[55] and that became a common starting point in much of the early twenty-first-century writing in the field.[56] To the extent that critical theorists do marginalize or ignore the body in their challenges to the liberal human or humanist subject, according to her analysis, they likewise ignore their own continuing indebtedness to problematic Cartesian splits between mind and body.

A second argument that Hayles advances against dismissing or marginalizing embodiment in favor of information is that such dismissals disregard the complex character of information theory itself.[57] More specifically, to the extent that writers have theorized the evaporation of bodies into code, they have incorrectly assumed that information is somehow real in a way that embodiment is not.[58] Or, put differently, any distinction between information and materiality produces, she states, "a hierarchy in which information is given the dominant position and materiality runs a distant second. As though we had learned nothing from Derrida about supplementarity, embodiment continues to be discussed as if it were a supplement to be purged from the dominant term of information, an accident of evolution we are now in a position to correct."[59] Not only does a scholarship against embodiment buttress liberal humanist theories of subjectivity, then, it also reinforces problematic hierarchies of real and not-real—ignoring the complex operations of discourse.[60]

Finally, in *My Mother Was a Computer*, Hayles develops a more nuanced approach to the question of embodiment[61]—linking it directly to agency,[62] and suggesting that any responsible theory must take both into consideration. Emphasizing that she has "not abandoned [her] commitment to the importance of embodiment," she notes that this continuing focus on bodies "requires repositioning materiality as distinct from physicality and re-envisioning the material basis for hybrid texts and subjectivities."[63] Or, as she argues in a different context,

> We are never only conscious subjects, for distributed cognition takes place throughout the body as well as without; we are never only texts, for we exist as embodied entities in physical contexts too complex to be reduced to semiotic codes; and we never act with complete agency, just as we are never completely without agency. In a word, we are the kind of posthuman I would want this word to mean.[64]

Like dismissing or ignoring embodiment, then, dismissing or ignoring agency may do a disservice to the field of critical science studies because it denies the complexity of nonhuman as well as human activities.[65] At best, it reinforces liberal humanist assumptions about individual consciousness, will, or desire. At worst, it allows these assumptions to muzzle any discussion of what Asdal, in reference to Latour, for example, describes as "field[s] for human and nonhuman agency," fields in which "the human subject is no longer in the center with its power to create worlds," and fields in which "nonhumans are also drawn in as co-producers."[66] The value of the science studies critique, in other words, rests squarely on the maintenance of embodiment, agency, and identity as points of analytical departure.

Nonetheless, one of the contributions that this computational history of suffragists' threatening speech makes to the fields of science and technology studies is to challenge these arguments that humans and their bodies—or that human, or for that matter nonhuman, agency—must always remain a part of historical narratives of language at work. Without rejecting the warnings of Hayles and others, these stories rest on the notion that—for methodological reasons if for no others—it is useful and necessary to sideline embodiment and to marginalize agency. Indeed, ignoring bodies and agency, at least for the sake of argument, can open up useful lines of inquiry that are not available otherwise.

More to the point, ignoring bodies and agency, and especially human bodies and human agency, respects the work and play of speech in a way that continuing to focus on them simply cannot—it allows for the possibility that linguistic activity can indeed occur apart from humans and apart from human intentions and desires. More broadly, it allows for the possibility that language might be detached from human and nonhuman speakers—not in a metaphorical or discursive way, but concretely and empirically. Ignoring bodies and agency, in other words, makes it possible to recognize *far more* of the physical and material things that speech or language might do. And, for the purposes of this book, ignoring bodies and agency likewise makes it possible to think about the *various* ways in which the speech of, for instance, suffragists might pose a threat. What this alternative history of speech promises, therefore, is a new trend in science studies—away from Latour's conclusion that speech may no longer be a purely human property, and toward an alternative conclusion that speech in fact never *was* a human property.

Chapter Three : Agency

Much of the writing on human and nonhuman speech, on information, computational languages, and machine code, on nature's speech, scientific speech, and ecological speech, and, hyperbolically, on suffragists' speech has been characterized by its indebtedness to various, multifarious, and often competing vocabularies of agency.[1] This chapter addresses a number of the more influential works on agency and language, describes how these interpretations of agency have played out in discussions of machine code specifically, and then begins to make the theoretical case that relying on these interpretations causes, at the very least, a significant methodological problem. This chapter thus acts, once again, as a foundation for the stories of suffragists' threatening speech that appear in the second part of the book. It serves as a theoretical jumping off point for the more empirically grounded argument that comes later—that threatening speech simply cannot be evaluated via analyses or discussions of agency.

Compiling a complete review of the late twentieth- and early twenty-first-century literature on agency is as daunting a task as compiling a review of the past four centuries of writing on threatening speech. There are, however, a few common themes that appear to unite much of the work on speech and agency, and it is these themes that work to structure this chapter. One frequent starting point in the literature, for instance, is J. L. Austin's 1969 *How to Do Things with Words*. Austin does not mention agency explicitly in this study, but the distinction that he draws between the "perlocutionary act"—that is, speech that produces a future effect—and the "illocutionary act"—that is, the "speech act" proper,[2] or speech that is, in and of itself, an effect—is implicitly reliant on what eventually gets defined as agency in the 1980s and 1990s.[3] Likewise, Austin's repeated return to the "dangerous" aspects of speech,[4] or to the problematic physicality of the speech act,[5] points, at least, to a type of sovereign or liberal agent at work.

As Judith Butler has noted in her reading of Austin, however, the link between this sovereign or liberal interpretation of agency and performative speech can pose problems. One of the more paradoxical aspects of Austin's work from the legal perspective, for instance, is that the illocutionary act—the speech *act* itself—is arguably the type of speaking least relevant to the will, intention, or desire of the subject. Whereas the perlocutionary act can to some extent be articulated in a linear story of a subject who, first, intends to speak, second, inaugurates speech, and third, produces certain desired effects as a result of this speech, the illocutionary act can be understood only within a discursive field, absent any linearity, and certainly absent any sovereign will.[6] The illocutionary act is necessarily an act of repetition,[7] an act that can only construct and situate a subject within an already existing linguistic realm.[8] In order for speech to *be* an act, therefore, intention and will—sovereign or liberal agency—must disappear.

One of the most effective concrete examples that Butler provides of this disintegration of the agency of the sovereign subject appears in her challenge to MacKinnon's work on pornography. When MacKinnon develops and extends the theory of the speech act, or speech-as-conduct, to the realm of pornography,[9] Butler argues, she does two things. First, she creates a space outside of U.S. First Amendment protections for political and legal response to this conduct. Second, and undermining the first, she eliminates the possibility of intentionality in the production of the pornography—the possibility, in legal language, of determining *mens rea*.[10] In order for pornography to be the bad conduct, the illocutionary *act*, that MacKinnon wants it to be, it must also be an act of repetition. The person or institution that produces the pornography thus cannot be the initiator of the bad conduct, cannot be possessed of an intent to cause harm, but must rather be one of many voices within a preexisting discursive field.[11]

Understanding pornography as a speech act, therefore, does open up an enormous—and, according to Butler, authoritarian—realm of political or legal redress. More to the point as far as MacKinnon's own project is concerned, however, (if less important to Butler's critique): extending the reach of speech-as-conduct to the sphere of pornography also destroys any chance of determining liability.[12] The sovereign individual possessed of agency is destabilized when brought to bear on harmful speech acts. Sovereign agents—those who spend their time speaking truth to power—as well as liable agents—those who must be assigned criminal responsibility—are both impossible figures when shifted into the realm of speech-as-conduct.

Butler's interpretation of MacKinnon's argument thus highlights the flattening function of agency in discussions of harmful speech. By operating in a framework of the sovereign subject's individual agency, MacKinnon does two things: she first insists on the simultaneity of linguistic and physical harm *and in the process* eliminates the possibility of any coherent legal narrative of this simultaneity. Agency in this way plays a dual role in MacKinnon's work—it raises the specter of physical and linguistic pain and suffering while eliminating any effective conversation about this pain and suffering. It is not just that irrelevant and/or parodic forms of condemnation and indignation are the most satisfying responses to harmful speech such as pornography. It is that, in the rhetorical field delimited by the vocabulary of liberal or sovereign agency, they are the *only* responses available.

Although these short-circuiting effects of agency are more overt in writing that valorizes sovereign subjects possessed of individual autonomy, more critical scholarship, reliant on multidimensional interpretations of agency, is also limited in this way. Butler's own theorization of the harm that speech might do, for instance, although nuanced, likewise disallows a complete description of its threatening character. Her book *Excitable Speech* begins with the point that any analysis of harmful speech must take agency into consideration. Indeed, in a precursor to some of the critical science studies writing on computer language and the environment, Butler's argument in the book rests on the idea that the harmful speech act assigns agency both to the speaking subject *and* to language—that the speaking subject as well as the words themselves are understood to "wound."[13]

Although the injurious potential of speech can best be understood by "untethering the speech act from the sovereign subject," and by "more fully acknowledging the way in which the subject is constituted in language,"[14] therefore, agency by no means disappears from the picture. Rather, agency is rearticulated in a more complex, and careful, vocabulary. The subject, for example, is neither a sovereign agent with a purely instrumental relation to language, nor a mere effect whose agency is purely complicit with prior operations of power. The vulnerability to the Other constituted by that prior address is never overcome in the assumption of agency (one reason that "agency" is not the same as mastery).[15]

An "injury" is thus according to this analysis "performed by the very act of interpellation, the one that rules out the possibility of the subject's autogenesis (and gives rise to that very fantasy)"; as a result it becomes even more necessary to "realize how inevitable is our dependency on the ways we are addressed in order to exercise any agency at all."[16]

Butler in this way challenges the idea that agency can be relevant only to self-conscious or purely active subjects, subjects with mastery over an inert or passive language, or subjects who both initiate and direct speech. Indeed, she insists that agency need not be tied even to a singular body possessed of consciousness. For her, the subject is a fragile figure, a figure constituted by language, and a figure whose agency is as vulnerable to the activity of language as language is vulnerable to the activity of the subject. It is, moreover, precisely this fraught relationship between subject and speech, mediated through agency, that gives to speech its threatening potential. Butler argues, for instance, that the fact that "linguistic injury . . . is, as it were, forced to draw its vocabulary from physical injury"[17] suggests an interaction that is far more than metaphorical. To the extent that the body is constituted by language, and to the extent that "it is by being interpellated within the terms of language that a certain social existence of the body first becomes possible,"[18] speech necessarily puts physical existence at stake. As she states in the conclusion to the book, "one need only consider . . . how the words enter the limbs, craft the gesture, bend the spine,"[19] to understand the bodily harm that speech can do.

This reading of the relationship between agency and harmful speech is without question convincing—especially to the extent that "harm" is understood to be nothing more (nor less) than "bodily harm." At the same time, however, its reliance on agency makes impossible any discussion of physically harmful speech that might range beyond subjects and their bodies.[20] It makes inconceivable and inexpressible any speech that might be also, and simultaneously, an assault on the environment, or any speech act that might be defined as a speech act to the extent that it alters the physical world. Moreover, this reading eliminates these alternative or additional interpretations of harmful speech by invoking an idea that is arguably at odds with Butler's usual interpretation of discourse—namely instrumentality. Put another way, the concept underlying Butler's theorization of agency—that the subject is the instrument of language as much as language is the instrument of the subject—does not eliminate the problem of instrumentality writ large.

Indeed, a separation of cause and effect, and of subject and object, remains necessary precisely in order to rescue agency as a viable concept:

> the gap that separates the speech act from its future effects has its auspicious implications: it begins a theory of linguistic agency that provides an alternative to the relentless search for legal remedy. The interval between instances of utterance not only makes the repetition and resignification of the utterance possible, but shows how words might, through time, become disjoined from their power to injure and recontextualized in more affirmative modes.[21]

Butler's argument thus disallows an analysis of purely illocutionary speech, of speech that is simultaneously act and effect,[22] or of speech that is itself an alteration of the environment because it is only in perlocutionary speech—in speech that produces later effects and in speech that returns relentlessly to subjects and bodies—that agency can be found. Whereas she provides an indispensable account of the *bodily* effects of speech, therefore—speech constitutes bodily experience or speech destroys intentionality—she does not get at the potentially broader *physicality* of the harmful or threatening speech act.

Linking agency to speech in this way in fact eliminates the possibility that speech *can* operate beyond the solely human realm. It is certainly the case that in this formulation the existence of the human subject who can speak, the existence of the human subject who can be wounded, and the force of the injurious speech itself are all reliant on a preexisting (and perhaps only marginally human) field of discourse—on a history of violent language that "exceeds in all directions the history of the speaking subject."[23] It is likewise true that the word-that-wounds is not a unitary event, but rather a repetition or a citation of a series of prior linguistic injuries.[24] At the same time, though, once agency becomes the framing concept in this reading, the only linguistic operation that can occur in practice is subjects speaking to other subjects, and then waiting for a response.[25] There is no performance absent an object and an indirect object, and speaking here becomes completely divorced from, say, the theory of information that ignored speaker, listener, and message in favor of system, and on which so many other types of language rely.

When Butler argues, for instance, that the "the speaker who utters the racial slur is . . . citing that slur, making linguistic community with a history of speakers,"[26] she is reinforcing both the instrumentality of language and its embeddedness in human subjects. What is important is not the speech itself, not the network, but the way in which this speech forges community among some subjects and excludes others. What is important is how the subject uses speech and how people respond to that usage. By emphasizing agency and instrumentality, Butler indeed suggests that this speech is the only type that can exist. Any other type of speech is quite literally "impossible,"[27] and thereby in and of itself unspeakable. And what makes it unspeakable is not just that it threatens the "dissolution of the subject," that it calls "the viability of the subject into question," or that it leads to "a sense that one is 'falling apart.'" What makes it unspeakable is that "if the subject speaks impossibly, speaks in ways that cannot be regarded as speech or as the speech of a subject, then that speech is discounted."[28] An interpretation of speech that understands performance to occur outside of the realm of human subjects speaking with other human subjects is simply not conceivable.

When agency is linked to harmful or threatening speech even in these more critical theories, then, speech seems able to operate only given the separation of subject and object or cause and effect. The invocation of agency turns speaking into something relevant to subjects and bodies, but completely irrelevant to systems, networks, or environments. The problem with this situation, again, is not that the search for agency is therefore somehow wrong or incorrect. Rather, it is that such interpretations disallow conversation about threatening speech beyond the narrow parameters of human subjectivity. Even among writers in science and technology studies, however, discussions of speech—including the speech of computers—seem inevitably to end with a reconfiguration of agency.

Hayles, for instance, is careful to avoid reducing speech to the linear or simple cause-and-effect models that appear in liberal or sovereign theories of agency, speakers, and their speech. A major theme in *Chaos Bound* is that in mathematics as well as in literature nonlinear problems began gradually to be recognized as significant "in their own right, rather than as inconvenient deviations from linearity"[29]—and that nonlinear functions in both fields "connote an often startling incongruity between cause and effect, so that a small cause can give rise to a large effect."[30] In *How We Became Posthuman*, Hayles goes a step further, invoking the work of Austin and Butler as she brings her analysis of speech to bear on computer language more specifically.[31] Moreover, her point in these passages is that as useful as Austin's and Butler's theories of performative speech have been, they are inadequate when it comes to describing computer code.

Contrasting "natural languages" with computer languages,[32] Hayles notes that "code that runs on a machine is performative in a much stronger sense than that attributed to language," and that whereas the "performative force" of natural language is "tied to the external changes through complex chains of mediation," computational language "causes changes in machine behavior and, through networked ports and other interfaces, may initiate other changes, all implemented through transmission and execution of code."[33] In short, when language becomes something that might operate outside the realm of purely human subjectivity, Austin's and Butler's theories of performative speech are necessary, but not sufficient, explanations of what exactly this language might be doing.[34]

Despite her adherence to philosophies of speech and language that question linear cause-and-effect frameworks and that move away from human subjectivity, however, Hayles nonetheless returns repeatedly to vocabularies of agency. In *My Mother Was a Computer*, for instance, she argues that the "feedback loops between artificial life forms and biological organisms" have led to "a crisis of agency," that language, although it is now being understood in new ways, is still "intimately connected with agency," and that it is incumbent upon scholars to think carefully about how "binary code," for instance, might and might not "challenge human agency."[35] She goes further, in fact, and advances a definition of "personhood" (if not humanity) that rests squarely on agency. "To count as a person," she states, "an entity must be able to exercise agency. Agency enables the subject to make choices, express intentions, perform actions. Scratch the surface of a person, and you find an agent; find an agent, and you are well on your way toward constituting a subject."[36] As careful as she is to repeat that agency in her analysis is "partial, complex, and intermediated,"[37] then, agency is nonetheless fundamental to her theory of speech and language.[38]

Indeed, her extended critique of Gilles Deleuze and Felix Guattari's work on dispersed subjectivity or *distributed* agency[39] rests to a large extent on their "radical reconceptualization of agency," in which "humans take on attributes of computational media" and "machines acquire biological traits."[40] In a 2001 article, Hayles makes the case that, like Richard Dawkins,[41] Deleuze and Guattari—precisely by seeking to "dissolve the role of agency altogether"—in fact "recuperate agency at crucial points."[42] In their description of bodies without organs, she states, they insist that the preservation of an organism's subjectivity in a "small" form remains necessary to the operation of the systems throughout which subjectivity more broadly is dispersed.[43] As a result, Hayles concludes, Deleuze and Guattari not only inappropriately "decontextualize our relations to each other and to the nonhuman world,"[44] but return inevitably to far more traditional, to some extent even Cartesian, interpretations of the active agent at work. To put the point bluntly, Hayles suggests that any theory of existence (or, for the purposes of this book, speech) that denies agency is necessarily reifying the human subject possessed of agency. Her point is not (or not only) that keeping human agency in mind in discussions of speech is some sort of political imperative; it is that ignoring or sidelining agency is analytically *impossible*. It is not that agency *should* be part of conversations about speech or language, but that it *must* be. In short, Hayles makes explicit the point implicit in Butler's analysis: any theory of speech that does not start and end with agency—and indeed human agency—is inconceivable as well as inexpressible.

Again, this book nonetheless rests on the idea that agency might be eliminated from at least some conversations about speech. The reason for this elimination, however, once more, is not that agency does not exist—or that it exists in some alternative form, say, inherent in objects or things,[45] that has not yet been effectively theorized.[46] The existence of agency or the way it may or may not manifest itself is irrelevant to its sidelining in the discussion here. The damage that agency does is instead methodological. Butler's return to human agency and human subjectivity, for instance, is detrimental because it disallows a full appreciation of the environmental character of certain modes of speech. And Hayles's argument that any analysis of language, including machine code, must explicitly refer to human agency or inevitably repeat liberal humanist modes of thought is arguably equally detrimental. Both—precisely via their invocation of agency—shut down certain avenues of conversation or ways of thinking about what speech might do. Both keep humans at the center of the argument—a move that is politically and perhaps even ontologically valid, but that, as will become clear over the retelling of stories of suffragists' speech, is in many ways methodologically disastrous.

As much as writing in critical science studies has been criticized for departing from traditional analyses of agency, then, in some ways it has actually not diverged far enough. Whereas some scholars have claimed, for instance, that it is politically irresponsible to extend "agency to the nonhuman and the technological" because doing so "perpetuates the tradition of denigrating human matter as dumb"[47]—and thereby makes it possible to ignore racist or sexist social structures[48]—this book operates according to the assumption that the extension of agency to the nonhuman is methodologically irresponsible for the opposite reason: because any recourse to agency at all detracts from multidimensional understandings of how nonhumans and humans together, as environments, might operate.

Or, put another way, although it is easy to chide writers in science studies for taking "political risks" in the name of the "intellectual stimulat[ion]" they derive from reconfiguring (or abandoning) agency,[49] such criticisms take their own, equally disturbing, *methodological* risks. These critics fail to recognize that maintaining an analytical framework that is not only outdated, but intellectually constricting, solely because this framework forces scholarship to remain faithful to patterns of thought that *some* may consider politically responsible carries its own ethical hazards. By making impossible any conversation that does not reinforce generally accepted theories of identity politics, such writing leaves important aspects of, in this case, threatening speech obscure. As a result, it ignores both the complex historical operation of threatening speech and the ways in which this operation continues in contemporary contexts.

Or, as Dennis Allen has put it in his discussion of identity, agency, and viral activism,[50] the "viral" aspect of this particular political activity can be appreciated only when given a move away from thinking of viruses ("both biological and cybernetic") "in anthropomorphic terms that imply a certain agency."[51] Indeed, such activity might best be understood precisely as "the dissemination of (genetic or computer-coded) information without an agent"—as behavior "which stresses the act rather than the identity of the actor" via "the replication of information."[52] As a result, methodologies that seek to describe this mode of political behavior in vocabularies of agency and identity are not only misguided, but arguably damaging. Viral activism, Allen states, does not "seem to be about celebrating the possibility of identity beyond identity

categories," its emphasis is "not on reworking one's own identity or altering our taxonomy of identity categories," and it is less to celebrate "the
anonymous activist than to gesture toward the complete irrelevance of
identity. To put it another way, I would argue that [viral] activism is
finally less about sexy 'secret agents' than about a radically restricted idea
of what an agent might be."[53] Indeed, Allen argues later on in his discussion that as much as scholarship that stresses "the artificiality of identity
categories" or manipulates "the plasticity of postmodern identity" may
"have a certain political efficacy, just as insisting on the validity of identity categories in order to argue for civil rights in juridical and govern-
mental contexts does, it is nonetheless true that the academic critique of
identity is still hopelessly fixated on identity itself."[54] In short, scholarly
approaches that return to identity and agency as the starting and ending
point of all analysis make it impossible to appreciate the complexity of,
here, this particular mode of political activity.

The same problem holds true for scholarship that addresses threatening speech—or, more specifically, suffragists' threatening speech—via
recourse to identity and agency. As valuable as Butler's critical, Hayles's
posthumanist, or the liberal humanist theories of speech have been in describing *some* characteristics of the harmful speech act and *some* of the
political implications of these characteristics, that is to say, these theories' reliance on agency has short-circuited more multifaceted descriptions of linguistic activity. More particularly, such scholarship has, once
again, made it impossible to address speech that does not take the human
subject as its central concern. Butler's theory effectively demonstrates the
shortcomings of assigning speech only to sovereign subjects whose
agency rests in their intention and will. But its rearticulation of agency as
something that (auspiciously) situates a subject within a given discursive
field relies on a continuing separation of cause and effect or subject and
object that is very much foreign to the environmental speech that is the
interest of this book. It disallows any linguistic activity that does not involve human subjects speaking to themselves or to one another.

Hayles likewise makes a convincing case that Austin's and Butler's
writing on performative speech is not sufficient when it comes to understanding the linguistic activity of nonhumans, and particularly computers. Once more, though, her argument that any refusal to recognize the
centrality of human agency masks a return to liberal humanist modes of
thought explicitly shuts down attempts to think about speech in its multidimensional, rather than narrowly human-centered, relation to systems

or environments. If marginalizing humans, or specifically humans possessed of agency, simply reinforces the universality or pervasiveness of both, then any approach that begins from such a position is doomed before it has even begun. Rather than accepting this pessimistic take on alternative interpretations of the speech act, this book therefore rests on the idea that leaving aside agency may not simply return scholarship to the realm of liberal, humanist subjectivity. It takes it as a given that additional, multidimensional analyses of threatening speech might become possible, at least, when agency leaves the picture. The point, once again, is thus not that looking for agency or reinterpreting agency is unethical; it is not that agency does not or cannot exist given contemporary technological conditions; it is simply that the repeated recourse to agency is detrimental to a broader understanding of the activity, operation, and execution of speech.

Chapter Four : Women's Suffrage

Although the women's suffrage movement in the United States and England is the case study on which this discussion of threatening speech rests, this book is not about women's suffrage per se. There is, however, a significant field of literature devoted to Anglo-American suffrage in its own right, and before getting to how historical conversations about women voting are relevant to the threats posed by speech and speaking more generally, it is worthwhile to recognize this work and how it might touch on the argument developed here. Of the six major themes from the past three decades of writing on suffrage that are highlighted in this chapter, the first five do not appear again in this book. The sixth theme—on how suffragists drew on nineteenth- and early twentieth-century race and class discourses in their work—does figure again obliquely in the conclusion to the book, but in an altered form, as one of many examples of writing that addresses the gendered nature of threatening speech. Again, though, given this book's reliance on an example that *has* generated such a great deal of scholarship, it makes sense to describe briefly at least some of the major debates, conversations, and questions that have been foundational to the historical study of women's suffrage. In doing so, it may become clear that a computational retelling of the suffrage narrative can be at least tangentially relevant to the history of women's suffrage writ large.

With that in mind, one of the key points that scholars of women's suffrage in the United States have made is that the fight over suffrage was simultaneously a fight over the meaning of contract, consent, and individual liberty in a nation-state that ostensibly rested comfortably and incontrovertibly on all three. When pro- and antisuffrage advocates debated the validity of defining adult women as citizens who nonetheless could not actively consent to their government, that is to say—and when each side drew parallels between marriage contracts and the social contract—the complexity or fragility of liberal democratic theory in the United States suddenly became apparent. The women's suffrage movement was thus, in some ways, a flashpoint for a multitude of fears and concerns about republican governance writ large.

Sarah Barringer Gordon's work on the role that polygamy in Utah played in national conversations about suffrage is a particularly effective example of the scholarly writing in this vein. The state of Utah granted women the right to vote relatively early on—after which the federal government revoked this right in the name of ending Mormon polygamy. As Gordon puts it in a 1996 journal article,

> the women's vote in Utah highlighted the central problem of consent in a political culture that embraced individual choice as the basis of state power. The apparent endorsement of polygamy by Utah women . . . served as a lightning rod for concerns about women's political participation and marriage that affected the country as a whole. . . . [T]hese analytically distinct, but often politically indistinguishable strands of political theory about the law of marriage and its relationship to the state coalesced in the 1880s to create a powerful logic of disfranchisement.[1]

As much as the nineteenth century might be called "'the age of contract,'" then, "when consent (to marriage, to employment, to government) governed the creation of relationships of authority,"[2] it might also be understood as a time when neat or harmonious interactions among these various contractual or consensual relationships came to be questioned. Antisuffrage advocates, especially, feared not only that "a separate political identity for women" might weaken the marriage contract, but that weak marriage contracts in turn might undermine liberal republican values.[3]

As the suffrage movement developed, that is to say, it gradually turned consent from a matter of political complacency or comfort into a matter of political concern. It demonstrated that theories of individual liberty and democratic governance were far more complex than many had admitted. Gordon brings this point into sharp relief in her 2002 book, *The Mormon Question: Polygamy and Constitutional Conflict in Nineteenth-Century America*. One of the themes that reappears in this book is that the federal government's interest in polygamy and suffrage in the western part of the United States was as fundamental to late nineteenth- and early twentieth-century shifts in U.S. theories of governance as Reconstruction in the South had been following the Civil War.[4] Once again, suffrage here thus operates as one entry point into a discussion of the roles that liberty (sexual, religious, personal), consent, and contract played on the national stage.

A second argument that is frequently advanced in the literature on the women's suffrage movement is that it and the rhetoric surrounding it can help scholars to understand not just sovereignty, democracy, and citizenship as they have been defined in a given national context, but also as they have been defined more generally—that nineteenth-century conversations about women's suffrage are as relevant to abstract political theory as they are to particular places and moments. In some cases, scholarship in this vein addresses the writing of specific individuals within the suffrage movement, describing how this writing might complicate definitions of sovereignty or citizenship. In a 2006 article, for instance, Teena Gabrielson suggests that suffrage advocate Mary Austin "proposes a transformation of the idea of citizenship: one that uses gender essentialism in order to establish women as co-sovereigns."[5] A decade before Gabrielson published her article, Seth Kovan, Sonya Michel, and Sandra Stanley Holton argued in various ways that the writing and activism of suffragists helped to shift citizenship theory away from liberal models reliant on consent or contract and toward socialist or quasi-socialist models reliant on labor.[6] Each of these writers, that is to say, implicitly or explicitly makes the case that the study of the suffrage movement might serve as a foundation for wider (liberal, socialist, nationalist, etc.) theories of democracy or sovereignty.[7]

Using the suffrage movement as a jumping off point for forays into abstract political theory is most common, however, among scholars who examine democracy and sovereignty through the lens of gender, or more broadly, identity issues. In a 2002 article entitled "Political Citizenship and Democratization: The Gender Paradox," for instance, Eileen McDonagh invokes the suffrage movement as a means of questioning the apparent dichotomy between "sameness and difference" or "individual equality and women's group differences" that has rested at the heart of much of the recent writing on feminist political belonging.[8] "Suffrage advocates," she argues, "invented a new, cultural justification for political inclusion, a paradoxical combination of liberal principles affirming the value of women's individual equality and ascriptive principles affirming the value of women's maternal group difference."[9] The women's suffrage movement operates here, in other words, as one example of the paradoxical—rather than necessarily dichotomous—character of gendered political citizenship.

But perhaps one of the most influential discussions of women's suffrage, gender, and democratic theory is Sandra VanBurkleo's *"Belonging to the World": Women's Rights and American Constitutional Culture.* At first glance, VanBurkleo's book is a context-specific analysis of women's rights—including, but not limited to, those rights sought by suffragists—in the United States. The book also, however, takes the history of women's rights as a starting point for developing a wider theory of gender, democracy, and—most relevant to the argument here—speech. Rather than addressing speech in its own right as something that might potentially cause harm, however, VanBurkleo understands speech as something necessarily empowering—as a tool or implement that has or has not been mobilized by women seeking to form public community with one another, or women seeking to "belong to the world."[10]

VanBurkleo thus devotes time in her book to describing how or why women have been silent (a bad thing) and how or why women have overcome this silence (a good thing).[11] From there, she develops a theory of sovereignty and citizenship predicated on the relationship between speaking out and the acquisition of rights. The suffrage movement thus appears in the book as one example of women using speech to enter the public sphere (via strategic use of their roles as wives and mothers), and thereby achieve political identities.[12] Although VanBurkleo's study does touch on some of the same issues that are of interest in this book, for the most part her project is therefore quite different. She is concerned less with the activity of speech itself and more with the activity of women who use speech, incidentally, as they gain rights. Her story is a political, and largely liberal, one; the story in this book is a linguistic and environmental one.

A third theme is related to a question toward which VanBurkleo gestures—whether the suffrage movement was in any way relevant to later women's rights movements. More specifically, many writers, responding to suggestions that the Nineteenth Amendment did little to advance gender equality in the United States, debate the validity of this amend-

ment—or the validity of the suffrage movement writ large—as a historical beginning of U.S. feminist politics.[13] For instance, Jennifer K. Brown
has argued that both "the heroic suffrage campaign" and the Nineteenth
Amendment itself "can and should be recognized as an affirmation of
women's constitutional equality."[14] In a more nuanced take on the relative relevance of the suffrage movement (if not necessarily the Nineteenth Amendment) to twentieth-century feminist projects, Sara
Hunter Graham's 1996 *Woman Suffrage and the New Democracy* makes
the case that later women's movements have in fact adopted many of the
activist tactics developed by nineteenth-century suffragists. Graham
continues, however, by arguing that the legacy of this adoption has been
a problematic one. Although the suffragists' move away from an activism
modeled on the work of bourgeois charitable foundations and toward an
activism of gender-based pressure politics was effective at the time, the
continuing reliance on pressure politics throughout the twentieth century inevitably compromised, Graham argues, later feminist movements.[15] At the heart of each of these studies, then, rests the question,
again, of whether women's movements in general profited from the
lessons—good and bad—of the suffrage movement.

A fourth trend in the suffrage scholarship answers this question
about the suffragists' legacy in a different way, connecting the suffrage
movement to later party political, left/right, or radical/conservative divides in the United States and England. Aileen Kraditor's foundational
The Ideas of the Woman Suffrage Movement, 1870–1920, published origi-
nally in 1965, to some extent set the boundaries for this conversation, arguing that the suffragists' ideological position gradually shifted from a
sort of radical egalitarianism to an increasingly pragmatic chauvinism at
odds with the ideals of the earlier activists.[16] By the 1920s, Kraditor argues, women's suffrage had thus become an essentially conservative political force. In a slightly different vein, Susan E. Marshall and Elna
Green have recuperated the conservative activism of the nineteenth-
and early twentieth-century women *opposed* to the extension of suffrage—recognizing that in this activism lies the roots of the more recent
conservative women's movements that have bolstered right-wing politics
in the United States.[17] Finally, scholars such as Martin Pugh have described in detail how suffrage associations played political parties against
one another and thereby altered to some extent the operation of—in the
case of Pugh's study—English parliamentary practice.[18] Here, in other
words, the suffrage movement's legacy is more incidental than it is delib-

erate—but it nonetheless remains relevant to conversations about later party politics.

In addition to these political and historical analyses of women's suffrage, there has also been a great deal of literature examining the suffrage movement through the lens of cultural studies or philosophy. A fifth theme that appears in writing on suffrage, for instance, describes how militant suffragists experienced their bodies or redefined embodiment. Although most of this writing takes the English movement as its example because English suffragists were generally (although certainly not uniquely) more invested in physical forms of activism and more likely to spectacularize their bodies than suffragists in other national contexts, it nonetheless merits mention here.[19] If nothing else, this trend in the literature touches on many of the same issues that the sixth trend, on suffrage and race or class identity, does.

Barbara Green's 1997 *Spectacular Confessions: Autobiography, Performative Activism, and the Sites of Suffrage, 1905–1938*, for instance, makes a convincing case that militant suffragists not only mobilized their bodies in new and spectacular ways, but that this mobilization changed the nature of spectacle in general, upset traditional modes of representation or narrative authority, and obliterated accepted divisions between public and private. By insisting that both their own and the antisuffragists' use of their bodies be politically and socially recognized, militant suffragists demonstrated the centrality of embodiment to political and social identity and activity writ large. When militant suffragists turned the mistreatment of their bodies in prison into stories written and published for mass consumption, for instance, Green suggests that they likewise invited public examination of ostensibly private spaces, mobilized new forms of narrative, and, again, turned political spectacle into something necessarily embodied. As a result, Green concludes, these early twentieth-century militant suffragists addressed many of the same issues that would preoccupy feminist activists a century later.[20]

This question of the relationship between militancy and embodiment in early twentieth-century suffrage movements has also been addressed from an alternative perspective, however. Laura E. Nym Mayhall, for instance, cautions against concentrating too exclusively on the spectacularization of the body, arguing that the movement "initiated multiple practices, not all of which focused on women's bodies in pain."[21] In an article published in 2002, Mayhall continues that although the "image of the tortured suffragette figures prominently in the canonical histories and autobiographies of the women's suffrage movement written by participants," excessive interest in this figure has detracted from a complete understanding of the wider implications of militant suffragists' practices.[22] "Militancy's implementation," she argues, "became a contest over the uses and utility of physical force in negotiations with the state."[23] In her 2003 book, *The Militant Suffrage Movement: Citizenship and Resistance in Britain, 1860–1930*, Mayhall develops this argument further, writing that the activities of suffragists can be understood only within the context of late nineteenth- and early twentieth-century radicalism and constitutional change more broadly defined. Once again, the implication here is that an exclusive interest in embodiment ignores the more fundamental transformation in theories of citizenship and political identity that the suffragists—violent as well as nonviolent—wrought.[24]

Both of these takes on militancy and embodiment, then, get at the new and increasingly complex forms of political belonging and political identity that the suffrage movement produced. In the first, Green reads the suffragists' spectacularization of their bodies as a demonstration of the fragility of traditional political relationships. In the second, Mayhall recognizes, but does not exclusively focus on, this bodily spectacle as a means of discussing how the suffrage movement irrevocably changed the character of modern citizenship. Each thus addresses questions that are relevant also to a final issue that appears in the suffrage literature, and that is worth highlighting in this chapter, namely the relationship between the activities of suffragists and the development of modern race and class hierarchies or identities.

This sixth theme takes as its starting point the repeated invocation or mobilization by many suffragists of late nineteenth- and early twentieth-century discourses of race or class inferiority and superiority. It then addresses the implications of this mobilization, describing, for instance, the role of suffragists from minority or marginalized backgrounds, or, alternatively, how the political theories and structures that the white, middle-class suffrage movement initiated were predicated on the maintenance of these oppressive hierarchies. In short, the writing that plays on this sixth theme describes both the intersection between the politics of suffrage and race or class politics and the wider repercussions of this intersection

This impetus toward tracing the relationship between the politics of women's suffrage and oppressive late nineteenth- and early twentieth-century rhetoric of race and class identity is not unique to scholarship that takes this relationship as its central problem. In 1978, for instance, Ellen Dubois described, critiqued, and analyzed the racist and classist positions taken by many prominent women within the suffrage movement in her *Feminism and Suffrage: The Emergence of an Independent Women's Movement in America*.[25] Gabrielson, Graham, and Buechler likewise take the overlap between the rhetoric of (white, middle-class) women's rights and the rhetoric of the inferiority of those outside of the white, middle-class norm as a starting point for their analyses.

Gabrielson, for instance, discusses the paradox of a democratic theory that simultaneously posited universal equality—based in "motherhood" and manifested in the vote—and an insistence on superior versus inferior "claims to citizenship."[26] Graham and Buechler, meantime, each in different ways forge links between the racism or classism of late nineteenth- and early twentieth-century suffragists and the complicated if not impossible legacy that their movement thereby left for later feminist practice—the former focusing in particular on the suffragists' tactical or strategic move away from abolitionist ideologies[27] and the latter discussing the inability of white, middle-class women in general to recognize race and class oppression in the way that they recognize gender oppression.[28] The extent to which the suffrage movement relied on and reproduced an awkward politics of race and class inequity has thus not gone unexamined in the broader literature in the field.

What makes the literature that addresses these issues explicitly and at length different therefore is, first, that it frequently focuses on the activism of suffragists who did not fit the white, middle-class norm, and second, that it seeks additional or expanded explanations for the seemingly inevitable racism and classism of prosuffrage speech and writing. Rosalyn Terborg-Penn, for instance, in her 1998 book, *African American Women in the Struggle for the Vote, 1850–1920*, makes the case that the activities of African American suffragists—although frequently marginalized or discounted by mainstream suffragists such as Susan B. Anthony and Elizabeth Cady Stanton—were vital to the success of the suffrage movement writ large. Unlike white, middle-class suffragists, however, who favored an increasingly narrow electorate based on education, race, or class *rather* than on gender, Terborg-Penn suggests that African American suffragists, recognizing the widespread oppression that existed at the nexus of race, class, and gender, sought a genuinely universal rights regime. Terborg-Penn thus concludes that the suffrage movement was never solely a white, middle-class phenomenon, but that those suffragists who did not fit the white, middle-class norm nonetheless had to negotiate the racist and classist assumptions of their colleagues as they strove to expand voting rights.[29]

Louise Michele Newman and Vron Ware approach the racist and classist nature of the suffrage movement from a different direction, focusing on the deeper structural indebtedness of mainstream women's suffrage ideologies to imperial race hierarchies. In her 1999 book, *White Women's Rights: The Racial Origins of Feminism in the United States*, for instance, Newman does not accept, as many other scholars have, that the suffrage movement's increasing racism and classism over the late nineteenth century was a response to pressing, if unsavory, strategic necessity. Instead, she notes both the simultaneity and the similarity of writing on evolutionary theory, writing on imperialism, and writing on women's suffrage and women's rights more generally. The democratic theory, the theories of citizenship, and the theories of equality and rights that developed out of the suffrage and women's rights movements, Newman argues, were not incidentally, but *inextricably*, bound up in the scientific racism of the late nineteenth and early twentieth centuries. As a result of this indebtedness to evolutionist and imperialist racist and classist thinking, Newman concludes, the suffrage movement could never seriously challenge gender inequities, much less make good on its initial promise of universal rights and equality.[30]

In her 1992 study, *Beyond the Pale: White Women, Racism, and History*, Ware addresses many of these same issues. Like Newman, her interest lies not in suffrage specifically, but in how feminist politics generally developed in opposition to, in tandem with, and alongside of racist or imperialist politics and policies. Ware's discussion of the complicated interaction or overlap between scientific or biological theories of race and late nineteenth- and early twentieth-century feminism, especially, prefigures Newman's book and is of particular salience to the writing on suffrage.[31] Terborg-Penn, Newman, and Ware indeed all add new dimensions to the historiography of women's suffrage—the first by complicating the usual story of middle-class, white activism and the second two by refusing to accept simple or superficial explanations for the more problematic directions in which the suffrage movement developed. Each is thus both relevant to the five other themes that appear in the literature on women's suffrage and indicative of the various alternative questions that discussions of the suffrage movement might raise.

Once again, since this book is not about women's suffrage or women's movements in and of themselves, most of the debates and conversations that have made up the bulk of this chapter do not appear in the following chapters. Whereas the literature on women's suffrage addresses philosophical, historical, or political issues to the extent that these issues shed light on suffrage itself, this book addresses women's suffrage to the extent that it might shed light on one philosophical, historical, and political issue: threatening speech. Indeed, even those works, like VanBurkleo's, that concern themselves with speech do so only in aid of a broader point about women's rights and women's political belonging. Here, instead, speech is the central concern, and women's suffrage is one of many possible entry points into a discussion of it. It is not speech that is the methodological tool in this analysis, but suffrage that is.

This inverted emphasis does not mean, however, that the scholarly literature on suffrage is completely disconnected from this book. If studies of the women's suffrage movement have been simultaneously studies of historical fights over contract, consent, and individual liberty, or studies of sovereignty and democracy in the abstract, then taking the suffrage movement as a case study of threatening speech is an effective way of linking speech back to these other issues. Likewise, if writing about women's suffrage has also been writing about later feminist activism, about twentieth-century party political divides, about embodiment or about identity, then so too might writing about the threatening speech of the suffragists be about these late twentieth- and early twenty-first-century concerns. The difference is that if this were a book *about* suffrage, there would be chapters devoted explicitly to engaging in these debates. Since it is not, its relevance to these debates remains largely implicit.

Conclusion to Part One: Ignoring Conventions

Although this computational history of threatening speech necessarily draws on a number of existing scholarly traditions, it also takes these traditions in new, and sometimes paradoxical, directions. On the one hand, for example, the writing on the physical harm that speech might do reaches many of its logical conclusions here. On the other hand, one of these conclusions is that environmental, as opposed to merely bodily, harm ought to be at the forefront of any discussion of speech. Likewise, as much as this history is a meeting point for various distinct theories of nonhuman linguistic activity—theories of nature's speech, of ecological speech, of machine code, and of digital languages—it evades the human identity, embodiment, and agency that operate, sometimes tacitly, at the heart of so many of these theories.

Indeed, while also situated within the past few decades' worth of work on agency, this computational history assumes not agency's reformulation or redefinition in more nuanced ways—not agency's extension to nonhuman objects or structures, or its dispersion over networks or grids—but the extensive methodological damage that a reliance on the vocabulary of agency, in any form, can do. In the same way, therefore, that the women's suffrage movement serves here as one example in a general analysis of speech—rather than speech serving as one example in a general analysis of voting or women's rights—the literature on agency serves here as one example of language brought into play for purely human purposes. Even when it is making the case that humans are not the only "persons" with agency, this literature—as the seven stories that follow make clear—nonetheless exists above all for the benefit of human bodies, human identities, and human subjectivity.

In addition to taking these traditions in new directions, however, the seven stories of suffragists' speech that make up the bulk of this book also fly in the face of many of the conventions that have founded these traditions. In concluding this prefatory section, therefore, it is worthwhile to explain why ignoring these conventions is an unproblematic move when machine code is taken as a linguistic norm. It is, after all, one thing for a history to play on or with the preexisting scholarly themes that frame it. It is quite another for a history to depart from these themes entirely. What these last few paragraphs of the introduction do, then, is discuss how it is not only possible, but necessary, first, to write a history of speech without adhering to an existing set of semiotic principles, and second, to write a history of systemic or environmental threats without recognizing the analytical categories that have developed in the field of science and technology studies.

With that in mind, one of the most deeply rooted principles in writing on threatening speech, harmful speech, speech and agency, or speech in general is that there are distinct, and crucial boundaries that must be maintained among "language," "speech," and "writing." Regardless of whether more traditional semiotic notions are taken as given—that language is an abstract or ideal system, of which speech is the practice and writing the mediated, absent supplement, or that symbolic representation and physical thing come together in (human) cognition to create meaning—or more recent Derridean ideas situating writing before or within language are the given[1]—the three concepts are always addressed separately. Even when Derrida places writing within language, or argues that writing—as "presence" rather than "absence"—brings speech into being,[2] for example, he both blurs the lines among language, speech, and writing *and also* plays up the fact that these lines still exist. The three concepts must remain separate in order for the rhetorical, ethical, and political moves that he initiates to be made.

Taking machine code as a linguistic model, and writing a computational rather than human history of speech, however, eliminates any need to rely on—or for that matter to address at length—these apparent distinctions. In part, this is because code operates in a distinctly shifted theoretical framework. As Hayles, for instance, has argued in reference to computational languages, if "writing," according to Derrida, "exceeds speech and cannot simply be conceptualized as speech's written form," then "code exceeds both writing and speech, having characteristics that appear in neither of these legacy systems."[3] The operation of machine code, in other words, upsets the formulas among language, speech, and writing far more efficiently than even Derrida and those influenced by him have done.

In part, however, these distinctions among language, speech, and writing evaporate for purely empirical or practical reasons. It is *in fact* the case that machine code is nothing more nor less than simultaneous language, speech, writing, and execution—all three are always present, in the semiotic sense of the word, and it is impossible to execute or perform code as speech across anything but likewise simultaneous symbolic and physical systems. There is simply no separation among the three. As a result, "language," "speech," and "writing" appear quite deliberately as interchangeable concepts in the following seven stories of suffragists' speech. Ignoring the traditional semiotic conventions about language, speech, and writing, that is to say—flying in the face of one of the best established traditions in the literature on threatening or harmful speech as well as in the literature on speech and agency—serves a specific methodological purpose in this book.

Doing so also reinforces a second deliberate conflation of what are ordinarily understood to be crucially distinct concepts—namely the conflation of "system," "environment," "physical world," "space," "network," and occasionally "nature." Once again, the various fields of scholarship on which these seven stories of suffragists' speech draw—including especially scholarship on nonhuman speech in the field of science studies—have developed around the position that eliding these concepts is, at best, an intellectually irresponsible move. "Nature" and "the environment," especially, have been held up as problematic terms—and indeed later chapters in this book go into more detail describing how the two *together* nonetheless underlie this computational history.

For now, it is simply worth pointing out that taking machine code as a linguistic model challenges, once again, the argument that maintaining a distinction among these concepts is a political, ethical, historical, or intellectual necessity. Put differently, once speech is no longer about humans transmitting messages to, conferring recognition upon, or communicating meaning with, one another, a linguistic system no longer need be defined narrowly as an abstract system of rules and principles, predicated on metaphysical human agreement, knowledge, discourse, or community. Far from it—a linguistic system must instead be a physical, mechanical, electronic, environmental, ecological, and yes, natural[4] *thing*.

Or, to get at this interpretation of "system" from another direction, when Hayles argues that computational language and machine code do not "allow the infinite iterability and citation that Derrida associates with inscriptions, whereby any phrase, sentence, or paragraph can be lifted from one context and embedded in another" because, unlike human writing, code becomes "unintelligible if transported into a different context—for example, into a different programming language or a different syntactic structure within the same language,"[5] she is implicitly referencing code's existence as a physical, mechanical, natural, and environmental—rather than abstract, social, rhetorical, or metaphysical—system. As much as Derrida's point about iterability and citation appears to suggest that the content or meaning of a given word is always contingent, that is to say, by making this point via the *decontextualization* of words, he is once again, if paradoxically, reinforcing the centrality of their content.

Contrarily, unlike Derrida's inscriptions, or for that matter Saussure's signs, computer language *cannot* be decontextualized. This is not, though, because computer language is too meaningful to be reframed or resituated. It is not because code defies iterability in its own right. Quite the opposite: it is because context (or environment, system, network, or space) is all that code is. It is nothing more nor less than the system on which it executes, and thus the process of decontextualization in the linguistic realm of code is an impossibility. As context rather than message, code operates simultaneously as system, space, and environment. Systems, environments, physical worlds, spaces, and networks thus not only can, but—once more—must, be interchangeable when machine code serves as the linguistic model.

The fact that the history told here not only departs from the scholarly traditions on which it also draws, but ignores many of the founding principles underlying these traditions, is therefore a deliberate methodological move. It is one further means of demonstrating that retelling stories of, in this case, suffragists' speech from the vantage point of machine code can usefully realign discussions of speech writ large—lifting these discussions from the narrow confines of debates about human subjectivity and dispersing them across human and nonhuman spaces and nonspaces. Indeed, as both the seven stories of suffragists' speech themselves and the arguments in the concluding section of this book suggest, the new methodology proposed here is useful not only for historiographical reasons, but as a means of explaining—and, more important, situating historically—a number of contemporary linguistic activities that seem to defy existing, human, analytical frameworks: the babble of the Internet, say, or the twenty-four-hour news and information cycle. Or, put differently, Weaver's telegraph girl was clearly not only a discreet and proper node within an informational system. She was one further iteration of a historically long-standing function that brings together speech, information, code, and the environment.

PART TWO : Reading Seven Stories of Suffragists' Speech

Each of the following seven chapters addresses a different characteristic of suffragists' threatening speech. These characteristics all appear with frequency in the popular and academic writing of the late nineteenth and early twentieth centuries, and all play with the idea that when suffragists speak, existing social or political—that is, human—relationships are threatened. Perhaps surprisingly, these characteristics are equally prominent in both pro- and antisuffrage writing—the potential threat posed by speaking suffragists as rhetorically valuable to those advocating the vote for women as it was to those opposing it. Indeed, these seven stories together produce a complex and multifaceted narrative of suffragists' speech as threatening speech, and in particular as politically or socially threatening speech. Each of these stories also, however, lends itself to readings that do not start with society or politics, and that do not assume speech to be solely a social, political, subjective, or for that matter human, phenomenon. Indeed, just as valid as these human-centered readings is one that emphasizes the environmental, systemic, or physical harm that suffragists' speech might do—a harm, once again, described prominently in both pro- and antisuffrage writing.

The chapters that follow invite such an alternative reading. Taking as a model not political, social, or subjective human speech, but physical, environmental, and computational nonhuman speech, these chapters begin to sketch a different, wider ranging narrative of harmful or threatening linguistic activity. At stake in these chapters is less how nineteenth- and early twentieth-century writers played on the theme of the socially or politically harmful public woman, and more how a particular mode of speech—a type of proto-machine code—came to be associated with suffragists, and how this mode of speech posed an increasingly dire environmental threat. These chapters, that is to say, take up the ignored systemic or environmental aspects of the story of speaking suffragists and make the case that these aspects are as key as human-centered ones to understanding what precisely speech might do.

If these systemic or environmental characteristics of suffragists' speech were so prominent in the writing surrounding the suffrage movement, though, why have they been ignored by scholars? In addition to proposing a systemic, computational, or environmental reading of the narrative of suffragists' threatening speech, the following chapters also set out to answer to this question. More specifically, they suggest that the reason that nonhuman interpretations of suffragists' speech have been marginalized is that the vocabulary of agency in which analyses of speech have ordinarily been articulated has obscured these alternative approaches. Methodological frameworks that start with agency, that is to say—even when agency is extended to nonhuman actors (or actants)— have made alternative, and in particular nonhuman, interpretations of threatening speech explicitly "impossible."[1]

Or, put another way, as important as the work that has addressed suffragists' speech from the direction of agency has been, this work has also closed down discussions of speech that do not refer back to human relationships and, more often than not, to human violence or oppression. The assumption underlying these chapters is thus that it might be useful, even if briefly, to ignore or abandon the intellectual frameworks that have made posing the problem of speech in the context of nonhuman beings or things or spaces—or asking whether the running theme of suffragists' threatening speech might be more complicated than it initially appears—unimaginable. By abandoning these existing frameworks, these chapters establish the possibility, at least, of entertaining equally useful, and more broadly defined, complementary interpretations.

In order to trace the contours of the alternative readings that make up the following chapters, and in order to sketch an outline of the argument against agency that underlies them, it is worthwhile providing one impressionistic example of the analysis on which they rely. With that in mind, in 1884, the *Boston Globe* ran an article by Joaquin Miller describing the activities of four suffrage advocates at the state capitol. According to Miller, the first of these advocates arrived at the hearing "with a whirr, a snap, consciousness and self-assertion, that at once was a sort of challenge to battle."[2] After this, "she ran around among the chairs and tables and men, like a little speckled hen that had lost her little chicken. Then she fluttered down beside the clerk, slammed down some books, and saying 'I am here to make a speech this morning,' proceeded to un-roll papers and write furiously."[3] The second speaker, Miller continues,

> dropped her spectacles, unfortunately, and as there were no spry young men on the platform, she had to get down on her hands and knees and feel about in the dim light and hunt for them herself. It took a good while feeling about, and she did not all the time keep her face to the audience. This made things look very awkward.[4]

The third, "a modest Scotch lady,"

> read her speech, which I could not hear, and turned in triumph to go to her seat. But alas for her excitation, she dropped the whole heap, split [sic] her speech all over the floor, and had to get down and fumble around and pick it up herself. Perhaps nothing in the world could have told so perfectly the unfitness of women for polit-ical work as this brave lady's attempt to speak. She tried ever so hard to fill the hall and be heard; but all in vain.[5]

Finally, as the fourth began to speak,

> the parasol handle rattled down on the platform, the alligator bag fell forward from the chair where she pitched it in general excite-ment, and she left a line of handkerchiefs and gloves behind her as she glided toward the desk. Her speech was delivered as she loafed with her right arm resting on the desk where she had de-posited a large white handkerchief. This slipped off two or three times, and gave her time to think up what to say next as she stooped to pick it up.[6]

Each of these passages is of a sort recognizable to anyone familiar with nineteenth-century sexual rhetoric. Each makes clear women's incapac-ity for political or legal speech, each treats the speakers with ridicule at best, hostility at worst, and each demonstrates the absurdity of women participating in electoral politics.

More pointedly, each of these passages seems tailor made for a scholarly analysis via traditional, human-centered interpretations of agency or identity. Miller, as narrator, deprives the speakers of any subject position as rational, self-conscious, liberal individuals. He refuses to consider or discuss what the speakers actually say, and instead attributes to them nonverbal noises, clattering, rattles, or ineffective silence. There is no mention of the speakers' words or their ideas. The article is devoted instead to their affect and physicality. Miller both infantilizes and dehumanizes the speakers (comparing them to children and animals). He sexualizes at least one by noting the "awkwardness" of her getting down on all fours with her back to the audience. The others are portrayed as disorganized, overwhelmed by their clothing and accessories, and unintelligible in the midst of their furious "excitation" and "excitement." In short, if we take Miller at his word, suffragists' speech is at best irrelevant, and at worst a threat to the political universe, because it is unruly, irrational, disorganized, and sexualized.

To the extent that this analysis via agency and identity would contain a critique, this critique might rest on two ideas: first, that Miller is incorrect in finding suffragists' speech threatening or ridiculous, and second, that it is an inappropriate move for him to deprive these women of their subject positions solely on the basis of their identity as women. Miller is operating in a discursive field that has already defined women as not quite subjects, and thus everything that these women say or do necessarily reinscribes them as not quite subjects within this field. Once such a critique were established, the conversation would then develop around questions such as how this inappropriate relationship among identity, difference, and subjectivity arose (and, if it were being normative, how to reimagine this relationship), or how these women succeeded or did not succeed in repositioning themselves as agents, especially given the relentlessness of this preexisting discourse.

To the extent that this analysis ranged further afield and addressed additional materials, it might also note that there is ample evidence that in fact many of these same (white, middle-class) suffragists made use of precisely the strategies that Miller used as they repositioned themselves as active subjects. In this and similar contexts, such an analysis might note, these mainstream suffragists appropriated narrative authority just as relentlessly as Miller did—asserting their agency, for instance, by consigning other marginalized (colonized, nonwhite, working-class) populations to the same nonlinguistic, infantilized, or nonhuman space to which they themselves had been so recently relegated. Again, the response to such a critique might therefore be how to reimagine or subvert these oppressive political, social, and discursive structures. Once the analytical framework of human agency and identity had been built up around these passages, in other words, there would be a set and finite field of questions to ask and also a set and finite field of positions that scholars might take. The conversation concerning these passages would run along established lines, and when new insights were elaborated, these insights would reinforce what we already know about the double-edged sword that is a coherent subject possessed of agency.

The following chapters recuperate some of the questions and answers that are left out of this existing conversation. As much as the narrator, the speakers, and the passages themselves define a universe of subjects and objects, of struggles for linguistic authority, or of active human agents and nonhuman, nonverbal incoherence, the next seven chapters start from the position that there are other ways of reading this article. One might, for example, take Miller at his word when he mobilizes the bird and animal metaphors. Rather than interpreting these metaphors as attempts to dehumanize women speakers and to deprive them of the uniquely human characteristic that is rational speech, they might also be read as descriptions of what Miller actually sees happening to the physical environment when suffragists speak. They might be read as the opposite of metaphors—of speech as something physical and as something that operates by altering the physical world.

Depicting the speakers as animals (or, more broadly, as part of nature or the environment), that is to say, may not merely be a snide means of undermining women's linguistic agency. Miller may not be simply shoring up his own subject position by destabilizing that of marginalized others. He may not, as many scholars have put it, be "identifying women with nature" in order to "legitimiz[e] their lack of political rights."[7] These passages also point to an alternative or additional take on speech that recognizes its systemic or environmental character. By divorcing suffragists' linguistic activity from any obvious human speaker, Miller might be expressing less a sublimated fear of the suffragists' human agency or human subjectivity, and more a quite overt fear of suffragists' speech as something that operates beyond agency, beyond subjectivity, and beyond human politics. His concern might be less political and more ecological or environmental. When he identifies suffragists with animals, therefore, he is not necessarily doing so in order to play up the difference between humans and animals, and in turn to exclude suffragists from either category. His purpose is not necessarily to transform speaking women into incoherent nonsubjects. His point instead might be that the speech he witnessed ignored any such simple categorization—of nature, human, animal, subject, object, speaker, or listener—in favor of systems, environments, or networks.

Moreover, reframing these passages in such a way opens up an arena in which other questions might be posed. One might ask, for instance, whether Miller's decision to focus on the meaningless noises that the speakers make, rather than on their words, is necessarily an effort to deprive these speakers of their narrative authority. Is his purpose indeed to depict a situation in which suffragists can make only rattling, clattering sounds without meaning, or might it be to posit that the act of making rattling, clattering sounds itself has potential, harmful effects? The content-free character of the speech that Miller describes might instead be read in the same way that the content-free character of machine code has been read—not as a linguistic activity limited by its absence of meaning, but as a linguistic activity full of information, and therefore full of physical potential. At issue might be less the ability of suffragists to make their points understood than the capacity of suffragists' speech to work a given system or network.

In short, then, when agency and identity are not the starting point for analysis, it becomes possible to move away from readings that take speech as a purely human quality and that take the alteration or deprivation of this human speech as an oppressive act. Moreover, once speech is detached from human existence, it becomes possible to recognize the other things that speech might do. It is these other things that are the concern of the following seven chapters. Regardless of whether one thinks of agency in the more liberal vein as something that self-conscious actors appropriate for themselves and deny or allow to others, in a more critical vein as a process by which subjects are formed or destabilized within a given discursive field, or in a posthuman vein as something distributed among human and nonhuman networks, it is antithetical to the repositioning that this book is undertaking. There is nothing wrong with reading the *Boston Globe* article as one further illustration of the discursive violence that underlies modern, liberal politics. But an alternative reading might open worthwhile lines of inquiry, and such a reading is impossible in a vocabulary of agency.

Once again, therefore, each of the next seven chapters is devoted to one characteristic of suffragists' speech that observers found harmful or threatening. The first chapter discusses how this speech was understood to pose a threat to secularism, the second evaluates the theme of the speaking suffragist as monster, and the third retells the story of the stuttering or repetitive suffragist. The fourth, fifth, sixth, and seventh chapters describe, respectively, speaking suffragists as witches, suffragists' speech as akin to voices heard by the psychotic or insane, the apparent devotion of suffragists to theory or philosophy run amok, and finally suffragists' speech as a variation on dream speech. Each of these chapters starts by pointing out the limitations that the vocabulary of agency presents to alternative readings of these stories. Each then goes on to link the threatening speech of the suffragist to a type of proto-machine code, and thereby to describe the threat posed by this speech as environmental or systemic rather than political, social, or subjective. The following seven chapters thus represent not only an alternative history of the harmful speaking suffragist, but also a jumping off point for rethinking more general writing on speech, gender, and the physical world.

Chapter Five : Antisecular Speech

Suffragists, according to one pervasive Anglo-American story, posed a particularly pernicious threat to the secular nature of democratic politics. In part, this threat arose from the fact that women in general were understood to be irredeemably "priest-ridden,"[1] and that both the methods and goals of the suffragists—women demonstrating in public spaces and women voting—were therefore necessarily the brain child of a disgruntled and power hungry religious establishment.[2] In part, especially in the United States, this threat arose more from religious identity than from religious belief. The extension of the vote to all women, according to such analyses, would allow Catholics and Mormons—who were ostensibly incapable of appreciating secularism in the way that Protestants were—to take political power, which would in turn upset secular and democratic institutions.[3]

This chapter addresses neither of these aspects of the narrative of the antisecular suffragist. Instead, it is limited to a description of how suffragists' speech undermined something that quickly came to be defined as secular speech. As these stories make clear, each variation on the theme of the antisecular suffragist rested on the idea that a particular mode of speech—in which humans communicated meaning to other humans—served as an implicit foundation for a secular ordering of the environment. And each variation on this theme in turn posited suffragists' speech as, first, a type of nonhuman code—frighteningly irrelevant to the communication of meaning—and, second, therefore, a means of fracturing this foundation. Reading stories of the antisecular suffragist as stories more specifically of suffragists' antisecular speech thus provides an additional entry point to understanding how one mode of speech as code might disrupt emergent secular theories of the environment.

In some ways, this chapter thus draws on the work that traces a connection between, as Elaine Graham puts it, "cyberspace" and "sacred space."[4] Just as certain trends in technology studies posit that secularism is as vulnerable as other modern structures and ideologies to late twentieth- and early twenty-first-century technological change,[5] this chapter suggests that secularism was similarly vulnerable to the late nineteenth- and early twentieth-century shifts in linguistic activity that evoked or preceded that change. Where it departs from this work is in focusing on linguistic activity alone.

This chapter's retelling of the antisecular threat, that is to say, does not rest on the idea that digital existence, like divine existence, offers an escape from a corrupt, material physicality—an idea that Graham and others have convincingly argued is no different from the liberal humanist desire to escape embodiment.[6] Nor does it rest on the more sophisticated notion that secularism reinforces the same human versus other (in this case, human versus God, rather than human versus nature, human versus machine, human male versus not-quite-human woman, etc.) dichotomies that more prominent modernist ideologies do, and that the cybernetic challenge to these dichotomies must likewise challenge secularism.[7] As much as these two takes on computation and secularism remain in the background of this chapter, its primary point is instead much simpler than that. It is that these stories of suffragists' antisecular threat are stories of particular type of language—computational language—overwhelming a particular type of speech—secular speech—and simultaneously altering physical environments.

Once again, though, in order to get at these linguistic aspects of the suffragists' antisecular threat, it is necessary to set aside analytical frameworks reliant on agency. As Talal Asad has argued, the current vocabulary of agency has in many ways limited effective discussions of secularism writ large—and to the extent that agency is understood particularly to promote rational self-consciousness or the reasonable avoidance of pain, its invocation has led to an uncritical acceptance of secularism as a modern good.[8] Even the most sophisticated writing on agency and subjectivity, he continues, assumes that "power—and so too pain—is external to and repressive of the agent," and that "the agent as 'active subject' has both the desire to oppose power and the responsibility to become more powerful so that disempowerment—suffering—can be overcome."[9]

As a result, the writing that takes human agency as its starting point produces an arena of "blame and pain" that turns "a world of apparent accidents . . . into a world of essences by attributing to a person moral/legal responsibility on whose basis guilt and innocence (and therefore punishment or exoneration) are determined."[10] This writing pays inadequate "attention to the limits of the human body as a site of agency," and it fails to recognize that there are multiple ways of engaging with pain, fate, or suffering.[11] These particular invocations of agency, in other words, are in part responsible for reducing a multidimensional issue—secularism—into a story, first, of condemnation, indignation, and redress, second, of purely human subjects possessed of purely human bodies, and third, of activity (happiness) versus passivity (suffering).

In order to avoid this reductive line of reasoning or discussion, Asad encourages his readers to keep in mind the complexity of the relationships among agency, secularism, and representation. He argues, for example, that "agents need not necessarily coincide with individual biological bodies and the consciousness that is said to go with them."[12] Moreover, taking the story of Oedipus's self-mutilation as an example, he suggests that "acts *can* have an ethical significance without necessarily having to be interpreted in terms of 'answerability,'" as acts articulated in a vocabulary of human agency must.[13] Indeed, "Oedipus suffers," Asad argues, "not because he is guilty but because he is virtuous."[14] Finally, Asad states, "the idea of representation underlying agency is rooted in a paradox: that who or what is represented is both absent and present at the same time (re-presented). Theoretical representation, when the actor's body makes present someone who is absent, exemplifies in a different way the same paradox."[15]

Like many of the science studies scholars writing contemporaneously, Asad thus chooses not to abandon agency as a methodological tool altogether, but rather to reimagine it or redefine it as a concept that might operate without recourse solely to human bodies, human consciousness, or linear models of speech and representation. At the same time, however, Asad's work suggests the possibility, at least, that it might be equally useful—methodologically if not necessarily ethically—to think about secularism without invoking agency at all. When he argues, for instance, that there is no necessary coincidence between agents on the one hand and biological bodies or consciousness on the other—and

that the insistence on this coincidence derails effective analyses of secularism—he implicitly raises the question of whether it is useful, then, to
try to reconfigure agency or representation to begin with. Perhaps the
more effective way to think about secularism—and especially threats to
secularism—is to leave aside not just the human body or human consciousness as categories of analysis, but also the agency that seems always
to refer or return to them. Doing so allows broader interpretations of both
the ethics of unanswerability and the paradox of representation—interpretations that recognize the nonhuman, and thus nonsecular, implications of both.

Indeed, the paradox of simultaneous physical presence and absence
that rests at the heart of "the idea of representation underlying agency" is
no longer paradoxical when agency leaves the picture and when speech
is no longer a purely human activity. Rather, a state of simultaneous presence and absence becomes a given, something assumed, because speech
is about systems, networks, and information—things that are always both
present and absent—rather than about speakers, listeners, and messages—things that (*unless* paradoxical) must be either one or the other.
The state of being that was paradoxical when linked to agency, in other
words, becomes common sense when divorced from it. Linguistic activity
that relies on simultaneous presence and absence ceases to be impossible
and instead becomes the norm—while the ostensible problem of representation loses its coherence or centrality.

Likewise, an ethics of unanswerability becomes fundamental when
speech operates outside of the realm of agency and operates instead in the
realm of computation. Since speech has little to do with statements and
answers, and everything to do with operations and executions, Oedipus's
suffering and virtue make perfect sense. When agency is no longer the
starting point of analysis, it becomes possible to recognize modes of speech
that not only undermine secularism, but that are irrelevant to it. Instead
of talking about secularism in the language of secularism—and thereby reinforcing the idea that no universe or environment except a secular universe or environment is imaginable—discussions of secularism might
finally rely on other terms. More to the point, these discussions might recognize that at least one apparent threat to secularism—the threat posed
by the speaking suffragist—was not necessarily religious, social, or political, but linguistic, physical, and environmental. Whether the speaking
suffragist assaulted secular interpretations of Christianity, secular rational-

ism, or secular institutions, this assault was predicated on a particular linguistic activity altering a particularly ordered physical environment.

Secular Systems, Environmental Systems, and Antisecular Code

It may seem strange to start a section on the suffragists' attack on secularism with a reference to Horace Bushnell, a clergyman and a great believer in the salutary influence of Christianity on politics. But in addition
to providing a vocabulary to antisuffrage advocates for a number of
decades after it was published in 1869, Bushnell's book, *Reform Against
Nature*, also makes clear that one of the fundamental threats that the
speaking suffragist posed was a threat to secular linguistic structures, and
thus to secular environments. As much as he and other religious figures
promoted public or political forms of Christianity, that is to say, they also
promoted modes of speech reliant on humans communicating meaning
to other humans, on linear models of representation, and on clear distinctions among the physical, political, divine (and proto-computational) spheres.

As such, to the extent that Christianity would be public or political,
according to Bushnell, it would promote speech acts undertaken by rational, coherent, secular human subjects who had a stake in conserving
secular environments. To the extent that Bushnell and others condemned the women's suffrage movement from what they called a Christian perspective, therefore, they condemned the linguistic and environmental implications of this movement as well. Indeed, Bushnell's book is
in many ways quite similar both to the antisuffrage writing that was produced later by self-described secularists and to the prosuffrage writing
that situated suffragists' speech within, once again, an explicitly secular
world. All three described suffragists' speech as a threat to secular speech.
And all three described how this speech—by valorizing systems and information over speakers and meaning—altered secular environments
and spaces precisely as it went into operation.

Near the end of *Reform Against Nature*, for example, Bushnell argues
that voting women will diminish the number of believing Christians in
the United States, and that this diminution will negatively affect state,
citizen, and believing subject. "For women to buckle on the harness of

political life and challenge the right to fight common battles with men," Bushnell states, is inappropriate, as is the replacement of women's "subject nature" with a "self-willed governing nature."[16] Indeed, the result of this change "will be . . . that only half as many women will accept the cross . . . and the count of Christian men will also be reduced, because the number that have Christian wives who have grace to win their husbands is reduced."[17] Finally, Bushnell concludes, "if this reform is carried . . . the number of them [husbands] that believe will be greatly diminished, and whole centuries of toilsome progress will be lost, as it were, in a day."[18]

Once again, Bushnell's argument seems far removed from any that might censure suffragists for threatening secularism. In addition to stating that voting women will reduce the religious population of the United States, he hints that government itself is a divine institution and that voting women will subvert God's arrangement of society. The way in which Bushnell sets up his argument, however, suggests that he likewise understands suffragists' speech to be a threat not to religious, but to secular, linguistic structures. Whereas it is true, therefore, that one reading of this passage is that Bushnell is making a commonplace misogynist point about how women's strength or capacity lies in their "subject nature"[19]—in their very inferiority or selflessness, or in their subtle influence over men—and that any attempt to become "self-willed" agents themselves will undermine this God given sphere of activity,[20] alternative readings are also possible.

If the question of agency is set to the side, for example, the role that speech itself, absent human intention or human agency, plays in this passage becomes apparent. In addition to talking about who ought to be subjected and who ought to be self-willed, Bushnell also talks, first, about who has grace and who has belief, and second, how grace and belief ought to be expressed. More particularly, he defines grace as something that women *have* and belief as something that men—via women—*do*. The situation that "centuries of progress" has produced, and that would be lost with the advent of women's suffrage, then, refers to a situation in which women, with grace, in the private sphere, influence men to believe, in the public. Bushnell is indeed talking as much about where grace belongs and where belief belongs—or how grace operates or how belief operates—as he is about where women and men, as humans, belong.[21] Grace, *intransitively executed*, belongs in the private sphere, whereas belief, transitively undertaken or transmitted (implicitly by some agent), belongs in the public.

Moreover, these references to grace and belief (or faith) are not carelessly chosen. In his previous work, Bushnell developed a complex theory of each, in which grace, synonymous with inspiration, could never be "some *thing* separate from God which, as it were, God gives to the creature in preparation for the divine indwelling."[22] Rather than operating as "an intermediary between God and the human person," grace was the immediate "presence of God," or, put another way, "the ever-present personal act of favor on the part of God toward the human person," on which humans themselves "have no claim."[23] Grace was irrelevant to sin, and irrelevant indeed to any human activity or desire.[24] Belief, contrarily, was according to Bushnell, less "the acceptance of something in spite of the lack of evidence," and more a "reasonable," "intelligent," or objective relationship with God.[25] Unlike grace, therefore, which existed regardless of human intelligence or action, and which suggested inspired speech acts *detached* from any human subject or object, belief was situated, indeed grounded, in humans and their reason—reliant on linear linguistic structures that maintained a clear distinction between human and natural or divine other.

Another way of reading Bushnell's argument is thus that the particular destruction that suffragists will cause is not just the destruction of the private, domestic sphere per se. Women's suffrage means not, or not just, the reconfiguration of men's and women's gender roles or the unnatural desire in women for activity at the expense of passivity. Nor does suffrage mean, alone, the diminution of the believing Christian population. In addition, suffragists raise the specter of grace—rather than belief—becoming public. Bushnell, in other words, fears the removal from public life of the self-conscious, reasonable, linear linguistic and physical relationship to God that is *belief*, and its replacement with the impersonal, unmerited, chaotic accident that is *grace*. He fears a public sphere reliant less on a transitive linguistic relationship with God and more on the intransitive operation or execution of God's language.

Put another way, Bushnell fears the advent of an antisecular public sphere resting on an antisecular mode of speech. He fears a public sphere in which the situated, structured, human language of belief—a language that distinguishes clearly between human and God—gives way to the free-floating, inexplicable, nonhuman language of grace. Whereas the language of belief reinforces humanity's distinctiveness from nonhuman others, including God, the language of grace is irrelevant to such distinctions. Whereas the language of belief is concerned with messages, their content, and their effects on speakers or listeners, the language of grace is concerned only with the act of speaking itself, with its operation or exe-cutability. Grace happens (or, in a more computational language, *runs*) regardless of human guilt or innocence, regardless of human conscious-ness or unconsciousness, and regardless of human activities, desires, or intentions. Whereas the language of belief is answerable, the language of grace is unanswerable. Whereas the language of belief assumes a distinc-tion between presence and absence, assumes the importance of represen-tation, in order to uphold its linear structure, the language of grace as-sumes a simultaneity of the two in order to uphold its nonlinear structure. As such, the operations of grace cannot be secular—and to the extent that Bushnell attributes such operations to the speaking suffragist, he is likewise attributing to suffragists' speech a fundamentally antisecular, be-cause *nonhuman*, quality.

In this alternative reading of Bushnell's condemnation of suffrage, then, humans, their agency, and their identity are less important than speech and its operation. In this reading Bushnell is not condemning the activities of the suffragists because they presage the entry of women into the public sphere, or because such activities, grounded in women's bod-ies, are necessarily unruly or productive of disorder. This is not a rehash-ing of the arguments that have been made before about liberalism's tradi-tion of exclusion and sexism. Nor is it a repetition of the arguments that emphasize the production, or death, of subjects or citizens within existing patriarchal discourses. Rather, what is at stake in Bushnell's analysis is a particular mode of *nonhuman* speech, and its capacity to assault a partic-ular mode of *human* public life that—despite its links to Christianity—is fundamentally secular. Suffragists' speech causes harm because it disman-tles linear modes of linguistic activity, promises a different kind of—non-linear—physical, environmental, and spatial order,[26] and thereby renders the secular human within a secular physical environment irrelevant.

The extent to which suffragists' antisecular speech worked on spaces and environments indeed becomes even clearer in the writing of commen-tators who did not have a direct stake in the Christian character of the state. Frederick A. Maxse,[27] for example, wrote in England in 1884 that women were far more prone than men to "dignifying mere impulse with the name of 'religious feeling,'" and that this "religious feeling [would], at the time of an election, be made use of (especially in the case of lonely women) to oppose all movements of progress."[28] In response to John Stu-art Mill's argument that "the Priest's" influence over women existed only because he "[the Priest] is the only person who speaks seriously to her," Maxse invoked what he understood to be women's fundamental nature:

> women are highly emotional, they fear death more than men, and they are weak. The Priest appeals to their emotions. He offers them access to celestial joys, he abolishes death, and holds in reserve a method of alarm which few women are strong enough to despise. The dead can never return to refute his words. What sort of a rival is the Politician with his meager fare of doubtful benefit to others?[29]

On the one hand, these passages present the argument about suffrage and secularism as an argument solely over the relative vulnerability of "free institutions."[30] On the other hand, however, they also hint once again at a different or alternative fear—a fear of suffragists' linguistic activities, and what these activities might do, physically, to secular spaces or environments.

When Maxse, for instance, argues, first, that women equate religious feeling with impulse and, second, that women are attracted to priests but not politicians because the former but not the latter promise to women an end to death, he is making a distinct case for a relationship between suffragists' antisecular speech and the dismantling of the physical world. According to Maxse, suffragists threaten not just the entry of the irrational (impulse, feeling) into politics, not just the entry of a vaguely defined opposition to "all movements of progress" into politics, but, most prominently, the entry, via *conversation* with the priest, of *immortality* into politics. What Maxse fears is, explicitly, first, priests speaking to women and women speaking to priests, second, the dead not speaking at all, and third, the advent in turn of a new physical as much as political order. Indeed, he accuses antisecular suffragists of the same "disdain for the mortality of the flesh," arising from the same reconfiguration of speech acts, that many have found problematic in "technophilic" "postbiological" writing.[31]

This refusal to take death seriously on the part of suffragists does not, however—as it seems to in late twentieth-century postbiological writing—necessarily point solely to their hope that conversation, or, broadly, language, will liberate them as individuals from an impure or finite flesh-bound existence. Maxse's argument only starts with discrete speakers ("priests") persuading discrete listeners ("women") that death may be abolished through the abandonment of bodies. After making this point, he then uses the abolition of death as a rhetorical entrance for describing a different mode of antisecular speech, one in which priests, women, and silent dead people *together*—operating as a system with what are arguably computational tendencies—do something not *for* individual subjects but *to* the physical universe: together, through their speech activities, they make the physical certainty that is death as open to question as the political problem that is voting.[32]

Maxse is thus effectively attributing to suffragists' antisecular speech the potential, like code, to go into a frighteningly physical operation. Like code, suffragists' speech is irrelevant to any linear structure of statement and response or of representation—an irrelevance that is explicit in the case of the dead who cannot reply to the priest, and that is implicit in the end of progressive political debate. Also like code, however, suffragists' speech operates here precisely to the extent that it disrupts physical structures or leaves these structures open to reorganization. The antisecular threat posed by the speech of suffragists is, in other words, simultaneously, even if implicitly, an environmental threat. Just as Bushnell saw in suffragists' antisecular speech the dismantling of linear linguistic as spatial orders, that is to say, Maxse sees in it the reorganization of linear political as biological systems.

Code as a Concrete Threat

By the end of the nineteenth century this fear of what suffragists' speech might do to the environment had left the realm of theory and entered the realm of irrefutable concrete evidence. In the United States, many local governments had granted women partial school suffrage, and a spate of articles in various newspapers had chronicled the dismal (antisecular) results. These discussions were more often than not articulated in a language of subjectivity, agency, or identity—but, once again, alternative readings also present themselves. An 1894 *New York Times* article, for instance, extensively quoted Windsor Terrace school trustee Ferdinand Roth to the effect that women's school suffrage "was not only a failure, but it was a most insufferable nuisance," that "the very class of women whose duty it was to come to the polls," the Protestant women, refused to vote, whereas "the ignorant and prejudiced classes of women," the Roman Catholics, "came in a great body, all voted against me, and told me so too in terms more emphatic than elegant." Moreover, "it was this latter class who tried to bring religion into the contest."[33] The article concludes with a quotation by another educational expert:

> my experience has taught me that wherever women get the right to vote, religion and other questions that have no business there are carried to the ballot box, the passions of the people are inflamed by the appeals of unscrupulous persons to the religious and racial prejudices of the people, to the great injury and detriment of the individual and community at large.[34]

Nearly twenty years later, Charles L. Underhill, of the Men's Antisuffrage League of Massachusetts, made the same argument at a hearing in the United States House of Representatives on the desirability of a suffrage amendment. Arguing that women's school suffrage in Massachusetts "brought into our politics and schools the question of religion, a question that man has always tried to keep out of politics," Underhill told the story of "a young fellow 21 years of age," who

> took the question of religion and carried it into his campaign for the school committee, and he got the women in his vicinity, in my district, to register, and he was elected. This year the women of the opposite religious belief have gone into politics, and have gone to the city hall and registered in order that they may get out and fight some of the other religions. . . . [T]hey had a fight on the school committee on religious lines, and they registered almost 10,000 women there, and they fought it out along those lines. . . . [T]he question of religion is going to predominate in our politics, because the women introduced it. It has been kept out of politics by the men.[35]

The theoretical fears articulated by Maxse have thus reached their practical conclusion in these passages: rational political progress becomes impossible when religious identity rules the polls. These school suffrage passages indeed seem inextricably linked to a rhetoric of religious (and class and race) identity. The apparently fundamental argument in both is that women's antisecularism, and thus women's suffrage, leads directly to religious, class, and race antagonisms—that the antisecular nature of suffragists' speech produces a politics of identity-based hatred. As long as men kept religion "out" of politics, these identity issues were muted in favor of the more important questions of education and civilization.

At the same time, however, it is telling that what serves as shorthand for this danger inherent in the suffragist's antisecular speech is the notion of "great bodies" or huge numbers ("almost 10,000") of people speaking at once in a sort of cacophony—making irrelevant, invisible, or meaningless the well-considered ideas of the thinking "individual" or "community." According to these analyses, in other words, the threat posed by the antisecular speaking suffragist is at heart a threat to distinct, specific human speech acts that might operate as a basis for community action. It is a threat to the idea, first, that speech might be grounded or embodied in an individual human, and second, that the field of discourse formed by this speech might produce a political community.

Put another way, instead of engaging in human-centered modes of speech—predicated on speakers, listeners, and messages with content—suffragists' antisecular speech in these passages defies human debate or conversation and ignores messages or content. The linguistic activity of the antisecular speaking suffragist indeed operates, according to these stories, beyond bodies or consciousness, in a realm of abstract numbers or immeasurable organisms. Or, more provocatively, suffragists' linguistic activities here privilege a theory of information that is explicitly "divorced from meaning," and linked rather to "randomness"[36]—a theory of speech predicated on executability rather than on message.

Although it is related to fears of mass democracy or mob rule, therefore, this variation on the story of the antisecular suffragist is also distinct from these early twentieth-century concerns. The problem with suffragists' speech is not just that the great body it creates is irrational, or that this body lacks discernment. The problem is that, like "grace" in Bushnell's analysis, this body is nonhuman—its activities sever any plausible link between individual human consciousness on the one hand and linguistic activity on the other. Once again, Roth is distressed not that the "great body" voted against him, but that it *told him so*.

And the reason that this seemingly redundant act is so galling to him is that, without human consciousness or bodily boundaries, the body or system that speaks is immune to any reply that Roth as an individual might make. The great body's speech is in this sense operational rather than conversational—its performance as much physical or environmental as it is political. In addition to eliminating Roth from the political sphere, that is to say, the antisecular speech of the suffragists also replaces an environment made up of bounded, interactive bodies with an alternative environment of one body or one system that encroaches, engulfs, expands, and defies interaction. It makes good on the computational, rather than political, religious, or sociological, promise at the basis of Bushnell's and Maxse's more theoretical writing.

Antisecular Theories of Electoral Politics

This alternative reading of the suffragists' linguistic threat to secular institutions thus implies, at least, that writers during this period were beginning to imagine a likewise alternative theory of electoral politics—a theory predicated on nonhuman speech, computational language, the impossibility of replies, responses, or answers, and the simultaneous disruption of environmental and political worlds. One of the more overt areas in which this theory of electoral politics played out was in the writing that posited women's votes, especially, to be identical to prayers offered up to God. Nineteenth-century prosuffrage advocates were particularly attracted to this line of argument, and frequently made the case that, to the extent that votes were prayers, women had as much of a right to vote as men had. In 1885, for example, the Reverend Charles H. Eaton suggested in an editorial in the *New York Times* that "woman" should have a say in the "the laws that govern her" precisely because women's "prayers to God" have no less effect than those "uttered by a man."[37]

A number of years earlier, John Weiss developed a more extensive theory of voting, based on the proposition that "a vote is a prayer," and that "a voter extols and offers up something to which he is devoted. He is a votary of ideas and measures, and hastens to lend his voice to the great supplication of a country as it gathers its life together into the special providence that answers prayers."[38] As a result, Weiss concluded,

> all the men should say, "If woman does not want to vote, still we want to have her vote: her moral judgment must be represented; her voice must re-enforce the feeble and tottering majorities of right. It is a matter of life and death to the country to let loose all the purity and truth we can command."[39]

This notion that voting, like prayer, is a unique mode of speech, beyond individual desire, appeared in the work of antisuffrage advocates as well. Although his position rested less on the idea that a vote is a prayer, and more on men's and women's fundamental natures, J. M. Buckley argued in his "Wrongs and Perils of Woman Suffrage" that casting a ballot "is not the mere dropping of a piece of paper, for it implies the whole mode of thinking, feeling, and acting, of which a vote is the concentrated expression . . . [T]o vote intelligently is to think and act in the imperative [masculine] mood."[40]

All three of these analyses follow familiar lines of nineteenth-century argument. Eaton links governance to human equality, Weiss subordinates women's desire to men's ("our") desire, and then men's desire to the greater good of the country, and Buckley states that governance is a natural masculine quality. But there is also more going on here than a simple rearticulation of the authoritarian theories of democracy that emphasized universal human dignity, the good of the state, or traditional modes of sexual behavior over the liberty of the individual. In addition to making these more established points, the three passages also describe a distinct, and arguably computational, relationship among suffragists' speech, women's votes, and secular speech.

In the first two passages, for example, a vote is "a prayer," whereas in the third, to vote is to act in the imperative mood. Women's votes, or votes in general, are thus imagined here first and foremost as speech acts that are purely operational, and that by definition invite no reply. They are as far removed from the realm of human agency as it is possible to be. In none of the three passages does voting have to do with embodied or self-conscious humans entering into some symbolic realm of politics, where choices and decisions lead in a linear way to foreseeable outcomes.[41] Like prayer, voting is a nonlinear invocation of the divine. It is both speech and operation. It is nothing more nor less than the running of a simultaneously political, physical, and divine code.

In the imperative mood, voting likewise becomes, by definition, an unanswerable physical act.[42] Like code, it is performative in the way that Hayles reading Austin understands performativity—it is a mode of speech that changes the system in which it operates not incidentally, but definitively, as a prerequisite to its definition *as* speech.[43] Indeed, if suffragists' speech turns votes into prayers, and voters into, as Weiss states, "votaries," then voters explicitly become tools, containers, instruments, or, more precisely, pathways or nodes for speech writ large. In the process, their existence as humans becomes less important than their existence as interchangeable conduits for a linguistic code that exists only to the extent that it alters the system or world around it.

These discussions of the antisecular quality of suffragists' speech can thus in many ways be read as precursors to a fundamental reimagining of electoral politics in the computational mode. They can be read as stories of language—political, physical, and otherwise—that operates itself, on its own, as an unanswerable thing, rather than being mobilized by human (or nonhuman) agents, as a tool in aid of communication, recognition, or representation. As a result, this reinterpretation of the story of the anti-secular suffragist can be read not just as a story of the oppression of women, of the problem of representation, or of the reification of traditional gender roles. It can also, and perhaps more profitably, be read as a preface to twentieth- and twenty-first-century theories of speech, computation, politics, and environmental space.

Conclusion

That these stories of suffragists and secularism did usher in a twentieth- and twenty-first-century theory of antisecular speech as computational speech with distinct environmental implications becomes apparent in more recent discussions of antisecular assaults on democracy. Most of these discussions do not address women or gender explicitly. Nor are they overtly concerned with the nonhuman, mechanical, or physical characteristics of antisecular speech. They do, though, make clear that the nineteenth-century harm caused by suffragists' antisecular speech is remarkably similar to the twenty-first-century harm that antisecular speech, more generally defined, has done. Indeed, in the late twentieth and early twenty-first centuries as well, narratives of antisecular harm only *start* with human agency or identity—before lending themselves equally well to a reading from the perspective of code.

In June 2005, for example, the U.S. Supreme Court ruled in *Van Orden v. Perry* that a monument depicting the Ten Commandments on the grounds of the Texas state capitol did not violate the Constitution's establishment clause—that is to say, the monument did not represent a threat to the secular nature of United States politics. Both this plurality decision and the opinions that dissented from it were couched, first and foremost, in a language of humans and human politics—each based on the assumption that antisecular speech potentially coerced free individuals, weakened American political structures, and produced divisive, identity-based violence.

Underlying the stories surrounding the case, in other words, were three questions: whether the monument threatened the individual citizen's capacity to make free choices, whether it undermined the state's capacity to produce public arenas in which these choices might occur, and whether it hampered the social collective's capacity to tolerate these choices and to build unity out of them. If the monument did pose such a threat, it was antisecular. If not, then it was not.[44] The ruling, its fallout, and the narratives driving it were thus, at least at first glance, very much in keeping with the rhetoric of agency and identity on which traditional discussions of law, rights, and secularism rely.

At the same time, however, it is likewise possible to interpret the discussion surrounding *Van Orden* from the vantage point of nonhuman linguistic activity. It is possible to emphasize the systemic, computational, and environmental aspects of the case, rather than its human and social aspects. Doing so makes clear that as much as the Supreme Court's rulings on secularism are concerned with choice, identity, or agency, they are also a legacy of an alternative narrative of antisecular linguistic threats. As much as antisecular speech in the twenty-first century might be defined via its work by, for, and against humans, that is to say, it also bears a striking resemblance to nineteenth-century suffragists' speech— altering physical spaces and shifting environmental systems even as it silences, empowers, frees, or coerces individuals.

Justice Clarence Thomas's opinion upholding the plurality decision in *Van Orden*, for instance, rests on a series of examples of incorrect designations of antisecular speech—of rulings that determined inoffensive monuments to pose antisecular threats. One of the most telling of these examples concerns "a park ranger" who "claimed that a cross erected to honor World War I veterans on a rock in the Mojave Desert Preserve violated the Establishment Clause, and won."[45] In referencing this ruling, Thomas argues that "if a cross in the middle of a desert establishes a religion, then no religious observance is safe from challenge."[46] He indeed uses the ruling as a means of driving home his point that such far-reaching or extensive definitions of antisecular speech irresponsibly draw attention away from the true (human, political) threats that antisecular speech might pose—threats, Thomas reiterates, to an individual citizen's choice, will, and belief.

Leaving aside what Thomas *intended* in making this argument, however—reading his statements within the nonhuman historical contexts and methodological frameworks suggested by this chapter's stories of suffragists' speech—additional threats lurking in antisecular linguistic activity begin to reveal themselves. For instance, the park ranger's claim is, according to this passage, a particularly absurd example of the exaggerated scope of the antisecular threat above all because of the *placement* of the cross, on a rock, in the middle of the desert. The fact that the cross is in a desert is repeatedly mentioned in the text, twice over the course of two consecutive sentences. What this passage suggests, therefore, is that if the cross does *not* change the desert—if the desert remains the desert, unharmed, unchanged, and incapable of being changed, even with the cross sitting in the middle of it—then the cross cannot pose an antisecular threat. Put differently, since the cross does not pose an *environmental* threat, it cannot pose an antisecular one.

Antisecular speech thereby becomes here not just speech that physically or financially coerces individuals, forcing them to act against their beliefs, interests, or wills, but (if implicitly) speech that changes, harms, or alters the physical world in which it is embedded. The cross in the desert does not change the desert. Using more provocative terms, the cross in the desert fails to execute—it fails to shift a physically defined space or system. It is therefore not only not antisecular speech, but not speech at all. The desert remains the desert, distinct from the cross—and in fact so much the desert that Thomas does not need to explain why being in the desert should render the cross so anodyne.

Once again, the purpose of rereading *Van Orden* in this way is not to insist that Justice Thomas *intended* to highlight the environmental, computational, or systemic aspects of threatening antisecular speech. Rather, it is to note that the environmental, computational, and systemic aspects of antisecular speech remain at least present in narratives of the harm that such speech might do, even if these aspects are not the central interest of those who speak about that harm. It is to make clear that, regardless of their focus on human agency, identity, belief, and will, the justices of the Court are also repeating, reiterating, and resituating nonhuman themes, divorced from agency, that are left over from the computational stories of the nineteenth-century. It is to demonstrate that fragments of suffragists' antisecular speech as code continue to operate—even if the environments and systems in which they are embedded include parks, deserts, or for that matter the steps of the Texas state capitol.

As delicate as it is, there does thus seem to be a link connecting the nineteenth-century rhetoric of the antisecular speaking suffragist to the twenty-first-century rhetoric of antisecular threats to the state. Although each *can* make sense within a framework of human agency, or for that matter, nonhuman agency, this framework is not the only one available.

Indeed, once the question of agency leaves the picture, a number of other ways of reading these stories of antisecular harm present themselves.

In particular, it becomes clear that stories of both the suffragist's and the monument's threat to secularism can also be read as stories of linguistic threats to physical environments. These are stories of a type of speech that not only allows for, but insists on, simultaneous presence and absence, on the irrelevance of representation, on the defiance of embodied human existence, and on the valorization of constantly shifting networks, systems, or environments. These are stories of a linguistic activity that occurs outside the realm of subject and object, outside the realm of human and nonhuman, and outside the realm of statement or question and answer. And finally, as a result, these are stories that perhaps explain in a more satisfactory way the ongoing humanist (or just anthropocentric) fear of antisecularism writ large—as well as the more distilled fear of antisecularism expressed in suffragists' threatening speech.

Chapter Six : Monsters (a Bridge)

Monstrosity has been a key component of much writing that challenges conventional models of humanist subjectivity and agency. Whether the monster demonstrates "the 'leakiness' of bodily boundaries," and thereby "the redundancy and instability of the ontological hygiene of the humanist subject,"[1] whether it exposes the "mingling of the subjectivity we attribute to characters, authors, and ourselves as users with the non-anthropomorphic actions of the computer program,"[2] or whether it "terrifies," semiotically rather than physically, "with its unprecedented deformation of the normal and its threat to the boundaries of conventional thought,"[3] it has been an effective means of emphasizing the impossibility of bounded, self-conscious human existence. Although this chapter rests on the assumed validity of this work, it does not continue in this vein. Subjectivity—whether Cartesian, hybrid, dissolved, or dispersed—is not its interest, and agency is an issue only to the extent that excessive methodological reliance on it has blocked conversation in other directions.

Instead, this chapter is limited to a rereading of the story of suffragists' monstrous *speech*, and to two methods by which this rereading might build a bridge between the previous chapter devoted to antisecular speech and the next chapter devoted to repetitive speech. The first of these methods is the further development of the argument that suffragists' speech terrified onlookers or observers *particularly* because it resembled an early type of machine code. Like narratives of their antisecular speech, that is to say, narratives of suffragists' monstrous speech were a means of expressing a more fundamental fear of a distinctly nonhuman

linguistic activity. The second method is the explicit discussion of one issue that might potentially cause confusion over the next chapters—
namely the role that nature plays in this book.

Although the system that suffragists' speech assaulted is usually described here as the physical world or the physical environment, there is
an implication at least—especially in the titles of the nineteenth- and
early twentieth-century work on women's suffrage—that what is really at
stake in discussions of women, speech, and the vote is something called
nature. Rather than ignoring these references to nature in the suffrage
writing, or dismissing them with the argument that the "nature" they invoke is a metaphor—a means of reinforcing convenient political or ideological positions—this chapter posits that it might be worthwhile to take
invocations of nature at face value. Other scholars have discussed or critiqued at length the political, ideological, and rhetorical uses of nature.[4]
This chapter instead asks what it might mean for nature *not* to be a purely
rhetorical concept—it considers the possibility that a distinct physical
system, nature, was indeed threatened by a particular linguistic activity,
suffragists' speech.

The natural, in other words, appears in this chapter in an unironic
way, as do the nineteenth- and early twentieth-century discussions that
describe the speaking suffragist as natural, unnatural, or in relation to nature. As much as these discussions appear to be straightforward examples
of nature used rhetorically to reinforce traditional sexual, social, or political hierarchies, that is to say, they also allow an alternative reading. Passages describing suffragists as horrific, sexually indeterminate monsters
need not be simply one further example of the rhetoric of nature undermining the agency of those who do not conform to normative political or
gender roles. They might also be, with equal validity, part of a well-
defined nineteenth-century theory of nonhuman language, proto-computational systems, and the environment. If agency is sidelined, it in fact
becomes clear that the threat that the monstrous speaking suffragist
posed was the same threat that a certain type of computational language
posed—to physical, rather than rhetorical, natural worlds.

Theorizing the Monster

The work of Latour and of Foucault lends itself especially well to this
unironic reading of nature and monstrous speech. In his *Politics of Na-*

ture, for instance, Latour takes the empirical rather than rhetorical problems posed by nature as well as monsters seriously—describing this fear of
the latter as, most commonly, a fear of the confusion of subject and object. He continues, however, by noting that if one detaches "the terms
'object' and 'subject'" from "their claim to describe domains of reality," it
becomes "possible to resist the *supposed monstrosity of their confrontation*.
What is a subject, actually? That which resists naturalization. What is an
object? That which resists subjectivization."[5] As long as "subject" and
"object" remain the primary means of describing "domains of reality," in
other words, being simultaneously subject and object is—or can be read
as—a monstrous notion. As long as the division between subject and object remains the fundamental division of reality, anything that resists
both naturalization *and* subjectivization is necessarily a monstrosity.

But if the distinction between subject and object evaporates—or,
more pointedly, if the rhetoric of human agency that valorizes subjectivity
and denigrates objectification is ignored—such simultaneity need not be
read as monstrous. By leaving aside this distinction, one can indeed read
the stories of, say, the monstrous "man-woman" or "third sex" that appear
with such frequency in the pro- and antisuffrage writing as something
other than examples of women's subject positions being undermined via
reference to their object status. If, that is to say, the collision between subject and object—or the collision between things that resist naturalization
and things that resist subjectivization—is not the methodological starting
point, the monstrosity of these figures might be linked to other qualities.
If the man-woman and third sex are described as monstrous not because
they upset conventional categories of subject and object, then their status
as monsters might be traced to other—linguistic—characteristics.

But what might these other, linguistic, characteristics be? One such
take on linguistic monstrosity appears in Foucault's discussion of law, nature, and the monstrous in his series of lectures *Abnormal*. In these lectures, Foucault defines the monstrous as "a breach of the law" that
nonetheless "does not bring about a legal response from the law."[6] He
elaborates on this point by arguing that "the monster's power and its capacity to create anxiety are due to the fact that it violates the law while
leaving it with nothing to say. It traps the law while breaching it."[7] A few
pages later, he continues that monstrosity

> is that kind of natural irregularity that calls law into question and
> disables it. Law must either question its own foundations, or its

practice, or fall silent, or abdicate, or appeal to another reference system, or again invent a casuistry. Essentially, the monster is the casuistry that is necessarily introduced into law by the confusion of nature.[8]

There are, then, two linguistic problems that the monster potentially poses, in this case with respect to legal structures. The first is that the monster's mode of speech is predicated, familiarly, on speech's unanswerability. The monster leaves the law, bluntly, with nothing left to say. Like the formless speaking numbers that so angered Windsor Terrace school trustee Ferdinand Roth, the monster's linguistic activity here, its breach of the law, makes interactive speech impossible. The monster assumes the validity of a linguistic system in which reply and response are irrelevant. Key to monstrous speech according to this first passage, then, is its capacity to execute or to operate—to breach or violate a legal or linguistic system—and thereby to leave speakers with no meaning to convey.

Second, and related, the monster demonstrates law's basis in casuistry. By being the natural exception to the legal or linguistic norm, the monster highlights, according to Foucault, the absurdity of applying general legal or linguistic rules to particular physical or natural cases (i.e., it highlight's law's casuistry). The monster plays up the senselessness of abstract rules in the face of concrete physical existence.

One conclusion to draw from this interpretation of monstrosity is that therefore any attempt to order or organize specific physical or natural cases according to legal or linguistic systems is impossible (or unethical)—and this is a reading of Foucault's work on monstrosity and taxonomy that has become relatively common.[9] This is not, however, the only conclusion that Foucault's discussion of the monster suggests. Indeed, rather than simply demonstrating the problems inherent in any impetus toward linguistic order or taxonomic structure[10]—and demonstrating thereby, more often than not, the problems inherent in the subjectivities that are derived from such an impetus—the monster as it is described here also points to the possibility of a complete reinterpretation of the relationship between language and nature.

Put another way, rather than showing that linguistic representations of the physical world are doomed to failure, the monster, according to this analysis, also shows that the only language that can work in these contexts is a language that is itself a physical or natural operation. The monster's role in highlighting the various problems of representation is thus not simply to point out that indeed there is an insurmountable gulf between language and what it describes. It is also to set aside the notion that language exists to describe or represent anything at all. The problem with language that the monster uncovers, therefore, is not necessarily *just* that language tries to be physical and fails. It is that language is not yet physical enough—that language remains impossibly reliant on message and meaning, while ignoring operation and execution. In addition to assuming a linguistic system in which speakers, their statements, and their responses or replies are largely irrelevant, then, monstrous speech here also appears as a sort of machine code—as a physical operation—that makes human language irrelevant because of human language's impossible reliance on description and representation.

As much as stories of the monstrous speaking suffragist—especially to the extent that these stories are articulated in a sexual vocabulary—seem to cry out for a reading via agency, identity, or subjectivity, therefore, they can also be read as stories of a horrific confrontation between two modes of speech. The theme of the suffragist as monster demonstrates not simply the staying power of oppressive theories of "the natural" that objectify some and allow others to maintain active human subject positions. This theme also points to a fear of linguistic systems that leave speakers with no message to convey—to a fear that language might exist not to the extent that it conveys meaning or *represents* the natural world, but to the extent that it physically *alters* the natural world. Moreover, it points to the fear that this second mode of language is in fact the most important one. The theme of the suffragist's monstrous speech is not simply a fear of the disorder that certain types of embodied speech might cause. It is a fear of an alternative order based on physical, rather than abstract, linguistic operations, in which embodiment and representation are largely beside the point.

Freaks, Men-Women, Chimeras, and the Third Sex

References to the horror of men and women somehow merging or losing sight of their proper places were common in the discussions surrounding women's suffrage from the mid-nineteenth century through the 1920s. Equally frequent were invocations of the monstrous nature of suffragists' speech. An 1869 review of Bushnell's *Reform Against Nature*, for instance, argued that if the "little book is read as it should be, it will quiet all minds but the few women [*sic*] who want to be men and can't."[11] In 1870, a *New York Times* article on the oddity of women's suffrage conventions described one woman suggesting "*sotto voce*, that at the next meeting they engage the two-headed girl to speak."[12] By the mid-1870s, the prospect of suffrage fomenting transvestitism or transsexuality appeared with increasing frequency in the form of passages in which, for instance,

> Dr. Z. RODGERS, recently from Chicago, appeared last night at the Woman's Suffrage Convention in this city [San Francisco], having one-half of his face shaved, the beard and whiskers remaining upon the other half, and announced that he did it in recognition of the fact that man was half man and half woman. He was arrested and sent to the insane asylum today.[13]

In a similarly surreal take on this aspect of suffragists' speech, the *Boston Globe* ran an article in 1894 discussing how "placarded boys" were "forced to speak on woman's suffrage" when the "Phi Sigma Rho fraternity of the Boston University law school"

> held an initiation and courted notoriety by parading their initiates through the streets. . . . [T]he company halted in front of a restaurant in newspaper row and made one of the blindfolded victims give a speech upon woman's suffrage to the passers by. Then the initiate was made to partake of milk from out of a nursing bottle. The company then crossed the street and gave a similar performance before The Globe building.[14]

Finally, in a discussion of the "grotesque element" of the women's suffrage movement, a writer critiques the excessively "free" character of the "free platform"—where "liberty may degenerate into license"—by emphasizing above all the "queer and crazy" figures who populate the environment surrounding the suffragists, including a "fearful little person" who was "dressed like a man, with a woman's hair streaming down her back, who flapped her arms like a bat."[15]

By the early twentieth century, the template thus already existed for conversations surrounding the monstrous speaking suffragist. In general, these conversations followed two paths. The first described the various ways in which suffragists' speech might twist or warp the human form in monstrous or abnormal ways. The second described suffragists' speech itself as fantastic, bizarre, and therefore monstrous. A 1909 *New York Times* article, entitled "New Woman a Freak, Says Bishop Doane: One Who Strives for Man's Work 'a Horrible, Misshapen Monster,' he Declares: Sees Suffragists' Doom," discussed a speech given by Bishop William Croswell Doane on the various evils inherent in the suffrage movement and women's movements more generally. Doane begins by following the first of the two conversational paths, arguing that "nothing but mischief and misery and confusion worse confounded can come from the attempt to make the two [woman and man] the same. The masculine woman, the effeminate man, like bearded women or a long-haired man, is a lusus naturae, a monstrum horrendum informe."[16] He concludes, however, with a detour onto the second path, addressing the "howling-dervish performances of the so-called Suffragettes," and the "hysterical clamor which is employed in the pursuit of this chimera."[17] The specifically "chimerical" nature of suffragists' goals and speech appeared with some frequency in his writing on the subject, the movement defined in a second article as a chimera because it was "all illusion and caprice."[18]

By World War I, each of these paths had reached its logical conclusion. The discussions of physical monstrosity, for instance, had resulted in extensive scientific analyses of the problem of the "third sex." As W. W. Gregg described it in a 1918 *New York Times* article, individuals who "live outside of normal marriage relations" or who "are not the parents of at least the minimum number of two or three children necessary to maintain the race," are likely members of "a kind of third or neuter sex and as in many respects comparable to that class of imperfect and sterile females in the insect world known as workers and easily distinguished in the hive or nest from the males and the queens or true females."[19] What Gregg wants readers to keep in mind about the emergence of this third sex, though, is less the interesting zoological lesson to be learned from it, and more its political consequences. As the article continues,

> if we bear in mind that the average male political leader and the average male voter have always belonged to the same non-third-sex class, while the new female political leaders are for the most part of the third sex and therefore not of the same class as the majority of those whom they claim to represent, can it be expected that the stream of legislation due to these women leaders will be practically determined, similarly as heretofore, in the case of men, by the views

of the average woman voter? . . . [T]he history of the suffrage movement in the past few years exemplifies at every turn the power of a
skillfully used minority to enforce its will against an unorganized
majority.[20]

The most straightforward reading of this passage is thus that there is a direct connection between the disintegration of a two-sex order and the
disintegration of a properly representative government.

The second path reached a similarly hyperbolic end point by World
War I. Here, however, the fear was of the monster that was suffragists'
speech emasculating the state, the electorate, or men themselves. To provide just a few examples: in an address to the New York State Senate in
1916, Senator Henry M. Sage reminded his colleagues of the horrors of
the woman who "gets the upper hand," asking them: "why didn't you recall the story of Samson and Dalilah [sic]? Remember what Circe did
when she got men under her control—she turned them into swine and
drove them over a precipice."[21] In 1917, an editorialist similarly argued
that "our first duty is to remasculinize America; and . . . to this end we in
this State must stand as a wall against the wave of effeminacy which now
threatens the semi-emasculation of our electorate."[22] In 1918, Mary G.
Kilbreth, a prominent antisuffragist, went a step further, stating that the
House of Representatives had been frightened into submission "by the
phantom female vote—the 'woman's vote' that the suffragists have never
been able to deliver," and that as a result,

> representative government has been wrecked; the people's repre-
> sentatives have been routed—stampeded—by the women politi-
> cians. A woman autocracy has been established in the nation's cap-
> ital. Will the people tamely submit to the yoke? The French dealt
> summarily with women politicians after the French Revolution, but
> the French are a virile race. Are we? Suffragists assure us we are not,
> and they are proving their case. . . . [I]t will be the task of anti-suf-
> fragists to use their ballots to put men in politics who have not yet
> lost all the male instincts of domination and sovereignty.[23]

In this final passage, therefore, suffragists' speech is simultaneously a
phantom, autocratic in the style of old regime France, and a direct threat
to "all the male instincts of domination and sovereignty."

And once again, each of these passages can effectively be read as an example of the unnatural monster mobilized rhetorically in order to deprive women of their agency. The man-woman is both threatening and despicable, both active subject out to destroy representative government or undermine the virility of the state, and passive object of contempt, disgust, or cold scientific inquiry. The speaking suffragist as sexually indeterminate monster is never quite coherent as subject *or* object, and is incapable therefore of operating as an agent or of overcoming her objectification.[24] The purpose of invoking the monster, given this analysis, is nothing more nor less than to expel the speaking suffragist from the human world of agency, identity, and human subjectivity.

According to such a reading, nature, or more specifically, the unnatural, is thereby a framework for thinking about metaphysical human existence rather than a framework for thinking about physical environments. Nature is understood to be a means of categorizing subject and object, and nineteenth- or early twentieth-century invocations of nature are understood to demonstrate nothing more than the oppressive or authoritarian implications of such categorizations. Regardless of whether this reading proposes the abandonment of nature altogether as an analytical concept, or a progressive redefinition of nature such that those deemed "unnatural"—because outside of traditional subject and object relations—become "natural," or such that the natural itself be endowed with agency, it reinforces the idea that any discussion of nature must be grounded in an analysis of human subjects and nonhuman objects. As a corollary, any discussion of monsters, monstrosity, and nature will seek, in this reading, to describe, or to critique, historical methods of defining who or what is a subject, who or what is an object, and who or what might be freakishly beyond such taxonomies.

If, however, human agency and subjectivity—along with the references to subject and object that agency and subjectivity seem to demand—are left out of the discussion, then these stories of the monstrous speaking suffragist can be read in alternative ways. In particular, these stories seem to point to a fear that suffragists' speech will alter or assault physical or natural *environments*—to a fear that the human modes of speech that represent nature and convey meaning will give way to nonhuman modes of speech that change nature and ignore meaning. Indeed, both strands in the narrative of the monstrous speaking suffragist—both the story of physically abnormal suffragist and the story of the fantastic, bizarre, or magical character of suffragists' speech—lend themselves to readings that highlight not the monster's potential disordering effects, but its potential to shift physical, natural, and environmental lines.

When the *New York Times* notes that an appropriate addition to the women's suffrage platform might be the two-headed girl or the half-shaven lunatic man, for instance, the point is not just that suffragists belong in a freak show. It is not just that suffragists' speech, like the freak, is incoherent, disordered, or out of place. These articles are also making a point about how precisely suffragists' speech operates. Suffragists' speech, in this narrative, is not in and of itself disordered, nor does it produce disorder. Instead, according to these articles, suffragists' speech executes a linguistic system predicated on physical, natural, and environmental change. The *New York Times*, that is to say, understands suffragists' speech *as* speech only when the concrete, physical exception—the freak—is, as code, quite literally added to the program.

Moreover, it is in these stories *only* speech, and not the speaker, that operates in this way. The extent to which the linguistic threat is based on the character of speech itself rather than on the identity of the women who are speaking, for instance, becomes explicit in the *Boston Globe* article, where it is specifically "boys" who now become nodes within the harmful linguistic system. Whereas it is true that the fundamental purpose of fraternity hazing is simultaneously to emasculate its victims and to reinforce preexisting gender identity hierarchies,[25] the hazing here also points to a fear of what, beyond or aside from politics, suffragists speech might do.

Indeed, by forcing the blindfolded initiate to talk, specifically, about women's suffrage—and by turning this speech about suffrage into the centerpiece of their disruption of the spaces around them—the fraternity is actually demonstrating the complicated and multidimensional *environmental* quality of this speech. The boy dressed and speaking as a woman, in other words, presumably against his will, demonstrates *both*, in a traditional misogynist way, the absurdity or undesirability of women occupying public space *and also* the capacity of suffragists' monstrous speech to alter and disturb the physical spaces within which it runs.

Suffragists' speech, according to these rereadings, then, is both speech and monstrous because it comes into effect precisely as physical changes or abnormalities appear. It is a linguistic system that rests on changes to a physical system—on adding the freak to the program. Or, put another way, whereas legal speech, according to Foucault, came up silent when faced with the casuistry that the monster introduced into the system, suffragists' speech executes only when this casuistry is revealed. It is only when abstract, general rules collide with concrete, monstrous exceptions that the necessity for this physical, rather than representational, mode of speech becomes apparent. Far from frightening its onlookers because it threatened disorder or an end to comforting taxonomies, therefore, this speech frightened its onlookers because it raised the possibility of a different sort of order, an order resting on information rather than knowledge, and an order predicated on the overlap—rather than distinction—between linguistic activity and natural or environmental change.

This aspect of the monstrous quality of suffragists' speech becomes more pronounced in Doane's address to the girl's school and in the scientific discussions of the third sex. In the first, there is the move away from excoriating this mode of speech as something that produces physical abnormality and toward doing so because it is fantastical, hysterical, bizarre, and chimerical. The repeated return to the chimera is particularly telling, in that it explicitly brings together these subjective and systemic, as well as physical and linguistic, threats. In classical mythology the chimera is monstrous both in and of itself—a vaguely female combination of various animal parts all operating together—and because its existence presages natural disaster. According to the popular early twentieth-century botanical usage of the term, the chimera likewise posed simultaneously physical, linguistic, subjective, and systemic problems. Unlike the "true" hybrid, which blends together two forms, a "chimera" is instead a "peculiar structure," in which two discrete plants both combine and remain distinct.[26]

To the extent that suffragists' speech is chimerical in these analyses, then, it is not just because it is illusory or fantastic. It is not just because it, itself, is a physical oddity. Suffragists' speech is chimerical because its individual physical oddity points to, presages, or produces systemic changes (for instance natural disaster). In the first, the monstrous combination of animal, human, and sexual forms becomes code for the likewise monstrous alteration or mutation of nature that is the catastrophic flood, earthquake, or volcano. In the second, this same monstrous combination of forms, unlike the hybrid's, is not about alterations to a specific plant, but about alterations to the taxonomic structure in which plants operate. Doane's rhetorical movement between the physical and linguistic threats posed by suffragists' monstrous speech, in other words, and his invocation of the chimera as the most typical manifestation of this threat, suggests as much a fear of systemic or environmental change as a fear of particular, specific, or concrete mutations and freaks.

The discussions of the third sex played similarly on this theme of monstrous suffragists' speech—likewise understanding it as something that adversely affected the physical environment, or as something that operated *as* speech only to the extent that it simultaneously altered physical systems, rather than as something necessarily abnormal in and of itself. Indeed, if the analogy to the sterile worker insect is taken at face value, there is nothing actually monstrous or unnatural about the existence of a third sex. As Danielle Allen has noted, the invocation of the hive of insects (or more specifically, the beehive) as a means of making a point about both politics and gender has a long history,[27] in which the worker bee is by no means consistently denigrated.[28] Moreover, Allen continues that this "image of the beehive" more often than not suggests a fantasy of order and "an integrated whole,"[29] rather than a terror of what havoc one element—the third sex—might wreak. The question then is why, in this context, in the midst of conversations about suffrage, the third sex or sterile worker insect should suddenly become something to fear or deride.

Given the long history of this metaphor of the political insect, it seems unlikely, again, that what is monstrous about the speaking suffragist, as a member of the third sex, is this figure's intrinsic abnormality or capacity to produce disorder. And indeed, as Gregg states in the *New York Times* article, the monstrous or destructive potential of the third sex is most apparent not in and of itself, but when considering what this group of false females will do to the world around them via liberal governance. Gregg particularly highlights the suffragists' total lack of interest in linguistic representation. Whereas speaking men can represent both men and true women, the third sex can represent no one—and, more horrific, representation is clearly *not the goal of their speech*. Gregg, in other words, fears suffragists as the third sex because their speech does *not* represent, does not *seek* to represent, and instead seeks to *act* or *operate*. Suffragists' speech is monstrous here, once again, because it is operational rather than representational. It is monstrous in the same way that machine code is monstrous.

Or, put another way, when monstrous speaking suffragists are described as members of the third sex, they pose almost exactly the same threat that Circe and Delilah—examples that also appear with frequency in the nineteenth- and early twentieth-century writing about suffrage—

do. The invocations of Circe make this association between suffragists' speech and changes in the physical world explicit: Circe changed, destroyed, or devastated nature precisely *in* speaking. The horror of Circe's language was quite specifically that it did not convey meaning and that it did not represent the environment. It instead changed or altered the environment. Indeed, as much as emasculation is key both to the initial classical story of Circe and to later citations of this story in the context of the suffrage movement, this emasculation need not be read as something having to do purely with human subjects or human agents. The emasculation theme, that is to say, is not just about what humans can or cannot do themselves, but about what certain types of executable language can or cannot do to the world.

Or, as Hayles writes in reference to the role that mutation might play in information theory as opposed to theories of human subjectivity,

> mutation is crucial because it names the bifurcation point at which the interplay between pattern and randomness causes the system to evolve in a new direction. It reveals the productive potential of randomness that is also recognized within information theory when uncertainty is seen as both antagonistic and intrinsic to information. . . . [M]utation is the catastrophe in the pattern/randomness dialectic analogous to castration in the presence/absence dialectic.[30]

Mutation, then, like castration (or emasculation),[31] both reveals, dialectically, the importance of absence (or randomness) in determining presence (or pattern) *and,* more important for this argument, it produces— via dialectic or binary revelation—alterations in the system. To the extent that emasculation is what mutants or monsters like Circe, the third sex, or the speaking suffragist accomplish, therefore, this emasculation does not simply indicate the weakening or impotence of the state, the body politic, or men themselves. More complex, the emasculating monstrous suffragist highlights the pattern/randomness or presence/absence dialectic and, in the process, highlights how these binaries are always on the verge of pushing systems in new directions. The castrating speech of the monstrous suffragists is as much frightening for the physical things it does to environmental and (unironic) natural systems as it is for the physical things it does to political states or to the human men who inhabit them.

When Kilbreth thus argues that suffragists' speech is simultaneously an imaginary phantom and a very real autocratic assault on male virility—and that the best way of dealing with it is "summarily," as the French revolutionaries did—she is making a distinct case about the relationship between this speech and the environmental or physical, in addition to political or social, system of which it is a part. Key to Kilbreth's analysis is that suffragists, or women voters more generally, are nonexistent phantoms. Not only are they are unimportant and negligible, but they are imaginary. Their *speech*, however, is monstrous, terrifying, and far from imaginary. Detached from human speakers, and once again ignoring meaning or representation, this speech alters natural systems. Kilbreth argues, in other words, that suffragists' speech is monstrous not because suffragists themselves, as not quite humans, are abnormal, and not because their speech is intrinsically malformed or out of place. Nor is this speech monstrous because it is directly responsible for the emasculation of men or the body politic.

Rather, Kilbreth's point is that suffragists' speech, like Circe's speech, does things to the environmental systems, and that, as a secondary effect, given these systems, men cannot be men, women cannot be women, and the government cannot be a government. The question of what men are or of what women are, of whether men or women can act or be agents, is *derivative*. Central to these passages instead is how suffragists' emasculating speech, upon going into operation, alters environments. It is the many monstrous ways in which the speech of these nonexistent, nonhuman phantoms will harm the world around it that concerns Kilbreth. Only after that issue gets discussed does she turn to the question of how, then, this environmental change might affect men, women, and men's society or government. Key is less how suffragists' speech might alter the *content* of what is, rhetorically, deemed "natural" and "unnatural," and more how this fundamentally nonhuman speech is expressed via constantly shifting concrete natural systems.

Conclusion

The rhetorical and political implications of juxtaposing the monstrous with the natural have been well studied. On the one hand, designating certain groups or individuals as unnatural monsters has been an effective means of asserting and reasserting oppressive dialectical relationships. Those deemed neither subject nor object, or those who exist monstrously beyond the normal or the natural, serve as backdrops for determining proper, normal, human subjects and proper, normal, nonhuman objects. Nature thus becomes a metaphor for ordered, liberal politics, while the monster or the freak becomes the liminal figure who marks or maintains this nature/politics line—the figure who keeps the metaphor in place.

On the other hand, the ongoing, historical *fear* of the monster suggests the essential paucity of this dialectic. Precisely because it is a borderline or liminal figure, the monster is also capable of blurring the line between subject and object, human and nonhuman, or normal and abnormal, and of thereby undermining political or social order. In this case, it is the monster who becomes the metaphor for a more inclusive postliberal politics, while nature becomes a means of rhetorically celebrating the end of oppressive taxonomies. Once again, both nature and monster thus operate solely in rhetorical and political realms.

Although the argument in this chapter is indebted to the conversations that have arisen out of these rhetorical and political interpretations of nature and the monster, it has also departed from them significantly. Predicated on the idea that the physical qualities of both nature and the monster need not be subordinated to their metaphorical qualities, it has posited that a way around this subordination is to rethink what role language plays in historical discussions of the natural, the unnatural, and the monstrous. If language itself might be defined physically or environmentally rather than rhetorically—as something that acts as a system, rather than as something that describes or represents systems—then monstrosity might likewise be approached as a linguistic or an environmental issue rather than as a political issue. Nature too might cease to be something political and instead become something physical.

Indeed, as this chapter has suggested, the story of suffragists' monstrous speech, especially in its relation to nature, can be read as the story of an alternative language producing an alternative, nonhuman order based in constantly shifting physical systems. It need not necessarily be read as the story of marginalized humans either producing political disorder or, carnivalesque and parodic, paradoxically reproducing political hierarchies. Likewise, the fear of suffragists' monstrous speech can be understood as a fear of particular or distinct characteristics of this alternative language. It can be understood as a fear of language that is indifferent to structures of statement and response, as a fear of language that leaves speakers with no message to transmit, and as a fear of language that exists not to convey meaning but to act or operate on nature.

Far from being a purely political effect, monstrous speech according to this analysis is, first, environmental, second, linguistic, and only then, as a derivative, political or rhetorical.

Once again, though, in order to read the relationship between monstrosity and nature as something more environmental and linguistic and less political or rhetorical, a now familiar methodological move must be made. Discussions of both the monster and the natural cannot both address these issues and also rely on frameworks that privilege subjectivity, objectification, agency, or identity as starting and ending points of analysis. In order to recognize alternative implications of stories of the monstrous, such human, humanist, or broadly biological issues must be sidelined.

And it is here that this chapter about the monstrous speaking suffragist forms a bridge between the previous chapter on suffragists' antisecular speech and the next chapter on their repetitive speech. Just as the vocabulary of agency made it difficult to get beyond the fascination with subjects and objects, and thereby to recognize the centrality of the physical environment to the depiction of monstrous speech, so too the vocabulary of agency made it difficult to recognize the centrality of the environment to writing on antisecular speech. And, as the next chapter makes clear, there is a similar methodological obstacle in place when reading stories of repetitive or hysterical speech. Although the chapters that follow, in order to avoid the baggage that the term "nature" continues to carry, refer more to physical or environmental systems than they do to natural systems, therefore, they also are wedded to the idea that naive approaches to nature, absent the focus on agency, are in the end perhaps more useful than the ironic ones that seem always to refer back to humans and human concerns.

Chapter Seven : Repetitive Speech

A third figure who appears frequently in nineteenth- and early twentieth-century stories about women's suffrage is the repetitive, compulsive, or babbling public woman, overwhelming her audience and the world around her with an ever increasing flood of words and information. Ordinarily, repetitive suffragists prompt mockery more than they do fear in the antisuffrage narrative—and in the prosuffrage narrative they are usually subordinated to the more rhetorically effective antisecularist or monster. At the same time, however, suffragists' repetitive speech, as a distinct linguistic mode, also operates at the intersection of two other familiar—and familiarly threatening—speech activities.

The first of these activities is, once again, machine code. The second is the older and more explicitly perilous speech act that is classical Greek *parrhesia*. Stories of suffragists' repetitive speech, that is to say, not only hint at unexpected similarities between twentieth- and twenty-first-century machine code and classical Greek parrhesia, they also suggest a linguistic world in which this speech—simultaneously code and parrhesia—assaults the physical environment. Stories of the repetitive suffragist are thus not simply variations on the theme of the nagging woman, the woman who will not shut up, or the woman with nothing worthwhile to say. Instead, they have deeper implications, and they open up new ways of thinking broadly about what speech might do to physical and environmental, as well as political, worlds.

Parrhesia and Code

In his series of lectures on parrhesia—etymologically, "speaking every-thing," or as he puts it in the title of the series, "speaking freely" or *Fear-less Speech*[1]—Foucault describes a number of characteristics of this dis-tinct type of classical Greek discourse. When engaged in parrhesia, for instance, the speaker is, according to Foucault, first and foremost "the subject of the opinion to which he refers."[2] On the one hand, therefore, parrhesia seems to privilege human speaker and human speech above all else—referring *only*, and hyperbolically, to humans and their concerns.[3] On the other hand, however, by defining the *parrhesiastes*—the one who engages in parrhesia—as both the subject who speaks and the subject who is spoken, Foucault is also, if paradoxically, at least hinting at a the-ory of speech that sidelines the human speaker. The parrhesiastes, after all, is not an active subject who produces passive speech. Nor is the par-rhesiastes a subject formed by discourse who in turn manipulates dis-course. Rather, the parrhesiastes is a subject who *is* speech. Or, put an-other way, parrhesia produces a total equivalency between speaker and speech.[4]

In effect, therefore, any hierarchy that privileges speaker over speech—any hierarchy, that is to say, grounded in assumptions of linguis-tic agency—dissipates when parrhesia is put into operation. In place of such hierarchies, indeed, occurs a situation in which speech equals speaker and speaker equals speech—or in which neither is subordinate to the other. Central to the execution of parrhesia is thus not the discrete speaker, listener, or speech act, but rather the linguistic *system* or *net-work*, composed of speakers, speech, and speech activities that goes into effect. Or, more pointedly, just as the machine running code is both the thing that speaks and the thing that is spoken, so too is the parrhesiastes.[5] Just as machine code is predicated on the simultaneity, and indeed over-lap, among speech, speaker, and act, so too is parrhesia. And finally, just as the machine running code executes a particular program whose sole purpose is the alteration of a physical or environmental system, so too does the parrhesiastes.

Indeed, this essential physicality of parrhesia becomes apparent in many of the additional characteristics that Foucault attributes to it as mode of speech.[6] When engaging in parrhesia, for instance, Foucault argues that "you risk death to tell the truth instead of reposing in the security of a life where the truth goes unspoken."[7] Parrhesia, that is to say, sets up a constant, if always potential, dichotomy between being "a truth-teller" on the one hand and being "living" on the other.[8] It assumes that the linguistic activity of speaking freely or speaking everything and the biological activity of living are not just linked, but inextricably intertwined.

The importance of speaking as a biological—rather than as a solely linguistic—activity is in fact so pronounced when engaging in parrhesia that the content, message, or meaning of the speech is less important than the physical activity that is speaking.[9] Both the "bad" and the "good" manifestations of parrhesia—"chattering"[10] or "having a mouth like a running spring"[11] in the first case, and existing as nothing more nor less than the one who speaks the truth in the second—are far more about speech as a physical or biological operation, resting on the constant sorting, storage, and reproduction of noise or information,[12] than they are about speech as a means of conveying meaning. Once again, therefore, like machine code, parrhesia here is only tangentially relevant to speakers transmitting messages to listeners. Like machine code, it is effective only to the extent that it defines or alters a physical system—in this case a living biological body.

At the same time, as much as Foucault's interpretation of the physicality of parrhesia returns back to humans with their bodies—and as much as this mode of speech seems physical only when it has something to do with biological life or death—its physicality need not be understood as a narrowly biological, or as a more narrowly human, characteristic. Although the most obvious reading of Foucault's work on parrhesia is that he is describing a form of discourse that brings together politics and biological life, therefore, this is not the only reading. In addition, Foucault also appears to be describing an activity whose physicality extends beyond biology and life, into the realm of code, where language is itself the operation of wider physical—biological as well as nonbiological—system.[13] As much as Foucault is, without question, discussing speech, subjectivity, and embodied forms of agency, that is, he is also discussing language and the environment—a discussion that becomes apparent, however, only when subjectivity and agency are de-emphasized.

In his analysis of the difference[14] between parrhesia and modern or Cartesian modes of speech, for instance, Foucault begins to connect the former with environmental, rather than with simply biological, systemic change. More specifically, he points out that "since Descartes, the coincidence between belief and truth is obtained in a certain (mental) evidential experience. For the Greeks, however, the coincidence between belief and truth does not take place in a (mental) experience, but in a *verbal activity*, namely, *parrhesia.*"[15] Ordinarily this Cartesian break is understood in an anthropocentric way to happen when the truth about the world becomes accessible (to humans) through external, objective, sensory evidence rather than through internal, subjective revelation. But this break also represents a shift in the relationship between the world and speech more generally defined. It represents a shift away from speech that *may* be grounded in human experience and toward speech that *must* be bound by human concerns.

Put another way, whereas for Descartes, belief and the speech that is derived from it are detached from the world's physicality—the physical world nothing more than the field in which belief is formulated—for the parrhesiastes, belief and speech are simultaneous with the physical world. For Descartes, speech, belief, and the world form a linear, hierarchical relationship, in which an inert, true, and verifiable physical world affects human belief, which in turn affects rational speech. Contrarily, for the parrhesiastes, speech, belief, and the world operate simultaneously as a dynamic and constantly shifting system.[16]

Although humans and their bodies are without question a part of this system, therefore, they are certainly not the only part, nor are they the most important part. Instead, the physical and linguistic activity that is parrhesia consists of systemwide operations or executions that are far more important than human existence, perceptions, senses, or life. Unlike the linear Cartesian relationship between speech and the world, which necessarily rests on human perception, human linguistic activity, and human bodies, the parrhesiastic relationship between speech and the world need not privilege any of these human attributes.

Intriguingly, it is nonetheless on the basis of this so-called Cartesian shift that Foucault argues that "*parrhesia*, in this Greek sense, can no longer occur in our modern epistemological framework."[17] And in one way, this point is undoubtedly valid. Given its nonlinear, system-oriented, message-poor, and information-rich physicality, parrhesia is in fact impossible in a modern framework that focuses on embodied human subjects exercising agency within a given discursive field. At the same time, however, parrhesia is quite *possible* in an epistemological framework that does not privilege human agency and human speech, and that does not concern itself with the agency of objects—in a framework, in other words, that takes as its starting point speech that looks like machine code, or language that looks like computational language. In this alter-

native, equally modern framework, speech activities that resemble parrhesia are not only possible, but indispensable.

More to the point, stories of threatening speech such as those that
populate the suffrage narrative suggest that a variation on parrhesia has
been very much at play in recent centuries. As the rest of this chapter
demonstrates, descriptions of the repetitive speaking suffragist in particular place this figure precisely at the points of overlap between the classical mode of speech that is parrhesia and the contemporary mode of
speech that is machine code. The repetitive speaking suffragist works simultaneously as machine and parrhesiastes, eluding theories of speech
based in agency, and very much present to those that look for physical or
environmental change. Like the machine and the parrhesiastes, the
repetitive suffragist is both speaker and speech—storing and sorting information physically rather than conveying messages subjectively. Like
machine code and parrhesia, suffragists' speech *can* affect human bodies
and biological life—but this is only to the extent that bodies and life are
part of the wider physical system that this speech alters. And finally, like
machine code and parrhesia, suffragists' speech assumes a nonlinear relationship between speech and the world, denying the centrality of human
bodies and human evidentiary experiences that characterize the so-
called Cartesian variation on this relationship.

Suffragists Speaking Freely

The extent to which speaking suffragists were identical to their speech—
and also, as a result, concerned more with the physical sorting, storing, or
reproducing of information than with the subjective transmission of
meaning—becomes most apparent in the writing that plays up this
speech as a compelled, compulsive, or repetitive barrage. In this writing,
two aspects of the speaking suffragist's tendency toward repetition get
highlighted: the first is how this repetition forces or compels further
speech on the part of the suffragist herself or those around her, and the
second is how it is in effect a physical assault. These aspects of the suffragist's repetitive speech were mobilized just as frequently by prosuffrage
advocates as they were by their critics. Indeed, advocates of a variety of
positions on the suffrage question recognized the potential, implicitly
computational, threat inherent in this mode of speech—and also its distinctly environmental character.

In 1881, for example, the Legislature of Wisconsin introduced a "joke" bill, "a burlesque upon the doctrine of woman's suffrage," stating that "the women of that state *shall* (not simply *may*) vote at the next general election" on the question of women's votes, with "a neglect on their part to vote . . . punishable by a fine of not less than one hundred dollars or by imprisonment for not less than three months."[18] Three years later, in 1884, a book reviewer for the *New York Evangelist* brought together this compulsive quality of suffragists' speech ridiculed by the Wisconsin legislature and its repetitive quality. In a critique of Elizabeth Cady Stanton's, Susan B. Anthony's, and Matilda Johnson Gage's *History of Woman Suffrage*, the reviewer played at length with the idea that excessive, repetitive, and compulsive speech was a distinctive and defining attribute of the suffrage movement. After discussing the book's lack of organization and general disarray, the reviewer eventually concludes, "if the history of temperance, the missionary, and other similar movements were written in this way and on this scale, there are no libraries large enough to hold the books, and human life would need to be indefinitely extended to enable anybody to read them."[19]

Once this aspect of suffragists' compulsive, compelled, and repetitive speech had been articulated, it appeared in a number of contexts and was invoked by a number of writers throughout the nineteenth and early twentieth centuries. It was not just that talk about women's suffrage had become "one of the noisiest of the day,"[20] or that the women's suffrage debate was like "a drum, a small instrument," that nonetheless "makes a great noise, and is heard afar."[21] It was that this noisy repetitiveness was both politically,[22] and, more so, physically dangerous. Under some circumstances, for instance, suffragists' repetitive speech was linked to their "fanatical faith in the omnipotence of legislation."[23] As the popular romance novelist Louise de la Ramée (Ouida), put it in 1896, suffragists' had little "sense of justice" or "freedom," and the universe they preferred was one in which "laws would be multiplied indefinitely and incessantly," and "the *infiniment petit* would be the dominate [*sic*] factor in politics."[24]

In other circumstances, the physical character of this repetition or reproduction of information was emphasized. As "A Man" wrote in the *New York Times* in 1910,

> I asked for a plain statement of "Why women should vote," done directly and clearly so the most ignorant layman might understand. I asked this because I knew nothing of the sort. If I had complained

at all my complaint would have been because there were already so many campaign documents a mere man couldn't find in them what the women really were trying to get at. There's a hysteria of documents. I was simply asking for a coherent statement when the women had become calm. But I see by the communication of M.W.S. that they are still raving and pouring forth their torrents of talk. She mentions 450 variegated styles of documents which will be mailed to me free; she adds that if I will call at headquarters I will be shown arguments from Lady Mary Whortley [*sic*] Montague to "Bill" Taft and the Brackett bill. . . . [I] have no inclination, even if I had the leisure, to go into this overproduction of gab, but I would like to see and read something brief and to the point. I am aware what a task I impose upon women when I ask them to be brief and to the point, but as they are struggling to be what they have never been before, might they not include this with the other?[25]

Once again, that is to say, the problem with women's suffrage, and more so suffragists' speech rested squarely with women's general and fundamental inability to stop talking.

Once again, though, it was not just antisuffrage advocates who told stories of suffragists' repetitive or battering linguistic behavior. Carrie Chapman Catt, for example, took the apparently burlesque notion that suffragists simply could not be quiet, likewise played up its physical implications, and ran with it. In her 1916 Presidential Address to the National American Woman Suffrage Association, Catt emphasized that the movement had reached a "crisis"—arguing indeed that even if it had not, "it is better to imagine a crisis where none exists than to fail to recognize one when it comes." She then encouraged suffragists to "take the crisis into victory" by "compel[ling] this array of lawmakers to see woman suffrage, to think woman suffrage, to talk woman suffrage every minute of every day until they heed our plea."[26] For Catt, the precipitation of the crisis thus required precisely the compulsive onslaught of repetitive speech—speech such that lawmakers as well as suffragists *could* see, think, and talk nothing else—that the antisuffrage advocates mocked or feared.[27] When Catt called on suffrage advocates to take the crisis into victory and to make their voices heard, her call was not to persuasion or discussion, but to an overwhelming physical, or at least sensory, assault.

Each of these passages, then, plays on the idea that suffragists' speech did something more than simply convey meaning. More so, it was a repetitive onslaught, compulsive and unstoppable, something that itself compelled further and more aggressive speech. Each of these passages can likewise be read to great effect through the lens of agency or identity. By diagnosing the women who advocate suffrage as compulsive, repetitive hysterics incapable of calm discussion or of making meaningful arguments, the antisuffrage writers have disqualified women generally from self-aware, sovereign citizenship. By undermining their attempts to appropriate linguistic agency, these writers have denied to speaking suffragists any space in which to operate as political actors. But by redirecting this rhetoric, and defining suffragists' repetitive speech as an instrument or tool that can be wielded at will for political purposes, Catt has likewise rehabilitated suffragists, and women generally, as self-conscious subjects possessed of agency. Even if the speech they wield is meaningless except as a weapon of battery, suffragists in Catt's universe find their agency— just as antisuffragists do—precisely in the act of speaking.

If agency and identity are de-emphasized, however, these passages also lend themselves to an alternative reading—to a reading in which this compulsive, repetitive speech, as a type of both parrhesia and code, overlaps completely with speaker, and in which it privileges the physical sorting and storing of information over the subjective transmission of meaning. According to every one of the antisuffrage passages, for instance, the speaking suffragist—whether personified by the *History of Women's Suffrage*, the noisemaker, the small drum, infinitely small and infinitely iterated legislation, or the hysterical M.W.S.—is both something that speaks through a kind of physical operation and also something spoken through this same operation. This interpretation of suffragists' speech is most obvious in the references to drums and noisemakers, instruments that by definition both speak and are spoken when they go into physical execution.

But "A Man," Ouida, and the book reviewer also hint at this peculiarity of suffragists' speech. Whereas "A Man," for example, accuses not suffragists themselves, but rather their *documents*, of hysteria, Ouida understands suffragists' speech as a monstrous, ever-increasing set of laws, while the book reviewer gradually shifts attention away from the potential damage that the *authors* of the *History of Women's Suffrage* will do to the damage that the massive, ever increasing *work itself* will do. Each thus demonstrates that the line between what speaks and what is spoken is by no means a clear one, and that what differentiates suffragists' speech from more appropriate modes of speech is in part this inability to distinguish the one from the other.

More than that, "A Man," Ouida, and the reviewer each also understand suffragists' speech to be doing unseemly and indeed physically or environmentally harmful things with information. The repeated return in the antisuffrage literature to suffragists' overwhelming or excessive speech, to their insistence on collecting and distributing ever more documents or facts, in other words, is not just a means of making a negative argument about the uselessness of their work. Nor is the point of this writing simply that suffragists' speech is meaningless and that their linguistic excesses obscure any rational case they may be making. In addition, and equally important, these references to the suffragists' linguistic excesses are a means of making a positive point about the physicality of the interaction between repetitive suffragist's speech and information. It is a means of placing suffragists' speech at the intersection of, first, parrhesia in the literal sense of "speaking everything" and, second, the machine code that exists fundamentally to sort and store data.

The M.W.S. whom "A Man" criticizes, for example, is criticized above all for the physically overwhelming manner in which she sorts, stores, and reproduces information—for her existence as nothing more nor less than a hysteria of documents. In addition, she is criticized for the physically frightening way in which she speaks everything and yet transmits no message—for her pouring forth of torrents of talk. The fact that "a mere man" (or human) cannot find meaning in these words or documents is thus arguably a secondary problem in "A Man's" analysis. More pressing is the fact that suffragists' repetitive speech here is not only nonhuman, computational, or parrhesiastic in its interaction with information—unconcerned with any human purpose and polluting the environment around it with ever more words and documents[28]—but also, according to speaking suffragists like M.W.S, validly so.

Similarly, by dissociating suffragists' speech from "justice" and "freedom"—the supposed interest of law—and turning this speech instead into the thing that overwhelms the political system with an infinitely small, yet infinitely extended, fractal sort of legislation, Ouida is not just warning of assaults on individual liberty. She too, like "A Man" is recognizing the fundamentally nonhuman quality of this speech—this speech that can continue processing information forever, that can overwhelm a system completely, but that is nonetheless tinier than anything measurable by human means. The problem with the suffragists' "fanatical faith in the omnipotence of legislation," indeed, is not just that it detaches law from human concerns like justice and freedom. It is not just that legal speech becomes something that might very well change the world. In addition, it is that suffragists' speech colonizes or infects legal speech in the name of alternative, nonhuman systems, operations, and environments. Speaking freely and speaking everything, suffragists in Ouida's analysis act, again, as machines running code.

Finally, the book reviewer is more overt about these threats inherent to the repetitive speech that operates, above all, through the storage or sorting of information. Once more, the basic message to be taken from the review is that suffragists talk too much, and that in the process they fail to convey any meaning. In addition, however, the reviewer explicitly mentions the specific problem of storage space or memory that arises from suffragists' repetitive speech—noting that this speech assumes a world in which libraries become infinitely large—*and also* the connection between this storage problem and the biopolitical nightmare of indefinitely extended human life ("human life would need to be indefinitely extended to enable anybody to read them").

The reviewer thus makes clear that speaking suffragists threaten, first, a shift away from human modes of speech, in which speaking is a finite activity that seeks to convey messages for subjective purposes—an activity that always keeps humans at the center of the linguistic universe. Second, speaking suffragists also threaten a shift toward a nonhuman mode of parrhesia, speaking everything, where such speech involves nothing more nor less than sorting, storing, and reproducing meaningless noise or information—and where if humans do play a role, it is solely as part of this informational system, their biological existence identical to the infinite and indefinitely extended work of speaking and sorting.

"A Man," Ouida, and the book reviewer thus all recognize that linguistic activity predicated on the sorting of information rather than on the transmission of meaning is not just physical in and of itself, but physically threatening to humans, and more important, to the environments of which humans form one small part. Or, in a different context, as Hayles citing Charles H. Bennet puts it, "the increasing awareness of environmental pollution and the information explosion brought on by computers have made the idea that information can have a negative value seem more natural now that it would have seemed earlier in this century."[29] What "A Man," Ouida, and the reviewer do not address, however, is the possibility that this linguistic activity can be as promising as it is threatening. As much as increasing amounts of information point to an increasingly chaotic system—in which humans and nonhumans alike might be buried or drowned in data—increasing amounts of information also promise a "transvaluation of chaos," where previously defined disorder can be read instead as a more complex or multidimensional order.[30] As much as the linguistic activity of the repetitive speaking suffragist terrifies in its nonhuman physicality and its alteration of systems or environments, then, it also opens up the possibility of a different sort of order.

And indeed, it is this promise of an alternative, chaotic, or nonlinear order *that rests on* a physically threatening, information-rich, and content-free speech that motivates Catt's 1916 reinterpretation of the antisuffrage writing. On the one hand, the crisis that suffragists' repetitive, compulsive speech will precipitate or force is, again, a type of physical assault—similar to the "truth event"[31] that Foucault describes in *Psychiatric Power* and that resembles in many ways the parrhesiastes speaking freely and speaking everything. In the same way that "the relationship between this truth-event and the person who is seized by it . . . is not a relationship of subject to object," and in the same way that "it is not a relationship within knowledge but, rather, a relationship of a shock or clash, like that of a thunderbolt or lightning,"[32] the linguistic crisis that Catt foretells is one that may very well harm or hurt human bodies, but that will happen nonetheless outside of the purely human realm of subject and object and within the broadly natural realm of the thunderbolt or lightning.

It is a crisis, in other words, not of altered understanding or of new knowledge, but of excessive, ever increasing speech, data, and information. It is a crisis of nonhuman memory or storage—a crisis that is reached when a particular linguistic activity (suffragists' speech) has stored or reproduced so much information or data that it has become identical to, or overwhelmed completely, the physical system of which it once formed only a part. When the linguistic activity has gone viral, when it has grown to the extent that it corresponds exactly with the physical system, that system is reduced to repeating a single strand of data—in this case talk about women's suffrage. Catt's point is not that speech about women's suffrage should make certain arguments or should persuade unconvinced opponents. It is that speech about women's suffrage—positive or negative—should be the only speech that exists, that it should colonize all parts of the existing physical and linguistic system.

Catt's belief, that is to say, is that if suffragists speak freely enough, if they sort, store, and reproduce enough information—regardless of any meaning or message that might be transmitted—they can then force a physical crisis in the preexisting system. They can, essentially, pollute or infect the existing environment such that it is transformed into something else, something uniquely devoted to the proliferation of the virus.[33]

Once again, though, on the other hand, this crisis is not, according to Catt, a bad thing. What this physical assault via language will do, according to her analysis, is help in the "transvaluation of chaos" that Hayles associates with twentieth-century information theory. It will precipitate a new, nonlinear order, in which the sea of meaningless information that so frightened and overwhelmed the antisuffrage writers becomes a source of infinite alternative environments. As much as they differ in their immediate goals, therefore, Catt and the antisuffrage writers do not differ in any fundamental way in their understanding of what suffragists' speech might do. Both describe the repetitive speaking suffragist as a figure who simultaneously speaks and is spoken. Both describe this speech as content poor and information rich. And both hint at the possibility that this speech might be a form, first, of parrhesia—speaking freely and speaking everything—and, second, of the machine code whose fundamental operation is the sorting and storage of information. The major difference between the two sets of writers is simply that whereas the antisuffrage advocates mock or fear this mode of speech, Catt and her colleagues insist that it is both inevitable and desirable.

Bodily Harm as Environmental Harm

As much as these stories of suffragists' repetitive speech operating at the intersection of parrhesia and machine code describe the nonhuman systemic or environmental implications of this speech, they also return frequently to human bodies or human subjectivity. Catt, for instance, couches her discussion of the crisis or truth event in a language, first of all, of human politics, and Foucault as well as the classical Greek writers he addresses understand parrhesia to be something that humans do in a uniquely human political realm. The fact that human subjectivity is the starting point for many of these stories, however, does not mean that it is also the ending point. Indeed, the writing that posits suffragists' repetitive speech—linked to code and parrhesia—as a specific type of human bodily harm can be read as a subset of a wider field that posits this speech as type of environmental harm. More so, bodily harm itself can be reread in this context as one aspect of a broader, network-wide, physical threat.

The way in which suffragists' repetitive or excessive speech might attack the human body is explicit in much of the antisuffrage writing. When Doane, for instance, writes in 1869 that the "issue and question of woman suffrage, like death, seems to have 'all seasons for its own.' It sows its tares, like the enemy, while most women sleep; and with a vigor and vigilance worthy of a better cause, the promoters of it are everywhere and all the time at work,"[34] he is essentially making the less poetic case that suffragists' speech, like death, cannot be avoided. Other antisuffrage writers, however, such as the historian, scholar, and environmental activist Francis Parkman, were more subtle in their discussions of suffragists' repetitive speech as a threat to bodies.

Throughout his 1879 essay "The Woman Question Again," Parkman expresses his fear that suffragists' speech will assault, first and foremost, suffragists' *own* bodies. Indeed, women in general, Parkman argues,

> have a feeling that because [voting] is unpleasant, it must be right. Many a woman is moved by this feeling who would be unmoved by temptation in the shape of ease or pleasure. Simply because her nature revolts from politics, she cannot entirely rid herself of an idea that it is her duty to take part in them.[35]

In a sympathetic review of Parkman's essay in the *New York Times*, this concern for suffragists' bodies is extended to a concern for Parkman's body as well, left open now to the onslaught of suffragists' speech. The reviewer in fact praises Parkman primarily for his "courage" at "dar[ing] the volleys of fierce reply which his contribution to the discussion is pretty sure to evoke," and the "abuse and the fusillade of stinging though harmless epithets, in which these combatants are wont to indulge."[36] The review then moves on to Parkman's linguistic sensitivity in the face of this attack. Parkman, the reviewer states, makes his case only "by the most decorous hints and gentle insinuations, and by no offensive plain speaking," thereby impressing "upon the mind the important functions with which nature has consecrated women and to which it has largely subordinated their activities."[37]

The writing of Doane, Parkman, and Parkman's reviewer is not, however, greatly distinct from the writing of the prosuffrage advocates that play on the same bodily themes. In a much later article in the *New York Times*, for instance, Thomas W. Palmer, a former senator of Michigan, is quoted as advocating women's right and entitlement to vote because "women will die for their convictions, ten to one, as compared with men. Who were the early Christians who were thrown to wild beasts in the amphitheatres because they would not give up their faith? The majority of them were young women."[38] Like Doane, that is to say, Palmer associates suffragists' speech with death, and like Parkman, he understands this simultaneously physical and linguistic attack to be largely self-inflicted.

Each of these descriptions of suffragists' repetitive speech, then, posits this speech to be a physical, and more specifically bodily, act with the potential to cause physical, and, again, more specifically bodily, harm. Doane and Palmer take this act of bodily harm to its logical conclusion in death. Parkman, contrarily, sees it in the fact that, for women generally, pain, pleasure, and speech are the same thing—and as a result suffragists' speech can never be anything but a physical or bodily experience. Suffragists do not revolt or recoil from some message they understand to be conveyed in speech; they recoil in revulsion during the very activity of speaking—an activity, however, that they nonetheless cannot resist. Finally, Parkman's reviewer juxtaposes suffragists' abusive, stinging, and fierce (though harmless) speech to Parkman's careful, thoughtful, and effective speech. Key to the suffragists' speech and missing from Parkman's, in other words, is its physical or bodily character. Whereas suffragists' speech batters like a weapon, Parkman's speech hints, insinuates, and persuades. In none of these passages is the content of suffragists' speech of any importance. Instead, suffragists' speech—like parrhesia—is distinct and recognizable by the way in which it acts on and through bodies.

Once again, though, as central as the human body may be in these stories of suffragists' repetitive speech, it is by no means the only arena in which this speech manifests itself as a physical operation. As much as these stories seem to revive classical parrhesia as a model for thinking about threatening speech, in other words, they also seem to be presaging twentieth-century machine code—operating on systems rather than being expressed by speakers—as a model for thinking about threatening speech. In the same way that, as Hayles notes, "recent trends within cognitive science and evolutionary biology . . . stress interactions between organism and environment"—recognizing that "a cognitive system" might involve "both human and nonhuman actors" or that "pressures" might "affect the system as a whole, causing it to self-organize in ways that no single actor may fully grasp"[39]—stories about suffragists' speech that appear to focus on the human body likewise emphasize the placement of these bodies within wider, nonhuman physical and linguistic systems.

Or, more bluntly, writing about the bodily harm caused by suffragists' repetitive speech can also be read as writing about the systemic, environmental harm caused by this speech. It can be read as a harm predicated on nonlinear, simultaneous interactions among speakers, speech, and the world—on interactions familiar both to the parrhesiastes and to the machine running code—rather than on linear, Cartesian interactions among speakers, speech, and the world. Humans with their bodies *may* be involved (or not) in these interactions, but their involvement is not the critically important issue that it appears to be upon an initial reading of these stories.

When Doane associates suffragists' repetitive or excessive speech with death, for instance, it is indeed possible to assume that the specific way in which it is like death is in its attack on biological bodies. A closer reading of the passage makes clear, however, that in fact the reason that suffragists' speech resembles death is that it is everywhere and at all times—that it is infinite temporally as well as spatially. Doane, that is to say, does hint that suffragists' repetitive speech is harmful because of what it does to humans, women, and their bodies. More than that, though, it is harmful because of its colonization and extension of existing networks and systems—because it replaces a linear relationship among speaker, speech, and the world, with a nonlinear relationship in which speech, like death, is everywhere within the world and indeed makes or destroys the world. For Doane, like Parkman, the story of suffragists' repetitive speech is thus a story of language assaulting the world.

Conclusion

One of the reasons that Foucault is so insistent that parrhesia is not possible in a modern context is that it can be so easily misappropriated or misunderstood. The classical Greek figure who risks his life or reputation to speak the truth—and *all* of the truth—to a more powerful, usually sovereign, group or individual is very attractive to modern, liberal citizens who believe in nineteenth- or twentieth-century variations on speaking truth to power. The problem with this false equivalency is that the classical Greek understanding of how truth, power, and speech interact is very different from the modern, liberal understanding of this interaction[40]—far removed from the realm of choice, liberty, or the sanctity of the rational individual's good conscience. In addition to making an epistemological point when he rejects the possibility of modern forms of parrhesia, therefore, Foucault is also issuing a warning: despite the attractiveness of classical Greek political models, be wary of trying to import them into alien frameworks.

This warning is well taken. In fact, in doing precisely what Foucault warned against—seeking modern examples of the parrhesiastes at work—this chapter has nonetheless stayed true to its spirit. Parrhesia, as this chapter has suggested, is impossible in a modern *human* framework. As long as human speakers remain distinct from their speech, as long as speaking involves humans persuading, convincing, or communicating messages to other humans, and as long as human bodies and human subjectivities are the only things threatened by harmful or dangerous speech, parrhesia is not a conceivable linguistic activity. More simply, as long as agency is at the center of conversations about speech, parrhesia cannot be.

At the same time, however, this chapter has also departed from Foucault's analysis by focusing on a type of speech that he ignored—nonhuman, or more specifically, computational speech. By shifting attention away from human-centered communication and toward system-oriented language, it becomes possible to rehabilitate parrhesia as a modern speech activity and to recognize it as a mode of speech that continues to provoke both faith and fear—just as it did in the classical Greek period. Narrowly, this rehabilitation of parrhesia within the computational realm is necessary to any multidimensional understanding of why suffragists' speech should have been so threatening. Unlike the perhaps intuitively obvious threat inherent to suffragists' antisecular or monstrous speech, the threat inherent to their repetitive speech is not so clear. And yet the story of the repetitive, compulsive, or overwhelming speech of the suffragist is one of the most prominent in the suffrage narrative. The only way to account for this discrepancy is to consider the possibility that what is at stake in suffragists' speech—just like what is at stake in parrhesia and machine code—is something beyond human bodies and human agency.

When both pro- and antisuffrage writers describe as threatening not just the strange equivalency between speaking suffragists and suffragists' speech, not just speaking suffragists' apparent inability or lack of interest in persuasion, argument, or the articulation of clear, distinct points, but also—and specifically—how suffragists' speech involves nothing more nor less than the sorting, storage, and reproduction of infinite amounts of noise and information, they are hinting at an essentially parrhesiastic *and* computational theory of language. When they go a step further and state that suffragists speaking freely and speaking everything produce a problem, fundamentally, of storage or memory—a problem that reaches its crisis when the linguistic and physical system in which this speech occurs is infected, polluted, or overwhelmed to such an extent that it can do nothing but reiterate a single line of code—they are likewise describing a type of speech that operates at the intersection of parrhesia and machine language. Neither of these aspects of the story of suffragists' repetitive speech is recognizable within an analytical framework based on human agency. Both, however, become immediately clear when parrhesia is brought into the modern, computational framework.

Similarly, as much as these aspects of suffragists' repetitive speech can be routed back toward discussions of human bodies and human subjectivity, the recovery of parrhesia within the realm of code demonstrates the poverty of such a move. Whereas it is true, for instance, that the so-called Cartesian shift from nonlinear to linear models of speech, belief, and the world has significant implications for theories of embodiment, it also has wider environmental implications. The bodily repercussions of the Cartesian moment are one, and only one, part of a wider set of repercussions. They are one small aspect of an environmental change in which speech ceased to interact with the world and instead became an effect of the world—an effect in turn based in human perception.

As the activity of the repetitive speaking suffragist indicates, however, this Cartesian shift was far from irreversible—alternative, nonlinear models of speech still very much available throughout the modern period. Indeed, to the extent that the speech of suffragists assaulted human bodies, this speech was very much divorced from the Cartesian model, and—more important—these assaults only affected human bodies to the extent that the bodies were part of a wider environmental system. Or, put another way, stories of the repetitive suffragist as parrhesiastes were likewise stories of the repetitive suffragist as machine running code—threatening precisely because they described so much more than human agency or human bodies.

And it is here that the more general implications of this rehabilitation of parrhesia within a modern computational—or proto-computational—field become clear. Despite warnings about the pitfalls of trying to use classical Greek models for modern political engagement, Greek "freedom" remains a traditional theme in American and other stories of liberalism and democracy. Rather than simply reiterating the point that this theme is historically invalid, epistemologically suspect, or anachronistic, however, it might be worthwhile to ask what it would mean if, in fact, some of these classical political ideas did have a role to play in modern, liberal structures.

What this chapter's revivification of parrhesia suggests is that these classical ideas are relevant—just not in the way that many commentators have understood them to be. If a parrhesiastes is to be found in the modern or contemporary world, it is not in the realm of electoral politics, not in the realm of politics more broadly defined, and not even in the realm of the human. The parrhesiastes instead belongs to the nonhuman, nonpolitical realm of the machine. Likewise, if parrhesia exists today, it affects not political systems, but physical and environmental ones. Or, alternatively—and perhaps more accurately—the speech activity that is parrhesia can be a human activity, can be a political activity, and can even be an activity relevant to electoral politics, but only to the extent that the human is one aspect of an environmental or computational system, and only to the extent that the political rests on the activities of machines. Inversely, therefore, what the rehabilitation of parrhesia posits is a human political universe in which speech performs physical functions rather than conveying messages or meaning.

Chapter Eight : Witches (a Bridge)

This short chapter acts as a bridge between the stories that precede it of repetitive suffragists and the stories that follow it of afflicted or insane suffragists. Like the first bridge chapter, this chapter focuses on a concept that appears throughout the book, but that is in danger of being misunderstood—in this case the concept of consent. Consent is a problematic issue to discuss in this context in that it seems central to the theories of speech and agency from which this book is distancing itself and also completely alien to the machine code that serves here as a model for suffragists' threatening speech. Rational human subjects consent or withhold consent. Nonhuman machines do not. Nonetheless, a case can be made that machines running code are in fact capable of consent. But, once again, this is a consent predicated on physical alterations to systems or environments, and recognizable only when agency has been eliminated as a methodological starting point.

In order to theorize the consent that underlies machine code, this chapter rereads a fourth set of stories common to the antisuffrage narrative—stories of suffragists' speech as witches' speech. It is without question true that rhetorically connecting suffragists to witches was one further means of marginalizing them and denying them access to the public or political sphere: if the suffragist could be linked to such an irrational, early modern or premodern throwback, then clearly she could have nothing to do with the work of modern, liberal citizens. The linguistic effects of this association, however, are also more complex than this simple interpretation of the suffrage-witchcraft association suggests.

This is because associating suffragists with witches also assigns to suffragists a distinct type of consent—a type of consent historically associated with witchcraft—that alters political, legal, or subjective worlds only by altering physical or natural worlds. The suffragist as witch, that is to say, consents to the social contract in a frighteningly physical way. Stories of suffragists' speech as witchcraft thus serve as an effective foundation for more general theories of consent absent agency, nonhuman consent, or consent in the computational realm. Just as the previous chapter questioned the anachronism of situating stories of suffragists' repetitive speech at the intersection of classical parrhesia and modern or contemporary code, therefore, this chapter questions the anachronism of finding in writing about suffragists' consent a link between early modern witchcraft and modern or contemporary machine code. At the overlap of these seemingly incommensurable modes of speech there is indeed a fruitful arena for rethinking the definition of threatening linguistic activity.

Tiny Consents

Near the end of his lecture series *Abnormal,* Foucault takes a detour into the realm of witchcraft and demonic possession. As a means of illustrating a more general point about the shifts and relationships between juridical power and disciplinary power, Foucault argues in these passages that there was an increasing distinction made, but also—importantly—an increasing connection developed, between witchcraft and possession throughout the seventeenth and eighteenth centuries. As for the distinction, Foucault notes that the consent of victims to their *possession* by the devil was much more "complex" than the consent of witches to their *pact* with the devil. In witchcraft, he continues,

> the witch's will is generally a juridical type of will. The witch agrees to an offered exchange: You offer me pleasure and power and I give you my body and soul. The witch goes along with the exchange and signs the pact: In the end she is a legal subject and it [is] as such that she can be punished.

Contrarily, in possession,

> the will is charged with all the ambiguities of desire. The will does and does not desire. . . . [T]he sensations are introduced through a

game of little pleasures, imperceptible sensations, tiny consents, and a sort of permanent slight connivance in which will and pleasure are entwined, somehow twist around each other and produce a deception.[1]

In this way the bodies of witches, Foucault states, likewise become distinct from the bodies of the possessed. The witch's body is "completely surrounded by or in some way the beneficiary of a number of magical powers," it is "capable of appearing and disappearing: it becomes invisible and in some cases it is also invincible."[2] The body of the possessed, conversely, is "a theatrical stage. . . . [D]ifferent powers and their confrontations manifest themselves within the body. It is not a body transported but a body penetrated in depth. It is the body of investments and counterinvestments."[3]

Foucault's point in making this distinction between witches and the possessed is to play up a more general distinction between juridical power and disciplinary power in the early modern period. The possessed, with their wills bound up in pleasure, with their bodies as sites rather than agents of power represent disciplinary subjects. Witches, with their self-conscious, rational choice, with their active, well-bounded bodies, with their sovereign subjectivity, represent juridical subjects. Once again, though, a second purpose of this discussion is to emphasize the association or overlap between juridical and disciplinary power—and likewise the overlap between the unitary, sovereign consent of the witch and the multiple, tiny consents of the possessed. More often than not, for example, as Foucault notes, it is the witch who is possessed by the devil and it is the possessed who initially agreed to the demonic pact.[4]

As a result, the role of consent in witchcraft becomes much more complicated than it first appears to be. Classical, juridical consent—the consent of the witch—is a single, self-contained, self-conscious act. Modern, disciplinary consent—the consent of the possessed—is repetitive, continuous, absent of will, and situated in bodily or biological pleasure. But each type of consent operates in tandem with the other, in the witch who allows herself to be possessed and in the possessed who signs the devil's contract.[5] More than that, each type of consent is based on an understanding of the body as something that operates beyond human subjectivity or sovereign (if not distributed) human agency. In each, the body is one part of a wider natural or supernatural system, and relevant to the act or activity of consent only in that it is part of this system. In the very act of their consent, witches and the possessed—or witches *as* the possessed—change the physical environment surrounding them. Their consent occurs as their bodies are mapped onto or transformed into the natural world—as they become the environment. Consent in this scenario is thus, first, a nonhuman or suprahuman affair and, second, a natural or supernatural—as much as a political or legal—operation.

Nineteenth- and early twentieth-century stories of suffragists' inappropriate understanding of consent and contract and of their similarity to witches hint at the staying power of these characteristics of witchcraft and possession. Each set of stories emphasizes the unique and uniquely environmental quality of suffragists' consent. Moreover, it is in the collision between these two sets that the most promising examples of nonhuman or computational consent are to be found. As criticisms of suffragists' redefinition of consent and contract give way in these stories to criticisms of suffragists' witchlike reliance on spells, talismans, or seduction, it becomes clear that at stake in the tales of the suffragist as witch is a particular linguistic activity—consent—that occurs only as natural and supernatural systems are altered. More telling, this is a linguistic activity very much familiar to the computer or machine—informational rather than meaningful, physical rather than subjective, tiny or insignificant but capable of infinite iteration or repetition.

Consent, Witchcraft, Code, and Suffrage

Consent was a problem that plagued all sides of the suffrage issue. Prosuffrage advocates argued that, without the vote, women had not consented and could never consent in the future to being governed, while antisuffrage advocates argued that by virtue of living within the borders of a given nation-state, an individual necessarily was in a constant state of consenting. Prosuffrage advocates thus seemed, at least, to adhere to the witch's juridical theory of consent, whereas antisuffrage advocates adhered to the political or disciplinary theory of consent surrounding the possessed. At the same time, however, this distinction was not as stark as it might seem—and indeed, much of the antisuffrage narrative assumed a certain overlap between the two. In 1894, for example, J. M. Buckley, describing the "wrongs and perils" of women's suffrage, stated that the proposition that men cannot represent women until they have legally consented to it is specious, but not sound. Who has ever been asked whether he consents to the government that exists here? That government was established before the present inhabitants were born. Under it the supreme power inheres in adult male citizens. The consent of the governed is and must be taken for granted, except as changes are made by constitutional methods, until a revolution arises.[6]

In her book, *Woman and the Republic,* published in 1897 and then reprinted in 1913 by the Guidon Club Opposed to Woman Suffrage, Helen Kendrick Johnson made a similar point. "The 'consent of the governed,'" she stated, "did not mean that every individual must consent to be governed somehow, by some scheme of government; for its laws were carefully framed so as to compel the external allegiance of those who never consent—the criminal and the anarchist."[7] Furthermore, "it is not true that American women did not, and do not, 'consent to be governed.' They have always consented loyally and joyfully . . . they showed their consent by their deeds. . . . [A]nd the Suffragists themselves consent to be governed every time they accept the protection of the law."[8]

If human agency were the starting point of analysis here, the basic message of each of these passages would be straightforward: suffragists do not understand the nature of political consent, and by insisting on explicitly granting or withholding their consent they are inappropriately introducing an archaic, juridical element into modern social contract theory. Whereas antisuffrage advocates understand agency to inhere in the disciplinary activity of (voting or nonvoting) citizens, suffrage advocates—according to these two criticisms—understand agency to inhere in a linguistic, and sovereign, acceptance or rejection of their roles within a given political structure. An alternative reading of these passages, however, absent agency, might locate the problem that Buckley and Johnson describe not in the suffragists' preference for one (archaic) interpretation of consent over another (modern) interpretation—but rather in the suffragists' introduction into the picture of a third mode of consent, a mechanistic or computational mode that brings the two together.

According to Buckley's interpretation of appropriate governance, for example, the consent of all individual citizens must be repetitive—men as well as women consented before birth, and continue to consent

throughout their lives, to an eternal social contract that placed government into the hands of adult men. The only two moments at which the
repetitive activity or ongoing state of consent might give way to a unitary
or juridical act of consent are, first, moments of constitutional change
and, second, moments of revolution. When suffragists insist on juridi-
cally consenting, or not consenting, to being represented by men, therefore, they are inappropriately and illegitimately attempting to bring these
two theories together. Buckley is arguing, in other words, that suffragists
are attempting to consent, simultaneously, in both the unitary and the
repetitive modes, and that this attempt undermines existing practices of
government.

Johnson engages in a similar rhetorical tactic. Like Buckley, she
notes, first, that the consent of the governed does not mean that all individuals must, via a unitary act or declaration, consent to their political
situation. She then continues in a slightly different direction, however,
arguing, second, that even those criminals and anarchists who "never
consent" nonetheless have effectively consented, and third, that nonsuf-
fragist women have also actively consented via their deeds. Finally, she
concludes that when suffragists insist on appropriating the juridical mode
of consent for women, they are being both hypocritical—having already
taken advantage of the repetitive mode of consent by operating within
the social contract—and dangerous, by introducing discontent into a
contented populace.

Johnson, in other words, also attributes to suffragists a damaging dual
mode of consent. Unlike content women, whose state or activity of consent is manifested in their deeds, and unlike even those who "never consent," whose de facto state of consent is manifested in their compelled allegiance, the suffragist, in Johnson's analysis, consents too much. She
both consents, by deed, to the social contract—taking unfair or hypocritical advantage of legal protection—and insists on consenting at the
same time via a declaration or juridical statement. Far from attributing to
suffragists a single, archaic mode of consent, therefore, both Buckley and
Johnson locate the threat that suffragists pose in their excessive, multiple, and ever expanding desire to consent.

The consent that antisuffrage writers attributed to suffragists was
thus a monstrous amalgam of unitary, juridical, linguistic consent and
repetitive, disciplinary, physical consent—a coming together of the consent of the witch and the consent of the possessed. When suffragists engaged in the act or activity that was consent, that is to say, they deliber-

ately and destructively failed to distinguish between masculine words and feminine deeds (as Johnson puts it) or between the tacit agreement of the individual citizen and the explicit agreement of the constitutional or revolutionary collective (as Buckley puts it). Suffragists' consent, as a result, was simultaneously linguistic and physical as well as simultaneously individual and collective. Not only did it operate through the tiny, physical consents of the disciplined body, but it turned these tiny, physical consents into explicit juridical statements of affiliation or denunciation. Suffragists' juridical, linguistic consent thus occurred only as bodies were put into play.

The extent to which these juridical statements of consent operated not only through the alteration of bodies, but through the alteration of the broader physical or environmental systems of which these bodies formed a part becomes clear in the discussions of suffragists casting spells or seducing the populace—discussions that more often than not run parallel to these analyses of consent. Indeed, the coming together of these two forms of consent within the witchcraft narrative gave the speaking suffragist's words a particularly potent, environmental quality.

Suffragists, for instance, were described by Gail Hamilton in one 1868 essay as interpreting the ballot as "a sort of talisman, with a power to ward off all harm from its possessor"—this despite the fact that the ballot was "a clumsy contrivance," in comparison with women's preexisting linguistic tools: "the pen, the fireside, and the thousand subtle social influences, penetrating, pervasive, purifying."[9] In the same essay, women who sought to use law to "sweep away vice" were warned that "into the empty, swept, and garnished house will enter seven devils more wicked than the first."[10] A few years later, in 1871, a second essay chided suffragists for being willing to give up "chivalrous deference," described as "the Koh-i-noor they now possess for the brassy, lacquered bauble contained in the ballot-box."[11]

Finally, in 1913, Mrs. Arthur M. Dodge, interviewed by the *New York Times*, described "the suffrage disturbance" as a type of "sex disturbance,"[12] the success of which was predicated on the sexual manipulation of men.[13] "Just so long as women clamor for 'political rights' and yet dress in garments that are the definition of bad taste," Dodge continued,

> all the votes in the world will not change the trend of sentiment in society throughout the whole population of the country. When I say that the suffragists rely after all on their sex and on the appeal of

their sex to men, I am repeating only what men on the sidewalks and in the club windows of New York said when the suffrage parade passed up Fifth Avenue in New York a week ago last Saturday.[14]

Unlike the asexual spinster or the monstrous man-woman who populated the earlier antisuffrage narratives, in other words, here it is the seductive, highly sexed, manipulative siren who represents the typical suffragist. Whereas before, suffragists were mocked for their inability to influence men, here they are both encouraged to do so—through "subtle social influences"—and also denigrated for doing so as they rely "on the appeal of their sex."

This does not mean, however, that the suffrage narrative had changed a great deal between the mid-nineteenth and the early twentieth centuries. When the first two passages, for instance, attribute to suffragists a belief in the talismanic power of the ballot—a belief that a particular speech act (voting) might pack a natural or supernatural punch—they are essentially arguing once again that suffragists inappropriately link physical deeds to linguistic expression. When these passages furthermore juxtapose this misplaced belief in the supernatural things that a vote might do with a reminder of the subtle, penetrating, and pervasive effects of feminine speech as it already exists, they are warning against any commingling of these two types of speech, and of the types of consent that go with them. The problem with suffragists' speech, in other words, is not, according to Hamilton, that talismanic speech might replace existing feminine speech, but that the two might overlap.

Regardless of whether Hamilton or the suffragists genuinely believed the ballot to be a talisman with supernatural power, that is to say (clearly neither did), the rhetorical positioning of suffragists' speech at this place between the talismanic and the pervasive, between the witch and the possessed, attributed to it the same damaging qualities that the discussions of suffragists' consent did. As long as suffragists remained caught at the intersection between the talisman and the thousand subtle social influences, their speech and consent produced untoward, clumsy physical effects. As long as this speech was both talismanic and pervasive, it combined the external, singular jolt of the former with the universal omnipresence of the latter. More to the point, as long as suffragists' speech simultaneously operated through deeds, through objects (talismans), and through subtle influences, its danger inhered not in its *redefinition* of consent, but in its *resituation* of consent across nonhuman or physical spaces, rather than within human or political bodies. Suffragists' speech turned consent into an environmental rather than a bodily, political, or subjective issue.

This alteration of consent via nonhuman, systemic, or witchlike speech becomes particularly pronounced in Dodge's discussion. On the one hand, her analysis redeploys the earlier antisuffrage strategies that defined suffragists in relation to their sexuality (or lack thereof) in order to deprive them of rational political identity. Whereas earlier on, suffragists were monstrously asexual, here suffragists are, like witches, hypersexual. In both cases, their essential characteristic is their bodily existence—and as beings solely defined by bodies and sex, they are ostensibly irrelevant to political speech, subjectivity, and agency. On the other hand, however, it is worth looking more closely at how Dodge comes to the conclusion that suffragists *are* so dangerously sexual. Rather than taking it for granted that Dodge is attempting to prevent suffragists from appropriating political identities, it might also be useful to ask more precisely what it is about the parading women that Dodge so fears.

The seemingly false dichotomy that Dodge sets up between seeking political rights and dressing in bad taste, for instance, may not be as incongruous as it initially appears. Nor is it necessarily just one further example of modern, liberal political identity resting on conformity to gendered codes of dress. In addition, clamoring for political rights and dressing in bad taste are two types of speech—linked to two types of consent—that the suffragists, according to Dodge, are inappropriately attempting to bring together. Whereas the clamor for political rights is a variation on juridical consent—an act that initiates a sovereign subject, who in turn actively agrees to participation in a given political structure—dressing in bad taste is a variation on disciplinary consent. It is an ongoing physical or bodily activity that is subtle, yet significant—but that just as inevitably situates a subject within a social contract. Suffragists' speech requires engaging in both.

More to the point, by engaging in both, by bringing these two incongruous modes of consent together, suffragists' speech also potentially shifts not just political structures, not just bodily boundaries, but—via the parade—entire urban grids. When Dodge decries not *just* clamoring for political rights, and not *just* dressing in bad taste, but, horrifically, doing both at the same time, and then *parading through the streets*, she is indeed making a distinct point about how suffragists' speech modifies the spectrum of consent and thus *in turn* physical environments. She is arguing that if suffragists' speech is simultaneously linguistic and physical, and if this simultaneity leaves suffragists in a constant (linguistic and physical) state of consent, this speech also poses a direct, if potential, environmental threat. Trapped at the intersection of the consent of the witch and the consent of the possessed, the parading suffragists described by Dodge must manifest this consent by flowing through the urban streets—demonstrating in a frighteningly overt way that consent need not have to do with the waiving of rights, need not have to do even with the transformation of biological or bodily space into political or legal space, but might instead be about streams of data running through networks, systems, or grids.

As much as Dodge seems to be implying (or stating outright) that suffragists' inappropriate speech and inappropriate consent are leaving them open to unmentionable forms of assault, therefore, the underlying fear that she expresses is of a type of consent that operates through networks, spaces, or grids, rather than, or in addition to, on specific bodies. According to Dodge, suffragists' speech involves a new, amalgamated, and monstrous form of consent—a form of consent that is just as inappropriate in its physical, systemic, and environmental implications as it is in its political, bodily, and sexual ones. Bluntly, it is a mode of consent more suited to witches and machines than it could ever be to human subjects. It is a mode of consent that occurs when information flows through, or on top of, rights and bodies, rather than when rights are waived, or bodies are disciplined. It is a mode of consent, that is to say, that evades humans and that ignores humans' political or biological concerns.

Conclusion

Of all of the different types of speech acts and activities that appear in this book, consent seems the most alien or irrelevant to code. In liberal legal theory, consent is a hyperbolically human concept. It is fundamental to the rule of law because it, and it alone, can make trespasses and violations functional or even ethical. Consent marks the line between sex and rape, between a visit and a burglary, or between surgery and assault.[15] The ability to consent is also the defining characteristic of the rational, active, liberal citizen who is so frequently held up in opposition to the underage, incompetent, or insane passive citizen. Highlighting the role of consent in stories of suffragists' witchlike speech and behavior—in stories of their predilection for talismans, spells, and seduction—thus serves two purposes in this chapter.

First, doing so demonstrates, again, the effectiveness of machine code as a model for discussions of speech at work. It shows that liberal, or simply human, theories of consent are not the only theories available—and that consent can operate as effectively across physical or mechanical systems as it does when embedded in human bodies. These stories of suffragists' threatening speech indeed gesture, at least, toward a nonhuman theory of consent that ignores the line between doing things to bodies, property, or identities and doing things within environments, spaces, or networks. They posit a theory that dismantles the apparent opposition between rational, capable, active citizens and irrational, incompetent, passive citizens. And finally, they suggest a theory that recognizes consent to be as much a mechanical activity as it is a bodily or political act. More simply, they begin to sketch a type of consent that might be executed by machines as well as by humans.

As a result, these stories also serve a second purpose. They forge a connection between consent as it implicitly appeared in the previous chapter on the repetitive speech of the parrhesiastes and consent as it appears in the next chapter on insane speech and its remedies. If a machine can consent, then so too can an informationally overwhelming parrhesiastes and an incompetent psychotic who hears voices. At stake is not the relationship between consent and subjectivity or citizenship, but rather consent and the environmental systems of which these subjects form one small node or part. Put another way, as much as stories about suffragists, consent, witchcraft, and particularly hypersexual witchcraft can be read in a framework of agency—as much as these stories can indeed be read as examples of suffragists marginalized and relegated to the irrational, hysterical, and apolitical sidelines—alternative frameworks of inquiry, absent agency, allow likewise alternative readings.

Perhaps the question to ask when reading these stories is thus not how suffragists were marginalized or relegated to these apolitical spaces, or how this marginalization might be prevented from happening in the future, but whether marginalization of this sort really makes any difference to the operation of consent. If consent ceases to be about human identity formation and instead becomes about mechanical or environmental change, the ethical implications of these stories change drastically. And just as parrhesia suddenly takes on modern or contemporary relevance when brought into the linguistic universe of machine code, so too the incompetent or insane not quite human subject ceases to be a cautionary tale in this universe, and instead becomes one variation on a perfectly acceptable norm.

Chapter Nine : Insane Speech and Its Remedies

Stories that posited suffragists as insane, demented, or unbalanced were widespread throughout the late nineteenth and early twentieth centuries—part of a more general discourse of feminine hysteria, and the product of a well-studied nineteenth-century trend toward pathologizing and medicalizing any activity, and especially any linguistic activity, that fell outside of an increasingly narrow norm. The purpose of this chapter is to emphasize, once more, that these stories are as much about altered and alterable physical systems—as much examples of the work of computational language on mechanical networks—as they are about marginalized or disciplined human subjects shattered by human language gone awry.

Taking the insane speech of the suffragists as another example of machines running code indeed opens up an arena for rethinking not just the damage that this speech might do, but also the fear or distaste with which *remedies* for this speech, either medical or political, were often met. One of the themes that reappears in stories of suffragists' insane speech, for instance, is that as necessary as a medical and political remedy might be to translating their information- or noise-rich gibberish into something recognizable and recognizably human, such a remedy by no means solved the more fundamental problems that their linguistic activities posed. Suffragists, even when cured, remained insane in these stories, their speech remained nonhuman, and the environmental threat underlying it remained very much in evidence. Even when the speaker was cured, in other words, her *speech* continued to run the same hysterical, demented, and above all, threatening, operations.

In order to address these aspects of suffragists' speech, this chapter therefore takes as a framework for analysis not only computational models but also an extensive rereading of a more recent, twenty-first-century iteration of the insane speech narrative. This iteration—the story of death row prisoner Charles Singleton—is arguably more relevant to late twentieth- and twenty-first-century theories of speaking machines than stories of the women's suffrage movement might be. But it also unquestionably hearkens back to the earlier suffrage narrative. As such, it serves as a useful link between the environmental interpretations of the nineteenth-century feminine hysteria that underlie this chapter and the late twentieth-century fears and fantasies of code run amok to which it nods. Singleton's story, that is to say, works at the intersection of both stories of suffragists' hysterical or insane speech and stories of machine language operating to the detriment of the physical world.

When in 2003, for example, the Eighth Circuit Court of Appeals ruled in *Singleton v. Norris* that Singleton could be required to take psychiatric medication rendering him fit for legal execution, this decision rested on the idea that Singleton's speech, like the speech of suffragists, was fundamentally information rich, but message poor—and that, as a result, it operated as a kind of infinitely iterated code on physical rather than political, legal, or subjective systems. The ruling highlighted the physical, distributed, and systemic, rather than embodied and human, character of insane linguistic activity.

Similarly, when the media discussion of Singleton's fate emphasized his transformation from a schizophrenic prone to hearing voices to a cured prisoner prepared for coherent speech and legally mandated death, this emphasis defined Singleton's speech as an activity—also like the speech of suffragists and machines—that was distinctly physical as well as nonhuman. It was, that is to say, an activity that operated beyond the usual linguistic categories of human and political or nonhuman and apolitical. And finally, when these discussions questioned the validity of Singleton's medical remedy in the form of a pill or injection, they mirrored earlier discussions questioning the suffragists' political remedy in the form of the vote—recognizing that nonhuman speech is not only unresponsive, but *irrelevant*, to any human impetus toward cure.

As much as Singleton's speech, once medicated, may have become recognizable to humans in a way that it was perhaps not before, in other words, it—like that of the suffragists—did not itself become more human, nor did it become less physical. As the widespread disgust with, on the one hand, medicating Singleton and, on the other hand, extending the vote to suffragists made clear, the remedy was not a remedy, and the threat that their speech posed remained a threat.

Singleton and the suffragists, even when cured, remained not just "digital subjects" as such subjects have been described by Hayles. They were not simply prone to infinite "fragmentation and recombination,"[1] and they did not simply communicate through applications running on top of programs running on top of code—rather than through the dredging up or exposure of interior humanist depths.[2] In addition, and perhaps more so, the speech of Singleton and the suffragists—detached from human speakers altogether—operated *as* speech via the same alterations to physical and environmental networks, via the same distributed effects, that it had implemented before the cure went into effect. The remedial speech of Singleton and the suffragists was therefore just as potentially harmful to the world as their insane speech had been in the absence of any cure.

Once again, though, rereading stories of Singleton's or the suffragists' insane speech and its remedies requires first abandoning analytical frameworks reliant on human agency. The vocabulary of agency here is unsuited, just as it was in previous chapters, to expressing the particular and peculiar environmental problems posed by both this mode of speech and its cures. By diagnosing insane speech and the medical or political responses to it as matters of human concern or human subjectivity, such analyses indeed prevent the full implications of such speech from being recognized. By ignoring the nonhuman, computational, and environmental character of this speech, and by leaving machine-oriented linguistic activity outside of discussions of threatening speech writ large, they consign interpretations of insane speech, hysterical speech, psychotic speech, and their remedies to a confined world of illness, pathology, and cure. They ignore the potential *effectiveness* of insane linguistic activity and approach it instead with horror, sentiment, or, at best, therapy.

Singleton's Insane Speech and Its Remedies

On January 6, 2004, the state of Arkansas executed Charles Singleton, and the problem that "artificial sanity"[3] had posed to the U.S. practice of capital punishment seemed settled. By deciding, first, that medication could cure Singleton of both his insanity and his incompetence for execution and, second, that death was only an "unwanted consequence"[4] of this cure, the U.S. courts determined that being made fit for political life and being made fit for biological death were by no means contradictory processes.[5] This coming together of Singleton's political life with his biological death has occupied much of the discussion surrounding the case. Among the central questions that Singleton's fate raised, for instance, were whether political life *can* be artificially induced or medicated into being, whether legal execution can or should depend so directly on this fragile form of life, and whether indicators of political life in the liberal tradition, such as consent to medical treatment, have any role at all to play in trials such as Singleton's.

This focus on human life and human death also, however, shifted attention away from two equally significant problems that plagued the case: what specifically the medication did to, or for, Singleton, and what the environmental implications of this medico-legal alteration to Singleton might be. For the most part, the medication itself seemed important only as an instrument in the hands of humans working on other humans. Singleton was schizophrenic; schizophrenia was an obstacle to legal execution; the medication alleviated Singleton's schizophrenic symptoms; Singleton thus became either actually or artificially fit for capital punishment.[6] The antipsychotic medication, in other words, was portrayed first and foremost as a tool for shifting Singleton from incompetence to competence—and this was either a miscarriage or a fortification of justice.

But the medication also did something more than this. It made Singleton capable of engaging in a particular mode of speech. When he was schizophrenic, Singleton was, according to the courts, both unfit for execution *and* unfit for speech. When he was on the medication, he could both effectively die *and* effectively speak. Far from serving in a mere instrumental capacity, therefore, and far from simply making death possible, the medication also opened up an alternative mode for thinking about the harm inherent in Singleton's speech and in speech more generally. By defining Singleton's tendency to hear voices as a harmful linguistic activity that, in turn, might be cured by granting him a capacity to produce speech, the courts were making a clear and deliberate distinction between what constituted threatening speech and what constituted nonthreatening speech.

Voices heard posed a threat. This threat rested, first, in the irrelevance of these voices to any human speaker, second, in their message-poor quality, and third, in the fact that these voices were simultaneously produced and recorded—part of a system surrounding Singleton rather than the acts of discrete speakers and listeners. Moreover, as will become clear, this threat was as much physical and environmental as it was legal, political, or subjective. Contrarily, the coherent speech that the medicated Singleton would ideally produce was nonthreatening. It could always be traced back to a single, discrete human speaker, its purpose was to convey meaning, and it assumed a linear or cause-and-effect relationship among speaker, speech, and listener. Once again, though, as much as Singleton's medication sought to grant him this capacity to produce human speech, the media narrative surrounding it and him denied this medication its fully curative properties. Even when it had been ostensibly medicated away, Singleton's *nonhuman* speech was still there, still running beneath the human translation, and continued to pose the same physical threats that it always had.

Put another way, whereas the human speech toward which the medication sought to move Singleton adhered to classical Aristotelian linguistic categorizations—with their emphasis on divisions among human, slave, and animal[7]—Singleton's insane speech, as well as his incompletely cured speech, inverted or exploded these categorizations. As Jacques Rancière has argued in summarizing these Aristotelian categories,

> The slave is the one who has the capacity to understand a logos without having the capacity of the logos. He is the specific transition from animality to humanity that Aristotle defines most precisely as participating in the linguistic community by way of comprehension but not understanding: . . . the slave is the one who participates in reason so far as to recognize it . . . but not so as to possess it.[8]

Of the three potential linguistic spaces available in the Aristotelian natural-as-political world, in other words, Singleton's speech was relevant to none. It had little to do with the space occupied by humans—who both recognize and possess rational speech. Nor could it occur in the space occupied by animals—who do neither. And finally, it was not a part of the space occupied by slaves—who recognize rational speech but do not possess it. Singleton's speech was simply not harmful in the way that any of these other linguistic activities might be harmful. It did not, for instance, silence or do violence to others, thereby transforming these others from humans into slaves or animals. Nor did it produce a situation in which

the human might be defined as "an animal whose politics places his existence as a living being in question,"[9] or a world in which a human's bare
life might become the essence of politics.[10] Bluntly, these Aristotelian
linguistic categories, with their reliance on theories of agency and identity, and with their relentless placement of the human at the center of
any linguistic activity,[11] could not effectively capture what Singleton's
insane or cured speech was doing.

If Singleton's linguistic activity *was* relevant to this classical linguistic categorization, therefore, it was only because it revealed the possibility of a fourth permutation of Aristotle's formula of speech and existence—a permutation that does not take the human as its reference
point, and a permutation that has more to do with environmental than
with subjective change. In addition to humans who both recognize and
possess rational speech, animals who do neither, and slaves who recognize rational speech but do not possess it, there remains the question of
who or what might *possess* rational speech but not *recognize* it.[12] Who or
what, that is to say, might hear rational speech, act upon or through this
speech, but not seek or desire to recognize the meaning of this speech?

One answer to this question is Singleton. A second answer, however,
again, is the machine running code. The machine running code is as
much defined by language as the human is; it is indeed perhaps more embedded in linguistic activity than any human—but its linguistic activity
is physical rather than rational, possessed, run, or operated rather than
recognized. More to the point, the machine running code is entirely
functional and healthy as it occupies this fourth space evoked by Aristotle's formula. The machine is not in need of cure, it is not the object of
pity, and it is certainly not the object of medico-legal intervention. The
only problem posed by its speech is that, like Singleton's, it always poses
a potential systemic or environmental threat.

Both Singleton and the machine running code are unaware, yet enveloped in speech. This speech is detached from any speaker, simply
there to be heard or to go into effect, comes from multiple directions at
once, and is irrelevant to dialogue or response. Both Singleton and the
machine running code are also, in the words of Latour, in need of a
"speech prosthesis"[13] in order to be understood within the human
realm—a pill, an injection, a program, or an application. But, fundamentally—and regardless of these potential prostheses—the speech of both
Singleton and the machine running code is environmental rather than
subjective. Both Singleton and the machine are part of—or are them-

selves—smart environments rather than speaking subjects. They are closer to John Searle's "Chinese room" as it was reinterpreted by Edwin Hutchins and described later by Hayles than they are to the fractured and shattered psychotic or schizophrenic of the literature concerned with agency.

As Hayles states, Hutchins found a way around Searle's relentlessly human-centered analysis of speech and intelligence—an analysis based in part on an ostensibly absurd scenario in which a man alone in a room, who does not know Chinese, passes nonsense messages in Chinese to Chinese speakers outside of the room, who think that this man does know the language, demonstrating that "communication in Chinese can take place without the actors knowing what their actions mean."[14] According to Searle, this hypothetical situation shows that only humans are capable of intelligent linguistic interaction because only humans would be able to distinguish between the meaningful messages that they produced intentionally and the random messages they passed along without purpose. According to Hutchins, however, what Searle has proved is not that humans alone can think, but that even if the speaker and listener do not know Chinese, the environment clearly does: "In Hutchins's neat interpretation," Hayles concludes, "Searle's argument is valuable precisely because it makes clear that it is not Searle but the entire room that knows Chinese. In this distributed cognitive system, the Chinese room knows more than do any of its components, including Searle."[15]

Although Hayles's purpose in this discussion is to describe the working of systems rather than necessarily to challenge the predominance of human-centered theories of speech, the example she invokes is an excellent way into a wider conversation about the environmental implications of Singleton's insane speech, the suffragists' insane speech, and insane speech more generally. Setting aside the analytical frameworks based on agency and identity that situate speech always with human speakers—and understanding speech, in turn, as something systemic and decentered in which, say, a room rather than a human speaker might engage—allows a multidimensional understanding of what insane speech might be doing. It not only rescues the schizophrenic or psychotic from being pitied or relentlessly cured, but also makes clear that this speech may be more than simply human, and may be relevant to systems that operate beyond the human.

As a type of nonhuman code, distributed throughout a system, working as the fourth permutation of Aristotle's formula, Singleton's and the suffragists' insane speech—precisely because it *was* physical rather than rational—was something that could alter environments and networks as much as, if not more than, it altered human politics. It, like the Chinese room, demonstrated the poverty of discussions of speech that do not range beyond identity, agency, and subjectivity. And above all, it demonstrated the value of discussions of speech that take up these nonhuman issues—the methodological and also *ethical* usefulness of situating speech beyond human concerns.

Psychotic Things and Linear Minds

One of the more effective ways in which the media narrative played up Singleton's nonhuman possession but not recognition of rational speech, and the environmental threat that such speech posed, was to describe his speech, his lawyer's speech, his family's speech, and the law's speech as a sort of integrated system operating as a unit to produce physical as well as legal change. Although the media reports appeared in many ways to set up an opposition between Singleton's (irrational) speech and that of his lawyer or his family, the fundamental purpose of much of the writing was at the same time, likewise, to tell the story of a unified linguistic network that operated beyond any dichotomy between rational and irrational speakers.

An extensive Associated Press report of Singleton's clemency hearing, for instance, begins with the point that although Singleton "didn't even want" the hearing, it was nonetheless "turned into a crusade for understanding a schizophrenic like him."[16] The report continues,

> Singleton's sister Sara argued that Singleton was attempting to commit state-assisted suicide by trying to waive his hearing and seek execution. And while doctors and other experts testified that schizophrenics hear voices and are delusional, Singleton interrupted, accusing his attorney of staring at him. . . . [H]e appeared exasperated as [his attorney, Jeff] Rosenzweig argued for clemency, repeatedly interrupted him and said "He does not speak for me. He speaks for himself." Singleton alleged that Rosenzweig and Sara Singleton were conspiring and that it was a money-making scheme for his lawyer. When given the chance to speak for himself, Singleton gave what was apparently stream-of-conscious remarks that

touched on the Bible and how he could hear the voice of his dead father. . . . [B]oard member Joe Franklin asked whether Singleton had recently received medication. Rosenzweig said Singleton had not approved a waiver of a new federal law that prevents disclosure of medical records. Singleton interjected that he has been receiving an injection once a month, but did not say what drug he was receiving, or its effect. Singleton tried to have the board cancel the hearing, but Rosenzweig said he pursued it anyway because state law doesn't require that only the inmate can make the request. The board was scheduled to meet later Friday in Little Rock to hear from those supporting Singleton's execution.[17]

A second discussion of the case also apparently contrasted Singleton's psychotic speech with the speech of his lawyer, his family, and the legal establishment. This article, on "the controversial fate of a condemned killer who believes his cell is possessed by demons," starts with a description of Singleton as "looking forward to dying because it will end his struggle with mental illness and silence the voices he hears in his head even when he takes his medicine."[18] "Deprived of medication," it continues, "Singleton descends into paranoid raving and stops eating."[19] The article then moves on to Rosenzweig's analysis of the situation, in which the lawyer asserts bluntly that Singleton "is mentally ill. There is no question about that," but that he "has a waxing and waning mental illness," such that it is impossible to know at precisely what point he is sane and at what point he is insane.[20]

Finally, a third article, on Singleton's last words, rearranges the relationship among Singleton's speech, his lawyer's speech, and the law's speech. Again, Singleton appears in this article as only marginally coherent, and the purpose of the reporting is seemingly to play up the contradiction between his linguistic activity and the law's linguistic activity. The article begins by noting that "the last words of Arkansas death row inmate Charles Singleton, executed Tuesday night, referred witnesses to a statement he had written by hand."[21] It continues that Singleton's only spoken words were, "I was going to speak but I wrote it down. I'll leave it up to the warden."[22] Finally, prior to printing the full text of the statement, the article concludes that "Department of Correction spokeswoman Dina Tyler said the statement was barely legible, so correction officials typed copies that were passed out after Singleton's death."[23]

It is both possible and valid to read these media reports through the lens of human or nonhuman agency. Such a reading might emphasize the clash or dislocation among the speech of the prisoner, the speech of the lawyer and family, and the speech of the law as a means of demonstrating the injustice of executing someone so clearly without political or moral identity. In the first passage, this reading might note, Singleton disagrees with both his lawyer and his sister, while his lawyer remains hemmed in by legal obstacles that stand in the way of his work for Singleton. Both Singleton's insanity and the law's abandonment of common sense are accentuated by the sane and rational labor of the lawyer.

In the second passage, once again, Rosenzweig's calm appraisal of the situation remains in direct contradistinction to Singleton's paranoid raving and the law's relentless condemnation of a person who believes his cell is haunted by demons. Finally, in the third passage, Singleton's illegibility is juxtaposed against the clear, typed copies of his speech, translated now by the correctional officials instead of the lawyer. Here, once more, the implicit question to be asked is whether Singleton is insane, incompetent, or without agency; the implicit answer is a resounding yes.

Alternatively, but still starting with questions of agency, a reading of these passages might step back from these apparent oppositions and ask how precisely they were developed by the reporters and the commentators. Such a reading might stress, for example, the rhetorical placement of the prisoner, the lawyer, and the law in the narrative of Singleton's hearings and death. Rather than accepting the idea of a collision or contradiction among the speech of the three players—an idea that assumes that each carried equal rhetorical weight—this reading might note that Singleton, Rosenzweig, and the court were far from narrative equals. Indeed, each is presented in the media accounts in a way that should be recognizable to any reader of post-Enlightenment era didactic fiction: Rosenzweig plays the role of the trustworthy and rational narrator of both the incompetent Singleton and the monstrous law—the last two framed, objectified, and undermined precisely as they enter the narrative.

Even as Singleton is "given the chance to speak for himself," for example, this speech—as well as the law's speech—is displaced and framed by Rosenzweig's story, and sometimes by his explicit exegesis. Whether we take Daniel Defoe's *Robinson Crusoe*, Mary Shelly's *Frankenstein*, or for that matter Henry James's *Turn of the Screw* as the model, we can see a familiar hierarchy here of narrative authority. Both the incompetent prisoner and the monstrous law are denied any linguistic agency by virtue of being objects of discourse. Their speech can only be the narrator's speech, and as such their speech serves only the narrator's purpose. In this type of analysis, the question is not whether Singleton is insane or incompetent, but whether Singleton has been the victim of discursive violence, and thereby deprived of his agency; once again, the implicit answer here is a resounding yes.

Although each of these approaches is, again, effective, neither gets at the full extent of the threat posed by the voices that Singleton heard, or by his linguistic activity more broadly defined. By focusing so exclusively on agency, these two interpretations and others like them ignore the systemic and environmental character, as opposed to the human character, of Singleton's speech. Attempting to fit this speech into one of the three classical Aristotelian linguistic categories, they deny the possibility that Singleton's linguistic activity might in fact be more relevant to the fourth permutation of Aristotle's formula, in which humans as well as nonhumans possess rational speech but do not—and do not need to—recognize it. In their search for meaning, these approaches do not consider the importance of noise, information, and physical effectiveness. They cannot get beyond speaking humans and into speaking rooms.

The initial passage, for instance, might be reread as, first, affirming that Singleton's desire to have or not to have a clemency hearing is beside the point and, second, emphasizing the superlative importance of "understanding a schizophrenic like him." Couched in such a way, neither Singleton's words nor his lawyer's words are interesting for any sense they may convey, for their truth or falsehood, or for their benefit as legal testimony. Indeed, the majority of the report is devoted to Singleton's "stream of consciousness" "interruptions" and "interjections." The speech of Singleton thus works in this passage *alongside* that of his lawyer and his family, as a system or as part of an operation, and is of interest only to the extent that it might interrupt, reroute, or halt the flow of noise or information.

By emphasizing interjection over message, that is to say, this narrative of the clemency hearing is likewise emphasizing systemic change over the transmission of meaning. Or, put another way, speech is evaluated here not according to whether Singleton, his lawyer, or his family might recognize or comprehend it, but whether Singleton—or these others—might possess and execute it. Important is not who speaks for what purpose, but whether speech, detached from speaker and purpose, might interrupt or shift the flow of noise and information, whether speech might perform an environmental function, and whether the linguistic operation in its entirety might be a coherent whole.

The irrelevance of Singleton's speech to meaning or recognition—the extent to which his speech neither can nor should be linked to rational choices, desires, or interests—indeed becomes particularly clear when his sister's argument that he is trying to commit "state assisted suicide" is marginalized. By noting but then dismissing Sara Singleton's point, the narrative makes clear that any discussion of Singleton rationally recognizing language, and using it to achieve a desired and subjective result, is alien to "understanding a schizophrenic like him." Sara Singleton's argument, in other words, leaves her brother's speech too well embedded in the world of recognition—as does any debate over agency, over whether Singleton represents himself, whether Rosenzweig represents Singleton, or whether the law represents either. At stake instead is the contingent or systemic effectiveness of this speech.

The two passages that follow this narrative of the clemency hearing also start with a nod to Singleton's choice or intention—his intention to die and "end his struggle with mental illness," or his choice to make his last thoughts known to others. But each then moves on to demonstrate the absurdity of rational choice in this linguistic context—Singleton's fundamentally "raving" or "illegible" speech—and then quickly engages in a description of the physical operation of this speech. In the first passage, Singleton's insanity is characterized by his refusal of language alongside his refusal of food. The medication must therefore force the prisoner simultaneously to talk and to eat. In the second, the physical character of Singleton's speech is more extreme—his speech goes into operation at the moment that his body ceases to operate.

Once again, though, as much as stories of Singleton's insane speech and voices heard were stories of physical harm, the stories of his *cured* speech and of the speech that resulted from the medico-legal remedy held out to him were almost more terrifying. These stories and reports made clear that the ostensible cure for Singleton's linguistic situation was by no means actually a cure—and that as much as the medication may have helped, as a prosthesis, to translate Singleton's linguistic activity into something recognizable by humans, it itself remained nonhuman, computational, and irrelevant to human dialogue or discussion. More to the point, Singleton's speech, still possessed but not fully recognized, remained harmful—the threat that it posed to political, legal, subjective,

and natural or environmental systems was just as prominent as it had always been.

A recurring theme in the Singleton narrative, for instance, was that
the court's decision to medicate Singleton into speaking was proof that
the United States (or the state of Arkansas) had become a totalitarian or
bureaucratic state of the sort criticized by late nineteenth- and early
twentieth-century writers such as George Orwell, Aldous Huxley, and
Franz Kafka. Orwell, Huxley, and Kafka were in fact repeatedly invoked
by opponents of the court's ruling, and although the basic dual message
behind these discussions was, first, that intrusive government control is a
bad thing, and second, that Singleton was a victim of such intrusive government control, there was a more complex lesson to be learned from
them as well. At stake in these discussions was not simply the distinction
between good and bad government regulation or care, but the distinction
between appropriate (human) and inappropriate (nonhuman) speech.

Over the course of a single article, for example, one writer moves
from George Orwell and his assertion that "only an intellectual would
believe something like that; ordinary people have too much sense," to
"the majority opinion, which sounds a little like an excerpt from Aldous
Huxley's *Brave New World*," to the question of whether "this is an excerpt from the annals of American law or something out of Kafka? And
just who's crazy here?"[24] The same writer concludes another piece with
the following: "now that the courts have done their worst, the fate of
Charles Laverne Singleton depends on Governor Mike Huckabee, and
whether he will show mercy. Or just some common sense. In this case,
he's got 48 hours to prove himself pro-life."[25] A second article starts with
the point that "time was when people read the works of Franz Kafka for a
sense of the surreal. Today they need only pick up the paper."[26] A third,
addressing a case that occurred alongside the *Singleton* decision, argues
that "critics of the government's position see shades of *1984*, the novel
by George Orwell that warned of brainwashing and other inhumane
abuses of dictatorial government aided by intrusive technology."[27] And
finally, a National Public Radio discussion of the story starts off with a
commentator's assertion that "it sounds like something Kafka would be
involved in."[28]

At first glance, the invocation of the Orwell-Huxley-Kafka triumvi-
rate seems an easily decipherable rhetorical move. The names of all three
have become shorthand[29] in political discourse for, first, the fantasy of a
clean dichotomy between individual and state, and second, unease that

this dichotomy is indeed so very much a fantasy. More specifically, they have become a means of articulating the apparent clash between an individual's freedom of consciousness or speech and a collective's regulation or domination of this consciousness or speech. Speech in these discussions is a simple thing, a tool that exists outside of, and can or must be used against, power. There is very little attempt to deal with the notion of speech as constitutive of power, and certainly no interest in other, alternative, and nonhuman modes of speech.

Again, though, the role that Orwell, Huxley, and Kafka play in narratives of Singleton's trial and death also points to something more than this. Whereas it is true, for instance, that the government's domination of the individual is a fear and a fantasy in all of these passages, this fear is seemingly secondary to the commentators' overriding *linguistic* concerns. Orwell, Huxley, and Kafka exist in these discussions first and foremost to play up the nonsensical, intellectual, crazy, or surreal turn that *language* takes when it runs up against the system of which Singleton (along with his lawyer, his family, and the law) is a part. The fear voiced by the commentators is thus not that a bad, totalitarian state might seek to regulate speech—nor is it that individuals might be deprived of their freedom of consciousness. If anything, it is quite the opposite: the fear expressed in this reporting is a fear that in a universe in which the *Singleton* decision can happen, speech itself necessarily becomes complicated, confusing, bizarre, or inexplicable. The fear is of speech suddenly out of an individual's control and—given that the human quality of "mercy" is equated with "common sense"—out of human control, but nonetheless continuing to operate. It is of speech that happens for physical, systemic, or environmental reasons rather than for the purposes of conveying messages or meaning among specific human speakers. It is a fear of the end of speech that might be mobilized for the purpose of human communication, dialogue, or care, and the beginning of speech that occurs beyond these purposes.

The invocation of Orwell-Huxley-Kafka in these passages, therefore, indicates by no means, necessarily, a desire for autonomy in speech or consciousness—nor does it indicate a desire for a government of individuals possessed of the untrammeled freedom to speak their minds. Rather, these references point to a yearning for an authority over, and a uniformity of, speech that will keep all linguistic activity within the controlled, rational, and human realm, rather than allowing it to venture in uncontrolled, nonsensical or nonhuman directions. As far as these writers are concerned, political authoritarianism is perfectly acceptable—preferable indeed to "nonsense" or the abandonment of "mercy" as "common sense"—provided this regulation and control will stave off the linguistic chaos threatened by what is essentially information-rich machine code. The role that the twentieth century's most popular antitotalitarian writers play in this narrative of insane speech cured or remedied, then, is as advocates for linguistic control in the hands of humans wed to linguistic self-control also in the hands of humans—as advocates for a regulated, reasonable harmony between the speech of the individual human and the speech of a humanistic law. They exist in these passages to plead for a world in which the question of "just who is crazy" might in fact be a meaningful one.

Because the alternative world is one in which this question serves no purpose. It is a world in which linguistic activity ceases to be a means determining which human is rational and which human is irrational, which human is making sense and which human is not, which human recognizes speech and which human merely possesses it, or which human is crazy and which human is not. It is a world in which speech, horrifically, can be far *more* than a human, legal, or political phenomenon. This alternative world, ostensibly criticized by Orwell-Huxley-Kafka, is one in which insane speech and ineffectively cured speech—or in which nonhuman speech and machine speech—are just as valuable as rational human speech. It is a world where machines running code, executing physical systems, are just as worthy of discussion as humans engaging in dialogue. And finally, it is a world in which Singleton's linguistic activity is of interest not because it is a cautionary tale but because it is and can be a model or a norm.

Suffragists' Insane Speech and Its Remedies

Taking Singleton's speech as a starting point thus opens up a space for rereading a number of stories of threatening speech—including the threatening speech of the insane, and sometimes, if ineffectively cured, suffragist. Like Singleton, the suffragists heard voices, and like Singleton's their insane speech gave them an affinity to machine code, placing them into the (implicit) fourth Aristotelian linguistic category. Like Singleton, suffragists hearing voices posed an environmental threat. And like Singleton's threat, the suffragists' threat rested on their operation as parts of a smart environment rather than on their existence as coherent human subjects; it derived from the dispersed spaces from which their voices emanated; and, finally, it inhered in the information-rich and message-poor nature of their linguistic activities. Also like Singleton's, however, the suffragists' cure—in the form of a vote rather than a pill or an injection—created as many environmental problems as it solved. As much as it translated suffragists' insane speech into something recognizable by humans, it by no means altered this speech's fundamentally nonhuman character.

One context in which stories of suffragists' insane speech appeared with frequency was in the antisuffrage writing that played on the theme of women not knowing or understanding what they really want. At the heart of this writing rested the idea that, since women were incapable of comprehending their real desires, and since most suffragists were women, any wish for women's suffrage must be fleeting at best and delusional at worst. And again, those who played on this theme unquestionably aimed at depriving women of political agency and undermining their political identity: an individual with no ability to discern genuine interest from irrational, transitory desire has no business engaging in political or legal decision making.

At the same time, however, an alternative reading of these stories is once more possible. Indeed, many of these discussions of women's confused desire—whether they attributed this desire to a charming feminine quirk or to hysteria, delusion, or psychosis—moved suffragists into precisely the linguistic world that Singleton would occupy a century later. The confused desire of the insane suffragist, for example, left her, in these stories, unaware and yet enveloped in speech, it detached her speech from the activity of human speakers, it made this speech irrelevant to dialogue or response, and it distributed it over distinctly physical or environmental networks. The confused desire of insane suffragists, that is to say, turned them into environments rather than subjects.[30] As much as the writing on suffrage and insanity *can* be read as writing about human subjects shattered or prone to mental breakdown, therefore, it can also be read as writing about, once again, a peculiarly environmental and nonhuman mode of speech.

One of the earliest proponents of the idea that suffragists who desire the vote do not actually understand or comprehend this desire was Bushnell, who wrote that although suffrage advocates were innocent of any intentional deception, they could not appreciate that the phrases "equal rights, natural rights, [and] rights of natural equality," if applied in an "over-absolute" way to the question of women voting, necessarily "take us more by their sound than by any properly discovered meaning."[31] As an (ironic) *New York Times* article a little over a decade later put it, arguments that women do not have an "inherent right" to the vote were mistaken, given the "notorious fact that woman (speaking of her in the abstract) not only has an inherent right to whatever she requires, but that she always gets what she asks for without ado," and that "there is nothing in the world, corporate or unincorporated, to which lovely woman is not entitled, provided only that she expresses desire for it and the right to it inheres in anybody."[32] The article then continues,

> literal people may ask, Why, then, does not woman have the right of suffrage? The answer is easy. She does not want it. Of course, it must be admitted that woman, or some women, think they want the ballot. But they do not really want it. . . . [T]hose who have studied this difficult and delicate subject declare it as their opinion that no woman really wants the right to vote, but that almost all women think they want that right. Philosophers have observed that the female desire is invariably kindled by that which is, or seems to be, unattainable. . . . [I]n fact, it is this longing for the unreachable that constitutes the chief charm of woman. . . . [O]nce the female ballot (if we may be allowed this clumsy phrase) were deposited, the voter would regret her choice and would demand the piece of paper back again. And eventually, in a wild delirium of incertitude, the fair voter would vow that she would not vote at all.[33]

The article eventually concludes by reiterating that "woman does not want the ballot. She thinks she does; and this, we admit, is almost like really wanting the ballot."[34]

By the early twentieth century, this theme appeared in a variety of contexts. Some writers simply repeated the idea that the advocate of women's suffrage was in essence "a woman who wants something and thinks it's the vote," whereas in reality what she wants is anything from "a pearl necklace, or house, or frock" to "an instrument of power."[35] Others drew on turn-of-the century scientific knowledge to explain this confused desire. Alice Hill Chittendon, for instance, warned that "feminine hysteria" was "no subject of jest," and that indeed this hysteria was directly responsible for "the fact that many of the women who have joined the suffrage ranks have no idea what suffrage is, or what its relation to government is."[36] As the physician Charles L. Dana put it in 1915, "no one can deny that the mean weight of the O.T. and C.S. in a man is 42 and in a woman 38, or that there is a significant difference in the pelvic girdle," which meant in turn that

> women are rather more subject than men to the pure psychoses. If women achieve the feministic ideal and live as men do, they would incur the risk of 25 per cent. more insanity than they have now. I am not saying that woman suffrage will make women crazy. I do say that woman suffrage would throw into the electorate a mass of voters of delicate nervous stability. . . . [W]omen seem, so far, to have taken in large measure the suffrage question, not intelligently, but obsessively. It is adopted as a kind of religion, a holy cult of self and sex, expressed by a passion to get what they want. There is no program, no promise; only ecstatic assertions that they ought to have it and must have it and of the wonders that will follow its possession. . . . [O]ften the active and aggressive workers and writers who think themselves so clever are definitely defective mentally. Measured by fair rules of intelligence testing, I should say that the average zealot in the cause has about the mental age of eleven. They look through a cranny and see a dazzling illumination beyond, which is to them the light of a new heaven, when it is really only the sublimation of an unoccupied "elan vital."[37]

Or, alternatively, as an article in Scientific American stated, "The brain of woman is four per cent smaller than that of man after deducting the factors of height and weight (Debierre), and woman's brain, as soon as it reaches its apogee, immediately begins to decline in weight, so that senile atrophy is manifested sooner than in man."[38] As a consequence, "the result of conferring suffrage cannot be positively predicted either one way or the other, since it would be injecting into our political system an entirely new factor."[39]

This question of the relative weight of men's and women's brains—and how this relationship might affect women's claims to, and desire for, suffrage—was, however, a contentious one, and one that was mobilized by prosuffrage writers as well.[40] Suffrage advocate Helen H. Gardener, for instance, willed her brain to Cornell University in 1927, in order to prove that women's and men's brains were equally suited to political activity. Dr. James W. Papez, the curator of the "Burt G. Wilder brain collection of the university," in turn confirmed in a report that Gardener's brain contained "a wealth of cortical substance" that was "equaled but not exceeded by the best brains in the Cornell collection, which includes those of a number of doctors, professors, lawyers, and naturalists."[41] Papez continued that Gardener's brain "showed unusual development in the lower forehead and eyebrow regions, which have to do with the higher thought processes," and that indeed, her brain as a whole was comparable "with that of the internationally known naturalist, the late Dr. Burt G. Wilder, through whose efforts Cornell . . . assembled its brain collection."[42]

There are, then, two prominent arenas in which stories of insane suffragists' confused desire are told—the first is the realm of rights rhetoric and the second is the realm of scientific rhetoric. Both sets of stories, however, link this confused desire to a particular mode of speech, attribute to this speech, in turn, a number of nonhuman characteristics, and finally, criticize or warn against these characteristics for the potential environmental or systemic—rather than necessarily subjective—harm that they might do. Bushnell and the *New York Times* article, for instance, each play on the now familiar theme that the nonsensical and message-poor speech of the suffragists is—precisely *because* of its absence of meaning—particularly and peculiarly apt to alter physical systems.

According to Bushnell, for example, the problem with suffragists' analysis of rights rhetoric or rights structures is not that equal or natural rights themselves make no sense, but that when they are expressed in the suffragists' relentless and overabsolute speech, they gradually lose their sense. When operating through insane suffragists, that is to say, words about rights are eventually deprived of content and turned into pretty sounds or noise. These words cease to carry any meaning and indeed move people only because they *have* been stripped of this meaning. Similarly, in the *New York Times* article, suffragists speaking about rights are made equivalent to suffragists falling into fits of delirium. Speaking, as it is described in the article, is explicitly a bodily activity—something that occurs precisely as the speaker falls into fits, rather than something that is produced as part of a rational dialogue. The language of rights thus becomes once again a physical, bodily language, without message or meaning, at exactly the moment that it is possessed (but not recognized) by the suffragist at work.

But the extent to which the insane suffragist's expression of rights rhetoric poses systemic or environmental, in addition to bodily or subjective, problems is also clear in both Bushnell's writing and the *New York Times* article. In each of these discussions, the confused desire of suffragists transforms not just their own speech about rights, but *any* speech about rights, into an information-rich, but message-poor, code. In both of these passages, that is to say, suffragists' speech alters the entire system or structure of, in this case, rights. Whenever suffragists' speech runs up against rights rhetoric or rights structures, these structures are irrevocably changed. According to these formulations, therefore, insane speech manifested in confused desire not only maps systems of rights directly onto women's abject, delirious bodies (a familiar move),[43] *but also* (less familiarly) maps these systems onto nonsensical spaces, systems, or networks.

Or, put another way, just as Singleton's discussion of rights during his clemency hearing was presented as a highly effective or evocative mode of speech that was, at the same time, totally absent any content, so too was the insane suffragist's discussion of rights highly effective and evocative but without any message or meaning. Likewise, just as Singleton and his speech were most threatening when understood as part of an extended system, so too the insane suffragist and her speech were the most threatening—and did the most harm—when their operation was understood to be embedded within, and synonymous with, alterations to an entire system of rights. As much as stories of Singleton's speech and the suffragists' speech do indeed point to incoherent or shattered human subjects, therefore, they also point to a mode of speech that is quite functional, and indeed threatening, when it is divorced from questions of human subjectivity or sanity. Possessing speech, but not recognizing it, Singleton and the suffragists engage in a linguistic activity that alters not just their own speech, not just their own bodies, but the entire physical and linguistic system of which their speech and bodies are a small part. As they speak, they turn not only the words that they themselves produce, but *all* words, everywhere, into contentless but nonetheless physically effective babble.

Indeed, the scientific discussions of suffragists' confused desire and insane speech—their hysteria and psychosis—emphasize this systemic or environmental threat more overtly than the discussions that took political rights as their starting point. When physicians such as Dana, for instance, argue, first, that suffragists understand the vote to be a dazzling illumination, the possession of which will work wonders, second, that the reason that they see the vote in this way is that they are ecstatic, obsessive, or psychotic, and third (if implicitly), that this is a bad thing, these physicians are elaborating a theory of speech that is predicated as much on the possibility of environmental change as it is on the possibility of subjective change. By insisting that what is wrong with voters who are psychotic or beside themselves is not that they might make an error of judgment, but that these voters believe their votes to be supernatural, Dana is suggesting that the damage such voters will cause is not only to themselves or to the political establishment, but also to the physical world that envelops them.

Ecstatic speakers who desire to "possess" speech that works wonders, after all, are not operating in a universe of human communication, dialogue, decisions, or foreseeable (even if sometimes regrettable) results. They are operating in a universe where speech is itself a miraculous physical effect and where what the human speaker can do is far less important than what words, executed, can do. Dana fears not that women might, if granted the vote, make bad decisions—his analysis has little to do with women's propensity to error or misjudgment. He fears instead that insane suffragists, if granted the vote, might, via their possessed rather than recognized speech, replace the rationally ordered human world of linguistic cause and effect, of human speakers doing things with their words, with an ecstatic or psychotic nonhuman world where words simply happen, linguistic cause *is* linguistic effect—and where speech exists and operates always for the sake of the system, and never for the sake of the speaker.

The fact that Dana himself presumably does not believe speech, or votes, to be capable of this type of physical operation or to be situated so inextricably within physical, rather than subjective, systems or environments is beside the point. The theory of speech that he is (perhaps inadvertently) elaborating is predicated precisely on speech as a systemic or environmental phenomenon rather than on speech as a human or subjective one. Bad speech, threatening speech, or harmful speech, according to his theory, is speech desired and possessed that, like the suffragists', can be identified by its nonhuman capacity to change systems and do work. Good speech, or nonthreatening speech, is speech recognized and free from desire that, like Dana's, can be identified by its human capacity to explain, communicate, and persuade other humans. Suffragists' insane speech is thereby, according to Dana, not just the *result* of a physical reality—the product of women's fragile biology—but it is also *itself* a physical reality.

This dual physicality of suffragists' insane speech is most pronounced, however, in the writing on women's votes and the relative weight of women's brains. Here, suffragists' speech becomes explicitly physical. Like the scientific objects described by Latour, the suffragist's disembodied brain in these passages necessarily possesses speech but does not recognize it—and, like the speech of these scientific objects, this speech possessed arises directly out of the object's physical existence.[44] Erasing any distinction between exterior and interior, the suffragist's brain is both externally there, in the outside world for anyone to measure and make talk, and also something uniquely inside the suffragist. Moreover, and more to the point, the suffragist's brain can likewise be possessed, processed, and turned into workable data—but on its own, unprocessed, it is no more *recognizable* as speech than any other field of information might be.

Like any scientific object distilled into pure data, the suffragist's disembodied brain, once weighed, requires, in Latour's words, a speech prosthesis in order to translate what it says into something understandable by humans. The fact, indeed, that there was such a fashion among late nineteenth- and early twentieth-century pro- and antisuffrage advocates for weighing women's brains suggests that this extra step in the process—the translation—was more than counterbalanced by the presumed effectiveness of the brain's purely physical speech. The nonhuman, physical mode of speech in which the disembodied brain engaged, in other words, was to many observers preferable to the potentially human mode of speech in which the suffragist might or might not engage when she was still alive and her brain was still inside of her. The possible harm inherent in the disembodied, nonhuman brain's speech was thus, for many writers, a risk worth running.

Once again, though, the speech of the insane suffragist's disembodied brain was physical not just in one way, but, like the ecstatic speech described by Dana, in two. In addition to being inertly physical, as the speech of all scientific objects is inertly physical, the brain's speech was also physical in its *operation*. Clear in the stories of the insane suffragist's speaking brain, that is to say, was the idea that this brain's speech was part of a wider, nonhuman cognitive and environmental system, and that this speech rested on constant changes or alterations to this system. The speech produced by the disembodied brain, unlike the speech produced by living brains that were still part of human bodies, was, for instance, binary. It had two possible modes—light or heavy—and its speech was nothing more nor less than *being* light or *being* heavy. To the extent that the disembodied brain spoke, it was precisely by *being* in one or the other of these physical states.

Moreover, depending on which side of the binary it occupied, the disembodied brain altered both political and environmental networks. When the brain was light, suffragists were delusional and their speech did harm. When the brain was heavy, suffragists were not delusional and their speech did not do harm. In essence, therefore, it was only when the disembodied brain was in the process of speaking a very basic type of binary code—when it was being light or when it was being heavy—that these systemic changes were executed. The speech of the disembodied brain was thus not just physical or bodily in and of itself—not just any object of scientific inquiry—but also a physical process. As a result, the translation of the disembodied brain's speech by scientists did not simply turn this speech into a message for human consumption, it also linked this speech back to a preexisting, *nonhuman* system that was already programmed to execute once the brain started speaking.

The debate over the weight of women's brains, over the relative psychosis or hysteria of the suffragists, and over the suffragists' confused or delirious desire, was therefore not just a debate over whether women possessed the intelligence, sanity, and self-control to be active citizens. In addition, and perhaps more so, it was a debate, sometimes in binary, over the relative merit or harm of a distinct type of speech—what appeared to be, and what was frequently designated, insane speech. This was a type of speech that manifested itself in voices heard, in babble produced out of nowhere but saturating everything, and in messages shattered or turned into fractured, meaningless noise. This was a speech that, like Singleton's, not only conjured up a mentally ill human subject, but also a fragile linguistic system—a system of rights, for instance, that itself was all too easily converted into a medium for evocative, pretty, and pointless noise. This too was a speech that enveloped, distributed, and disintegrated the speaking subject into nothing more nor less than an environment. And finally, this was speech that was defined, identified, or evaluated according to its frightening and irrational capacity to do work and to change *things*, rather than according to its capacity to transmit meaning or to change *minds*.

Again, though, as much as this speech might be distinguished as the speech of insane, rather than sane, humans—it can also be distinguished as the speech of nonhuman systems divorced from human subjects. Indeed, the fact that much of the writing on insane suffragists and their confused desire seems motivated less by pity or by the desire to help and more by fear, or at best mockery, indicates that suffragists' actual sanity or insanity was less of a defining characteristic of their speech than it might initially appear to be. Or, put another way, as much as mocking or hostile discussions of suffragists' confused desire and insane speech were a means of depriving these women of political agency, these discussions also hinted at a more fundamental terror of a particular mode of speech—a mode of speech, once more, with a peculiar affinity to mid-twentieth-century machine code, and a mode of speech with a unique and frightening capacity to assault the physical or natural world.

Like Singleton's insane speech, the suffragists' insane speech seemed to cry out for a remedy or cure. At the same time, however, just as observers deemed Singleton's medical cure in the form of an injection or pill to be ineffective and in fact harmful—even as it translated his words for human consumption—the suffragists' potential political cure in the form of the vote was also frequently criticized for trying to mask the non-human and threatening character of their speech. Although the vote might indeed make the suffragists' misdirected, hysterical, or psychotic desire—and the insane speech that went with this desire—meaningful to other humans, it could not alleviate the environmental threat that this speech posed. Nor could it turn this speech into something relevant solely to human subjects rather than to physical systems. At the heart of these stories of insane speech cured via the vote, therefore, was the conviction that this remedy was not only useless or unjust, but damaging.

Between the 1880s and the end of World War I, for instance, a number of articles and essays linked the vote, first, to the destruction of women's personal liberty, second, to the dissolution of preexisting linguistic systems, and finally, to the alteration or destruction of preexisting physical systems. In some cases, these essays simply warned women that "insisting on their imaginary right to vote" would lead to their inevitable "imprisonment."[45] In others, however, writers forged a direct relationship between voting as a cure for an earlier, uniquely feminine mode of speech and the pernicious, continuing influence of the suffragists' nonhuman variation on this feminine mode of speech. In these passages, the vote did indeed turn suffragists' speech into something, for the first time, humanly understandable—but this remedy by no means benefited suffragists, women more broadly, political structures, or the natural world.

As one antisuffrage advocate argued, "since granted the ballot our status as women has changed. We have lost our old power of petition which we had as a non-political body, and we must use our new power or be treated as nonentities. . . . [I]f rule by the people is to be restored, rule by the suffrage lobby must be overcome by women."[46] Writing in a similar vein in 1915, Everett P. Wheeler, the chair of the Man-Suffrage Association Opposed to Woman Suffrage, argued that the "lawlessness and disorder" existing in the state of Colorado at the time was the direct result of women voting—"of the constant interference of women politicians to harass the Executive; and by hysterical appeals, and what can best be described as nagging, to keep him from decisive and manly action."[47] In the same year, Judge Edgar M. Cullen suggested, first, that men "prize justice more highly," while women "will be apt to prize most mercy," second that "indiscriminate mercy may lead to anarchy," and finally, that "it should always be borne in mind that mercy to the wicked is often oppression of the good."[48] Finally, in 1918, the Women's Anti-Suffrage Association issued a number of statements warning that women's votes forced presidents and politicians to veer away from common sense and to repudiate or contradict themselves, making their words or promises meaningless or nonsensical.[49] At the same time, more generally, women's votes threatened to end the American multiparty democratic system and replace it with "a nonpartisan female machine."[50]

In each of these passages, the vote thus posed a danger both to women themselves and to law and politics broadly defined. And each of these passages can thereby serve well as an example of the traditional story of women's incapacity to operate as rational political agents. At the same time, however, the vote is also presented in these stories as a type of cure for a particularly problematic mode of speech—a linguistic remedy that plays the same role in relation to women's confused desire that the medication played in relation to Singleton's schizophrenic symptoms. These passages, that is to say, are also examples of a different narrative— a narrative not of politics and women's subjectivity but of computational speech and nonhuman systems.

When antisuffragists argued that women who voted lost their previous power of petition, for example—and that this was an undesirable state of affairs—they were not just making a claim about the proper sphere for women's usefulness or describing appropriate versus inappropriate forums for women's political activity. In addition, they were arguing that the petition and the vote were two distinct *types* of speech, that the vote was an unwanted and ineffective remedy for the petition, and that as much as voting focused suffragists' speech into something politically understandable, it also hid the continuing threat to democratic "rule by the people" or multiparty liberal democracy that suffragists' speech had always posed.

Antisuffragists were suggesting, in other words, that replacing the confused desire that had manifested itself in the amorphous yet direct form of the petition with the coherent political speech that manifested itself in the concentrated yet indirect form of the vote simply meant replacing one overt mode of threatening, nonhuman speech with another covert mode of threatening, nonhuman speech. The only difference between the two was that whereas the "nonpolitical" petition saturated a given system with speech at least linked to desiring humans—women ideally voicing their desire in a repetitive, iterative, nonlinear way to politically or socially powerful men—the vote, while ostensibly making this desire politically meaningful or coherent, saturated a given system with speech delinked from humans altogether. Whereas the petition, according to antisuffrage advocates, was minimally relevant to human activity—persuasive if not necessarily comprehensible—the vote, although comprehensible and therefore a remedy for the petition, was completely irrelevant to human activity. The vote was not about human persuasion or dialogue. Instead, it turned women-as-humans into "nonentities," except to the extent that the speech of these women-as-humans was incorporated into the preexisting, self-executing system of which the vote formed a part.

Furthermore, the vote as a cure for, specifically, suffragists' speech introduced into this system a malfunction, precisely as speaking women were incorporated into it. As a result, the system ceased to have anything to do with its initial purpose—rule by the people or multiparty democracy—and became something alien, uniform, and irrelevant to human governance, a nonhuman "machine." Like Singleton's medication, therefore—which allowed him to ignore his nonhuman voices and to speak meaningfully to humans, but which, in the process, also demonstrated the "crazy" and "nonsensical" potential of linguistic systems writ large—the suffragist's vote allowed her to ignore her nonhuman desire and to translate her speech to humans, but, upon its execution, demonstrated the potential for the system it operated to turn into a meaningless, self-contradictory, machine. The cure represented by the vote, that is to say, was identical to the cure represented by the pill or injection—both made insane speech humanly comprehensible, but in the process, both simultaneously privileged and damaged systems while marginalizing or trivializing human linguistic activity.

Wheeler's and Cullen's analyses of the vote as an ineffective cure for suffragists' speech emphasize similar difficulties that arise from this remedy. In each of these essays, the underlying problem with hysterical, nag-ging, or for that matter merciful women voters was—familiarly—not that such women would use their votes unwisely, make bad decisions, or take their duties lightly. Instead it was that the vote as a cure drove legal, po-litical, and linguistic systems into "anarchy." It was that when suffragists' confused desire was remedied with the vote, the speech that resulted was unrelated to the "manly" (human) act of making a decision,[51] and was in-stead aimed at an infinite, meaningless linguistic activity that always re-mained just outside of human control. Just as Singleton's cure threatened to turn all language into chaotic babble, then, the suffragists' cure in these stories did the same.

Moreover, just as the antitotalitarian descriptions of Singleton's in-appropriate fate rested, paradoxically, on a fear of the *disintegration* of au-thoritarian and uniform (but human) speech, and the replacement of this authoritarian speech by inexplicable, nonhuman speech gone out of con-trol, these liberal democratic narratives criticizing states that cured women through the vote did the same. As much as antisuffragists con-demned suffragists' votes-as-cure for being coercive, authoritarian, sub-ject to political machines, or indifferent to the views and needs of indi-vidual citizens, that is to say, the underlying fear that motivated this writing was a fear that one kind of machine language might overwhelm or incorporate another kind of human language.

Even Cullen's inversion of the "mercy" discussion—in which suf-fragists are threatening *because* they are merciful (as opposed to Huck-abee being threatening in the context of the *Singleton* decision because he is not)—points to this fundamental concern. Particularly worrisome about suffragists' mercy is its "indiscriminate" nature—the extent to which it is out of control and detached from any specific context or situ-ation. Worrisome about suffragists' mercy, in other words, is that it de-rives not from a specific human sentiment sparked by a unique human scenario, but from systemic and environmental qualities. Suffragists' mercy leads to anarchy and disorder because it is a generic mode of oper-ation or a behavior, rather than a distinct human deed or act.

Indeed, it is arguably because the vote was so disturbing as, specifi-cally, an ineffective cure for a particularly damaging mode of speech, that the prosuffrage rhetoric of the inevitability of women's votes was so roundly condemned. When antisuffrage advocates attacked suffragists for their aggression in positing women's votes to be inevitable or a fait ac-compli—"something rather of a providential than human purpose,"[52] or "a fundamental fact, for which no justification was necessary, and from which there was no appeal"[53]—these advocates were not simply chiding suffragists for refusing to engage in balanced dialogue. Likewise, when prosuffrage advocates like Catt took this criticism and used it to the advantage of the movement, arguing that the coming of votes for women was "not a prophecy; it is a statement of fact"—that "it is as if a tremendous telepathic wave were sweeping the entire country bearing with it to every woman in every State the message that victory is at hand and within our reach"[54]—their point was that since women's suffrage ought to happen, it must happen, regardless of individual cavils or quibbles.

Both of these interpretations of the coming suffrage are positing the vote as, first, a remedy for suffragists' confused desire and, second, just as damaging, just as nonhuman, and just as environmentally harmful as this desire. On the one hand, the vote, again, works to focus and to translate suffragists' insane speech to humans—it takes what was once a collection of incomprehensible voices coming from everywhere (women's desire) and turns these voices into a pointed, coherent, and singular cry with a pointed, coherent, and singular message. On the other hand, however, the vote nevertheless remains outside of the realm of human communication or dialogue—unrelated to linguistic activities such as appeal, dialogue, or persuasion. It is, again, not a means of transmitting meaning so much as a physical effect, an operation brought into execution.

More than that, the type of operation that the vote-as-cure executes involves the alteration of a massive system via small, repetitive, or iterative physical changes. It is, for instance, a telepathic wave that bypasses as irrelevant any human articulation and that sweeps the country precisely as it changes each and every specific woman-as-node. Or, alternatively, it is a fundamental fact that occurs at both the level of the infinitely small and the level of the infinitely large—prompting not discussion but systemic change. Like suffragists' insane speech manifested in their confused desire, then, the cure for this speech, the vote, appears in both pro- and antisuffrage writing as a mode of speech detached from human speakers or meaning, irrelevant to human acts or responses, and working in a broad, distributed system that itself shifts or changes whenever this speech is initiated. As superficially comprehensible to humans—and thus superior to insane speech—as the vote may appear to be in these narratives, it remains very much an environmental rather than human phenomenon, far closer to computational code than to human linguistic activity.

Conclusion

Rereading stories of Singleton's insanity and cure alongside stories of the suffragists' insanity and cure thus provides an alternative way of thinking more generally about insane speech, voices heard, and their remedies. When separated from the realm of human identity or agency, speaking chaotically and hearing nonhuman voices need not necessarily be pitied, attacked, or held up as cautionary tales—indeed, they need not be understood as symptomatic of an illness or a disease at all. Rather, insane speech and voices heard can be read in these narratives as perfectly functional and effective variations on computational speech—sorting and reproducing information as a means of executing widespread systemic change. As such, these linguistic activities are without question threatening and potentially harmful: like the other aspects of suffragists' speech as computational language that appear in this book, they also replace the transmission of messages and meaning with the production of noise and the shifting of systems, they disperse language over environments rather than situating it in speakers, and they thereby privilege changes to physical spaces over actions on the part of human subjects.

But, as these stories also make clear, the medical, legal, or political cure for this speech is just as potentially damaging as insane speech itself. Translating this nonhuman linguistic activity for human consumption, and trapping it within the realm of human subjectivity, these remedies by no means alter its fundamental character. Both the speech and the voices remain nonhuman, remain physical, and remain dispersed throughout smart environments. Both continue to alter, transform, or assault systems even as they succeed in communicating messages. Like the speech of the disembodied brain that was both physical itself and a physical operation—both speaking to humans in binary and, in the process, altering networks—cured speech continued to transform environments even as it became relevant to human communication.

Or, to put it another way, those whose insane linguistic activity was ostensibly cured were operating as much in the fourth category of Aristotelian linguistic existence—where rational speech can be possessed but never recognized—as those whose insane linguistic activity remained unchanged. Both had more affinity to machines running code than to humans doing things with words.

And indeed, this methodological shift makes it possible to reread a variety of takes on threatening speech and its remedies. In 1927, for instance, the same year that Helen Gardener willed her brain to Cornell University, the Supreme Court issued an influential decision—*Whitney v. California*—that addressed precisely this sort of curative or remedial speech. As Justice Louis Brandeis argued in his opinion in this case, advocating (good) speech as the remedy for (bad) speech,

> Those who won our independence . . . believed that freedom to think as you will and to speak as you think are means indispensable to the discovery and spread of political truth . . . that the greatest menace to freedom is an inert people; that public discussion is a political duty, and that this should be a fundamental principle of the American government. . . . [B]elieving in the power of reason as applied through public discussion, they eschewed silence coerced by law. . . . [I]t is the function of speech to free men from the bondage of irrational fears. . . . [I]f there be time to expose through discussion the falsehood and fallacies, to avert evil by the processes of education, the remedy to be applied is more speech, not enforced silence.[55]

This passage is particularly relevant given the antisuffrage position that Brandeis took a number of decades earlier, in 1885. Arguing in a moot court situation against extending the vote to women, he read at that time a "petition, written by Miss Dewey," stating that "'the common good will be lessened by the voting of women on political questions.'"[56]

Essentially, therefore, speaking is for Brandeis, on the one hand, the cure for irrationality—with free speech, more speech, or increased speech, "not enforced silence," the only means of discovering truth. On the other hand, however, as the silenced and absent Miss Dewey makes clear, women's participation in this sort of public dialogue is also a threat to the common good. How is it possible to advocate both more, or increased speech, and also, simultaneously, the salutary silence of a significant portion of the nation's population?

There are a few straightforward ways to solve this problem. One is to recognize that a great deal of time had elapsed between 1885 and 1927— certainly enough time for a thinker like Brandeis to change or hone his ideas.[57] A second is to note that as inclusive, rational, and indebted to theories of equality and liberty as this passage is, one need not assume that Brandeis, or any of his colleagues, had women in mind when they described the importance of making "men free to develop their faculties."[58] All of these justices, after all, were writing in the context of late nineteenth- and early twentieth-century assumptions about gender identity—even if *Whitney* itself was a case involving, specifically, women's speech.

A third means of resolving the apparent contradictions between these two positions, however, is to leave aside Brandeis's intention in writing, and to approach his opinion like that of Justice Thomas in *Van Orden*. It is to resituate his words within the computational realm of the speaking suffragist in order to ask an additional question of the text: what are the broader, environmental, or mechanical repercussions of imagining speech as a remedy? One such repercussion is that speaking itself becomes as much *medical* as it is social, its healing function psychological and physical (a cure for irrationality) at the same time that it is political (a cure for tyranny).

A second such repercussion is that when speech does become a medical cure in this way—whether in Brandeis's world, the suffragists', or in Singleton's—it can no longer be evaluated according to the meaning it conveys. Its behavior or *work* supersedes in importance its content or message. When speech becomes the remedy for everything from insanity to despotism, that is to say—when, for instance, Singleton is medicated into speech and thereby ceases to hear voices, or when the inert people is invigorated by speech and thereby released from bondage—speaking itself takes on value as an effect in itself rather than as a means of transmitting meaning or conveying messages. Content and message become irrelevant to its remedial or curative potential.

As much as Brandeis, like Thomas, clearly attributes speech solely to human speakers, therefore, and as much as his interest, like Thomas's, is in how language might serve as a tool for humans within legal or political systems, the implications of this opinion—once it is read against the backdrop of suffragists' speech—also extend beyond human speakers, human law, or human politics. Once speech becomes something that, divorced from meaning or content, *can* do work—and that is valuable precisely to the extent that it does this work—then a new range of speakers and a new spectrum of speech enter the picture. Scientific objects, smart environments, and, above all, machines running code become just as linguistically and ethically crucial as humans expressing desirable or undesirable political ideas appear to be.

Moreover—and perhaps more worrisome from an anthropocentric perspective—machines running code become arguably *more* crucial to these linguistic and physical systems. After all, if the cure for bad, threatening, or insane speech is the production of more speech, then machines can speak infinitely longer, from infinitely more directions, and for infinitely more environmental or systemic purposes than humans ever can. Just as defining speech as a cure or remedy—as something that does work—turns machine code into a legitimate linguistic activity, therefore, the machine running code shows up the uselessness or meaninglessness of speech as a cure for irrationality. Any line between rational and irrational speech becomes irrelevant.

It is worth emphasizing again that neither Brandeis nor the pro- and antisuffrage writers took these threats inherent in machines running code into consideration in their writing. The fact that stories of suffragists' insane speech and cure played on so many of the themes that later stories of machines running amok with their code would, however, nonetheless suggests that these late nineteenth- and early twentieth-century reinterpretations of effective speech, threatening speech, and useful speech can be linked at least tenuously to the later emergence of computational language. If nothing else, it makes sense to include references to this language in discussions of suffragists' linguistic activity and suffragists' speech. Doing so, once more, allows an unexpected resolution to the apparent contradiction between Brandeis's insistence, first, that ever increasing speech is a remedy for tyranny, and his insistence, second, that women's participation in public discourse undermines the common good.

If suffragists' speech does indeed pose the same threat to the idea of speech-as-remedy that machine code does—if it potentially overwhelms the fragile linguistic system that this cure promises—then silencing suffragists is *in fact* a necessary precursor to expanding (human) speech. Rather than simply assuming that Brandeis changed his mind about the value of speech, therefore, or that, by excluding women from the Aristotelian category of speaking human, he relegated them to the category of silent animal or slave, it may make sense also to read Brandeis's writing from an additional methodological perspective—a perspective that allows, once again, for the existence of an implicit fourth category of Aristotelian existence. It may make sense to recognize that hidden within Brandeis's opinions is the suggestion, at least, that human, animal, and slave are not the only three linguistic options available.

Whereas it is without question true, therefore, that this alternative reading still (at least according to liberal theory) leaves suffragists, or women more generally, in a politically undesirable place—not human—it also provides a different explanation of why this place is undesirable.

Rather than interpreting the equation between women and nonhuman things as an example of women deprived of a particular and peculiarly human political agency, it becomes possible instead to interpret it as an example of women associated with an effective, and frighteningly relevant, mode of speech—a mode of speech that comes into its own when rationality ceases to be of any political, legal, or environmental interest. In this way, this alternative reading also allows a series of more radical or far-reaching questions to be posed: Singleton's story read from the perspective of machine code raised the question of whether insane speech is something to pity and cure or something to hold up as a model or norm. The suffragists' story from the same perspective raises a similar question: what, then, is so desirable about being human at all?

Chapter Ten : Rampant Theory (a Bridge)

A theme, not just in nineteenth-century discussions of women voting but in more recent analyses of scholarship by or about women, is that women's political or scholarly speech is excessively theory laden, that it is too intellectual, or that it flies in the face of common sense.[1] The late nineteenth- and early twentieth-century literature that condemned the work of suffragists as convoluted or mired in abstraction indeed finds a distinct echo in the recent literature that condemns the work of feminist theorists for the same reasons.[2] This bridge chapter, however, rereads these stories of the suffragist trapped in theory with an eye, once again, not toward their political or subjective implications, but toward their physical and environmental ones.

Mocking or hostile stories of speaking suffragists' inability to bow to common sense, that is to say, need not be read simply as further evidence that "common sense" has frequently been used to reinforce normative political or social structures that exclude or marginalize various identity groups—thereby depriving members of these groups of their agency. In addition, or alternatively, these stories of suffragists' inappropriately abstract speech also point to a fear of what a particular mode of nonhuman linguistic activity—the production, codification, and proliferation of improbable information, detached from human needs or human interests—might do to the physical, rather than political, world. Indeed, many of these stories of rampant theory can be read as variations on the theme of suffragists' speech as a type of overwhelming, information-rich, and message-poor code.

The spatial and temporal threats posed by this code, however, become far more explicit in the discussions of theorizing suffragists and common sense than they have in the stories of threatening speech that appeared in previous chapters. According to these narratives, for example, abandoning common sense and engaging in abstract theorizing are tantamount to sorting, storing, and reproducing not just excessive information, but excessively *improbable* information. Prefiguring the mid-twentieth-century information theorists described by Hayles, late nineteenth- and early twentieth-century writers thus condemned suffragists' theorizing as much because, increasingly improbable and therefore unwieldy to transmit, it took up disproportionate amounts of physical space and time as because it was confusing or difficult to understand.

Or, to put it another way, critics of suffragists' abandonment of common sense and their tendency toward abstraction were anticipating a computational world in which "efficient coding [would] reserv[e] the shortest code for the most likely elements . . . leaving longer codes for the unlikely ones," or where "improbable elements . . . [would] occupy the most room in the transmission channel," with "fewer . . . sent in a unit of time than probable ones."[3] They were also anticipating the underside of this computational world, where infinitely improbable messages—viral noise—caused as much physical damage as they passed through physical systems, as they did intellectual or subjective damage when they reached their ostensibly human endpoint or receiver.

Stories of suffragists' rampant theory can therefore be read as stories of speech so improbable that, when coded, it demanded almost infinite space and infinite time to operate. They can be read as stories less about the human, political implications of transmitting bad information than about the environmental implications of transmitting improbable information—about codes saturating spatial and temporal environments, or about codified speech proliferating and thereby infecting, ingesting, or polluting space and time. Stories of suffragists' rampant theory and abandonment of common sense, in other words, addressed the physical and environmental threats posed by computational speech almost more directly than did other, similar discussions of suffragists' threatening speech. At stake in these stories was the way in which excessively improbable theory and abstraction could become not metaphorical, but concrete physical and environmental, operations.

It is here that a second argument underlying this chapter becomes relevant. Specifically, one of the results of reading stories of suffragists' rampant theorizing from this alternative perspective is that the relationship between abstraction and embodiment shifts. Or, more precisely, embodiment ceases to be relevant to conversations about abstraction. This sidelining of embodiment, however, can easily be misinterpreted, both because bodies have been so central to recent theories of speech and also because ignoring embodiment has more often than not meant ignoring various important questions that have been raised in the fields of gender and sexuality studies. Like the previous bridge chapters, therefore, this chapter also addresses an issue—embodiment—that is relevant to this book, but whose relatively insignificant role in it is in danger of being misunderstood. More particularly, it explains why embodiment is not playing the central part here that it might be expected to play—and it makes the case that the abandonment of embodiment in this context is not irresponsible, but in fact necessary to the alternative readings of threatening speech on which this book rests.

Bodies

The methodological dangers of ignoring embodiment—especially in the discussions of information, code, or cybernetics that draw on the work of posthumanist thinkers—have been described in detail by a number of scholars. In an analysis of writing and intellectual property, for instance, Hayles expands on her earlier warnings about how cybernetic fantasies of disembodiment reify the liberal or Cartesian imagery of a distinction between mind and body,[4] by describing the more general "gender implications of an evaluation that places abstraction above embodiment."[5] "The men producing these discourses" about intellectual property, she argues,

> had in mind the male writer, whose creative masculine spirit gave rise to works of genius that soared above their material instantiations in books. Thus a hierarchy of values emerged that placed at the ascendant end of the scale the disembodied, the creative, the masculine, and the writer who worked for glory; at the lower end of the scale were the embodied, the repetitive, the feminine, and the writer who worked for money.[6]

In addition to potentially reinforcing problematic liberal, humanist definitions of the subject, therefore, ignoring embodiment can also create an artificial and oppressive hierarchy of transcendent, masculine creativity and embodied or material, feminine work. An additional problem

with privileging abstraction over embodiment, that is to say, is that doing so denies or denigrates the physical or material world and, in the
process, relegates women to this physical or material mode of existence.

By focusing, however, on stories that describe suffragists' (and, more
generally, women's) speech as harmful because it, *more* than "masculine"
speech, is disembodied and abstract—and by noting that the harm
caused by this disembodied, abstract speech is understood in turn to be
physical, material, and environmental—this chapter begins to trace an
alternative route around the body, a route that does not run into the liberal, humanist, and misogynist pitfalls that many others do. In the stories
that constitute this chapter, abstract or disembodied speech is harmful or
powerful, once again, precisely *because* of its physical and material implications. Abstract and ungrounded to the point of infinite improbability,
such speech overwhelms physical environments, taking up infinite space
and infinite time as it spreads and proliferates. The reason that bodies are
marginalized in this chapter and also throughout this book, therefore, is
not that the material, physical universe is less worthy of interest than the
abstract, intellectual universe—earthbound rather than transcendent.
Instead, it is that the scholarly focus on bodies above all else draws attention away from the wider materiality or physicality of speech and linguistic activity. It is that theories of speech that do *not* ignore embodiment run the risk of ignoring the rest of the physical world.[7]

Just as other chapters have mentioned the bodily repercussions of
reading suffragists' speech as machine code, therefore—in the form, say,
of the parrhesiastes whose speech is nothing more nor less than biological life and death, or manifested in the insane, desiring suffragist falling
into fits of delirium—so too does this chapter. But, also like previous
chapters, this chapter addresses bodies only as a precursor to descriptions
of the more important environmental and systemic aspects of suffragists'
speech as machine code. Yes, in other words, human bodies are part of
the physical world. But they are not necessarily the most important or
most engaging part—and they are certainly not the only part worthy of
attention by feminist scholars.

Improbable Theory, Common Sense, and System Failure

A number of writers throughout the late 1860s and 1870s made the case
that the philosophical foundations of the suffrage movement in the

United States were flawed. In general, this argument rested on the idea, popularized by Bushnell, that suffragists were excessively enamored of "French" thought, "the cheap imposture of philosophy," an "infection" to which even early American Revolutionaries were briefly exposed.[8] One antidote to such French thinking was to invoke common sense, as one later writer in 1909 did, via references to "cool and [analytically] deadly" English writers such as Jeremy Bentham.[9] Another antidote was to write, as Parkman did in the 1880s, that French philosophy in the hands of American writers led not just to individual confusion, not just to national frailty, but to a discordant relationship between "man" and "earth":

> Our critics' idea of government is not practical, but utterly impractical. It is not American, but French. It is that government of abstractions and generalities which, as we once said before, found its realization in the French Revolution, and its apostle in the depraved and half-crazy man of genius, Jean Jacques Rousseau. . . . [T]he government of abstractions has been called, sometimes the *a priori,* and sometimes the sentimental method. We object to this last term, unless it is carefully defined. Sentiments, like principles, enter into the life of nations as well as that of individuals and they are vital to both. But they should be healthy, and not morbid; rational, and not extravagant. It is not common sense alone that makes the greatness of states; neither is it sentiment and principles alone. It is these last joined with reason, reflection, and moderation. . . . [O]ut of the wholesome fruits of the earth, and the staff of life itself, the perverse chemistry of man distills delirious vapours, which being condensed and bottled, exalt his brain with glorious phantasies, and then leave him in the mud. So it is with the unhappy suffragists. From the sober words of our ancestors they extract the means of mental inebriety.[10]

This inappropriate relationship between suffragists' excessively abstract speech and the "earth" or the physical world was indeed a widespread theme in the antisuffrage "common sense" writing. Catherine Beecher, for instance, argued in 1870 that "whatever theories metaphysicians have originated," there are "general truths," which are "often called 'common-sense' or 'principles of common-sense,'" and that "the great mistake of those who are urging 'woman's right' to the ballot" is that they do not apply "the principles of common-sense to practical questions."[11]

The most fundamental of these principles of common sense, according to Beecher, was that "civil law . . . is to be enforced by physical power," that "civil law always implies rules, penalties for disobedience, and *physical* power to enforce them; and whenever this power is lost, then civil government is at an end"; as a result, "the law-making and executive powers have always been given to men rather than to women and children, because men are 'best adapted to' these duties by their superior physical power."[12] As another 1870 essay on suffrage and common sense put it, the "plain every day common sense principle" militates against women voting because no "person has a natural right to vote, no more than they [*sic*] have a natural right to fly or to swim."[13]

In the later nineteenth and early twentieth centuries, discussions of speaking suffragists trapped in abstract theory or abandoning common sense took a familiar biological turn. In 1894, for example, Buckley wrote that although "a physician may evoke smiles and compliments from advocates of the suffrage for women by declaring that he knows of no anatomical or physiological impediment to the assumption by women of the duties of political life," the "common sense of the race" makes clear that such duties are not a part of women's sphere.[14] In an essay on the "scientific aspects of the woman suffrage question," Mary K. Sedgwick continued in this vein by arguing, first, that suffragists "forget that the practical handling of [political] problems differs entirely from the theoretic treatment of the same," and therefore, second, that "we weave a new tyranny about ourselves if we assume . . . responsibilities more fitly left to those better adapted to bear them, both by nature and experience," or when we allow theory to "overturn nature and government."[15] Indeed, she concludes, "they who defy natural law inevitably in the end suffer overwhelming defeat."[16] By 1912, various articles attributing the suffrage movement to "feminine hysteria" linked this hysteria directly to "much false theorizing."[17]

The question, then, is why this "false theorizing," this denial of common sense, came to be linked so securely to suffragists' inappropriate relationship to biological and physical force or to the biological and physical worlds. One answer to this question, once again, is that connecting suffragists' penchant for abstraction to their misinterpretation of the physical universe is a quite effective means of depriving them of political or legal agency. Each of the passages above—whether they attribute to suffragists a mental inebriety, whether they attribute to suffragists' theoretical speech the rejection of natural law, or whether they blame theory for producing both feminine hysteria and misfired activism, in one way or another deprive women of coherent, active subject positions. Each makes a connection, first, between the speaking suffragist's delight in abstraction and her unintelligibility, and second, between her unintelligibility and the abnormality of her participating in politics. Each leaves the suffragist marginalized, apolitical, and without a public identity. According to this reading invoking agency, each passage also indirectly prefigures much of the recent work that cautions against ignoring embodiment—hinting that the fundamental problem with suffragists' obsession with abstraction is that it denies the importance, or even the existence, of material reality or the physical world.

A reading that relies less on agency, however—or less on how these stories of abstract, overly theoretical speech allow only a circumscribed arena in which women might embody coherent political identities—leads to alternative conclusions about what exactly was wrong with suffragists' theorizing. By starting not with what role the speaker plays in these passages, but instead with what role the "physical" or the "natural"—ostensibly ignored by these speakers—plays in them, such a reading shifts attention away from the relationship between abstract speech and human subjectivity and toward the relationship between abstract speech and the environment. As much as this antisuffrage writing seems to be equating the speaking suffragists' denial of common sense with a denial of the physical world, that is to say, it is also equating their denial of common sense with a linguistic *assault* on the physical world. By focusing less on what humans are doing in these stories and more on what the environment is doing, it in fact becomes clear that, far from an inert thing that speaking suffragists ignore at their peril, the physical world is a dynamic system that suffragists' speech overwhelms and potentially destroys. At the heart of this writing is the frightening *improbability* of suffragists' theorizing, its attendant demand for ever-increasing space and time, and the consequent systemic or environmental failure that it portends.

When Parkman, for instance, moves seamlessly from Rousseau's half-crazy political theory to the fact that sentiment, principle, and reason together support effective nation-states, to the tendency, finally, of perverse humans to distill the "fruits of the earth, and the staff of life" into a damaging drug, he is not moving solely in a world of metaphors or human subjectivity. He is also making the case for a direct link between mistreating the earth and half-crazy theorizing. Against the political *and* environmental balance represented by sentiment, principles, and reason, there is the political *and* environmental imbalance represented by French philosophy. Parkman's point is not—or not just—that suffragists will never participate effectively in politics because women get drunk off of theory.

Also, and perhaps more so, he is arguing that theorizing suffragists misunderstand and do damage to the environment—their theory abuses and depletes "earth" and "life" as it is distilled and reproduced. Although Parkman's vocabulary is more biological or botanical than it is computational, therefore, he is very much prefiguring the problems with which information theorists would struggle a few decades later. Suffragists' speech is so improbable as to be, like Rousseau's, "crazy," and as a result of this improbability, it—like inefficient or deliberately damaging code—saturates, depletes, and destroys the physical system in which it operates. The fact that this system is explicitly the "earth" merely emphasizes the fundamental connection between suffragists' speech as machine code and suffragists' speech as an environmental threat.

Beecher's point that theorizing suffragists do not heed physical reality and Buckley's and Sedgwick's points that theorizing suffragists themselves are physiologically unnatural work along similar lines. Beecher's repeated insistence, for example, that law not only relies on physical force but, more pressing, does not exist *without* physical force, is both a commentary on what law is *and also* a commentary on what physical force or the physical world is. The suffragists' tendency to dissociate physical force from law or politics is frightening to Beecher, that is to say, not just because this dissociation undermines law's coercive power. It is frightening because it leaves her italicized *physical* available and open to any and all systems or orders, including, but by no means limited to, the legal and political. It turns physical force into something potentially diffuse, scattered, or dispersed.

Unlike Parkman, who attributes to suffragists' abstract and improbable speech the depletion of the physical world, therefore, Beecher attributes to suffragists' abstract and improbable speech the detaching of the physical world with its physical power from its (in her analysis) properly legal or political ordering principle. Both, though, describe a direct connection between abstract and improbable theory on the one hand and, first, political harm (the weakening of the nation or the unenforceability of law), and second, environmental or systemic harm (the abuse of the fruits of the earth or the dispersion of the "physical"). Theorizing suffragists' denial of common sense thus does not just harm nations or civil governments, it does not just deplete the biological or botanical world, it also distends and weakens the physical world more broadly defined. It turns Beecher's physical reality into an amorphous absence of structure, potentially diffused over multiple political and nonpolitical systems.

Indeed, Beecher's implicit argument about the physical harm that suffragists' abstract speech might cause sets as much of a foundation for Sedgwick's argument about suffragists' tyrannical theorizing as her explicit warning concerning the likely legal or political damage it might cause. Without question, that is to say, Sedgwick, like Beecher, is making a political point when she states that the suffragists' denial of natural law and common sense will force "us" potentially to "weave a new tyranny about ourselves." As Sedgwick and Beecher both note, when legal order is abandoned, the classical result is an unhealthy state ruled by the personal whim of tyrants.

In addition to this invocation of classical tyranny, however, Sedgwick, like Beecher, is also describing a "new" tyranny—as much environmental as it is political. This is a tyranny that is produced directly from suffragists' "inspired" and yet "theoretic" linguistic activity, and that operates by weaving and *enveloping* us as much as it does by coercing or *forcing* us. It is a tyranny, in other words, of excessively abstract or improbable speech that works as an environment as much as it does on or through human individuals or the classical, and human, whim of the tyrant. And finally, it is a tyranny that therefore will be defeated not because humans agitate against it or against the individual tyrant but because "nature and government," as physical and political subsystems that have been incorporated into this new environmental tyranny that defies "natural law," will fail.

Late nineteenth- and early twentieth-century stories of theorizing suffragists drunk on abstraction, denying common sense, and violating natural law were thus as much about systems overwhelmed and incapacitated by the physically demanding transmission of improbable information as they were about defining political women as insane or impractical because of their uniquely embodied subject positions—and thereby disqualifying these women from public or legal personhood. Once again, as much at stake in these passages were the systemic or environmental implications of transmitting improbable information as the political or subjective implications of transmitting bad or incorrect information. In order to recognize these wider physical or environmental, as opposed to—or in addition to—political or biological, aspects of the story of speaking suffragists' rampant theory, however, the embodied human or nonhuman agent needs to be sidelined. Indeed, the frequent appearance of these same computational and environmental themes—of improbable theory codified and overwhelming systems—in prosuffrage writing only makes sense when agency, and particularly embodied agency, is not the starting point of analysis.

Despite the fact that John Stuart Mill—as early and influential a writer in the prosuffrage camp as Bushnell was among the antisuffragists—condemned those who *refused* to consider women voting for being mired in "theory,"[18] other prosuffrage writers turned the denial of common sense and the emphasis on abstraction into a virtue and a threat. In response to Beecher's arguments, for instance, Mary E. Everts, a self-styled "plain, country farmer's wife," took it upon herself to state "some 'common sense' views (or uncommon sense views, if you choose to call them such)" on the issue of women voting.[19] Rather than making a straightforward case that the suffragists in fact had something called common sense on their side, however, Everts argued that "if those desires for further useful action are contrary to 'common sense' then I pray God to give us more just such desires, more just such uncommon sense."[20] Further on, in developing what looks very much like a commonsense reply to Beecher's "physical force" argument—suggesting that if the mustering of force is the only prerequisite for political activity, then "the horse . . . might well take precedence over man"[21]—Everts takes an unexpected detour and concludes with a distinctly nonpractical point: "the true reformer . . . hesitates and fears not to promulgate true reformatory principles knowing that their adoption will benefit humanity sooner or later. Their motto is, 'Let right be done although the heavens fall.'"[22]

Similarly, in response to Parkman's insistence on an environmentally sound balance among sentiment, principle, and reason, Caroline H. Dall argues that such "masculine common sense" has little to do with the work of suffragists:

> "Faith is indispensable to achievement," concludes Mr. Parkman; "but faith must not quarrel with common sense." Certainly not; and all the more because faith has nothing whatever to do with common sense, and would be very unhappy in her company. In faith, women have undertaken this work; in faith, they are to execute it,—a faith born of God, nurtured in prayer, and to be made manifest in work, in spite of ill-health, discomfort, or discouragement.

That such faith can be carried into fact in spite of masculine common sense, and in defiance of all anciently understood conditions of
fitness, is one of the most valuable lessons that men are to learn
from the women of the future.[23]

Indeed, Mill as well, upon a closer reading, does not seem to be making a
straightforward case for the suffragists' common sense, even as he attributes—echoing the misogynist advocates of intellectual property law discussed by Hayles—"theory and speculation" to "man" and "practical tal-
ent" to "woman."[24] In order to come to his conclusions that "a woman
seldom runs wild after an abstraction," and that "women's thoughts are
thus as useful in giving reality to those of thinking men, as men's
thoughts in giving width and largeness to those of women," for instance,
Mill argues that it is precisely feminine "intuition" that allows women to
see "much more than a man of what is immediately before her."[25] He
then continues that it is, again, this "intuition" that produces in women
a "sensibility to the present," rather than to the future, and an ability to
"discern and discriminate the particular cases" rather than to develop
general theories.[26] And finally, if paradoxically, it is still this "intuition"
that allows women to perceive, again, "the present," "the real," "actual
fact," or "objective fact," and that prevents them from speculating on
"comprehensive truths."[27]

On the one hand, then, a number of prosuffrage advocates explicitly
stated that abandoning common sense and adhering to theory, faith, or
uncommon sense was a virtue to be encouraged. On the other hand, it
was only by invoking female intuition that writers like Mill arrived at the
conclusion that it was men's speech, not women's, that was excessively
abstract. Both of these positions thus emphasize more than they refute
the argument that suffragists' speech was effective (or threatening) because it was either impractically theoretical or because it was—grounded
intuitively rather than sensibly—detached from masculine logic. More to
the point, all of these passages explicitly or implicitly link these qualities
of suffragists' speech to distinct shifts and changes in the physical environment—changes predicated on, first, the improbability of this speech
and, second, on a prefiguring of the systemic effects that improbable
speech as code might have.

Mill's point that intuition is the basis for suffragists' grasp of objective reality, for instance, is based on three assumptions about how suffragists' speech operates. The first assumption is that the concrete or

grounded reality that suffragists' speech brings to men's abstract thought is a reality based not in the evaluation of empirical or sensory evidence but in the immediate apprehension—regardless of the senses or intellect—of the world as a wholesale system. The second assumption is that suffragists' speech is powerful above all in its tendency to "discern and discriminate . . . particular cases"—in its tendency to sort and store numerous discrete bits of data, without ever condensing this data into a more compact general theory. On the one hand, that is to say, suffragists' speech is mapped intuitively onto the world writ large. On the other hand, it operates by separating, storing, and organizing each and every minute aspect of this world as a discrete and distinct element.

Finally, Mill's third and perhaps most important assumption is that suffragists' speech has a distinctive, nonlinear relationship to time—it is always "immediate" or within "the present." Unlike male speech, therefore, suffragists' speech is without time and temporally nonlinear; it is always in the moment. It is likewise derived from a nonsensory, nonintellectual, and intuitive apprehension of "reality" as a whole. And finally, it is most effective in its processing, storing, and reproducing of distinct, unrelated pieces of information—information that, because of its particularity, requires more and more memory as it is encountered and engaged. Suffragists' speech, in other words, is temporally as well as spatially infinite. By collapsing all time into the immediate present, it saturates all time, and by apprehending reality as a whole—but as a whole that nonetheless must be infinitely sorted into smaller and smaller cases or bits of information—it saturates all memory or space.

As much as Mill is attributing to speaking suffragists a healthy fear of abstraction, therefore, he is also operating in exactly the same rhetorical space as those who described suffragists' speech—for better or for worse—as a type of pure and unfettered theory. His analysis of the way in which suffragists' speech exists in time and space is indeed quite similar to that of Dall in her discussion of the *irrelevance* of common sense to this speech. Like Mill, Dall also sets up a peculiar temporal framework in which suffragists' speech will operate. By insisting that only the abandonment of common sense, and the proliferation of faith, will allow, first, present suffragists to defy ancient strictures, and second, present men to learn from "the women of the future," Dall is arguing, just as Mill did, that one key quality of suffragists' speech is its irrelevance to temporal linearity. More threatening, she is attributing to suffragists' speech the potential to collapse all time into the immediate present. By abandoning common sense—precisely by *being* improbable—Dall is suggesting that suffragists' speech can and will take up all the time in the world. In Dall's analysis, that is to say, suffragists' speech works as a type of inefficient code, taking up potentially infinite amounts of time, just as in Mill's analysis, this speech worked as a related type of inefficient code, taking up potentially infinite amounts of both time *and* space.

Dall's conclusions in this way take the temporal and spatial qualities of suffragists' speech described by Mill to their logical conclusion. Because it is uncommon, unexpected, and improbable, this excessively theoretical speech overwhelms and saturates time. And in the process—as Everts likewise makes clear in her claim that the abstract theory of right must prevail even if the heavens should fall—this speech poses a distinct systemic or environmental threat. Rampantly abstract and theoretical, suffragists' speech ignores linear human time and finite human space in favor of nonlinear computational time and infinite computational space. Its saturation of temporal and spatial systems—or its demand for infinite time and space to operate—can thus be both "bad," as the antisuffragists argued, in that it denies the possibility that any transmission will eventually end, but also "good," as the prosuffragists argued, in that it demonstrated the frightening physical capabilities and possibilities that in fact did inhere in pure theory.

Conclusion

There have been a couple of analytical slippages in this chapter that are worth identifying and explaining in these last few paragraphs. First, and most difficult, these rereadings of the stories of suffragists' rampant theory have brought together the mathematical improbability that underlies twentieth- and twenty-first-century information theory and the aesthetic or rhetorical improbability that nineteenth-century writers and speakers attributed to suffragists into perhaps uncomfortable proximity. Mathematical improbability carries no moral or political judgment—certain letters, for instance, are less likely to occur in certain languages than other letters, and therefore in a codified transmission involving these languages, these letters will be designated "improbable" and will be assigned longer codes than their more common counterparts.[28] There is as little emphasis on strangeness, oddness, or for that matter insanity in these mathematical attributions of improbability as there is in the aesthetic or rhetorical attributions of improbability to, say, ideas or ideologies.

Second, the systemic or environmental damage that theorizing suffragists' speech might do has appeared in this chapter as both the sort of damage that occurs during the transmission of information—taking excessive or infinite time to complete—and also the sort of damage that occurs during the storage of information—taking excessive or infinite space to process or organize. The systems that fail as a result of suffragists' theory are thus not necessarily related to one another. Each of these two slippages could easily lead to the conclusion that the relationship between the potential threat posed by theorizing suffragists' improbable speech and the potential threat posed by the slow transmission of improbable code is purely metaphorical—that rereading these stories through the lens of computational code rather than through the lens of agency is an interesting exercise, but hardly relevant to environmental, physical, *or* political realities.

What this bridge chapter has in part tried to show, however, is that it is precisely in these two slippages that the concrete, nonmetaphorical relationship between suffragists' speech and computational language becomes clear. One point to keep in mind, for instance, is that in both mathematical information theory and in the nineteenth- and early twentieth-century suffrage writing, the designation "improbable" is a subjective one. It is true that information theorists will ordinarily try to see to it that the subjective designation matches an objective or true improbability—that in codified English, say, the letter *e* is not designated as highly improbable—because the result would be a saturation or devastation of the lines and systems of transmission. But such designations are by no means certain, and one very easy way to cause incremental yet widespread damage to a system is to switch such designations around. Indeed, a frequent element that has nonetheless been designated "improbable" will cause far more harm than an infrequent and therefore "truly" improbable element will—its viral potential, that is to say, will be infinitely greater than the viral potential of a less common improbable element.

It is therefore worth emphasizing that neither pro- nor antisuffrage writers chose to alleviate the threat posed by suffragists' rampant theory—especially as it proliferated in the later years of the nineteenth century—by simply describing it as, now, probable or common (because frequent). Instead, the uncommon, unusual, strange, or crazy—the *improbable*—character of suffragists' theorizing became more and more central in stories of theorizing suffragists' speech, common sense like-wise became increasingly distant from the activity of the suffragists, and as a result, the systemic threat inherent in this linguistic activity grew exponentially.

And indeed, it was precisely the viral potential of this speech with which prosuffrage advocates of a variety of backgrounds played in their writing. They too highlighted the improbability of suffragists' theory, turned it into something valuable in its uniqueness—even as it prolifer-ated, expanded, and was infinitely repeated—because it *could* pose this systemic threat. The relationship between the harm caused by theorizing suffragists' speech and the potential harm done by information theorists' improperly labeled improbable elements was thus *not* purely metaphori-cal. Separated as they were by a number of decades, suffragists' speech and computational language could and did pose the same systemic, non-human threats.

Moreover, as both Parkman and Mill make clear, these threats were spatial as well as temporal—not just systemic, but environmental. And it is here that this chapter's conflation of the transmission of information and the storage of information—or of the damage done by improbable el-ements sent through lines or systems and of the damage done by improb-able (or, in Mill's language, "particular") elements processed in mem-ory—becomes relevant. One of the characteristics that binds together computational language and suffragists' speech in these stories is that each blurs the line between space and time. As the sorting of particular or discrete bits of information gradually clogs storage space or memory, the transmission of these bits of information likewise becomes encum-bered. Similarly, as the transmission of improbable elements (packed with information) gradually slows down systems, the storage of this in-formation becomes increasingly difficult.

There is thus an affinity between Parkman's antisuffrage argument that suffragists deplete the earth as they distill their theory and Mill's pro-suffrage argument that suffragists' speech is effective in its capacity to process particular cases, to sort discrete bits of information, and to col-lapse all time into the present. Each attributes to suffragists' speech a fun-damentally computational quality. Each assumes that suffragists' speech operates—either productively or destructively—by saturating and re-configuring simultaneously spatial and temporal systems. And finally, each thereby understands suffragists' speech to be, at least in part, a dis-tinctly nonhuman activity. By reading these stories of theorizing suffragists and their inappropriate relationship to the physical world from the direction of the *world*, rather than from the direction of the human speaker, therefore, it becomes possible to trace their environmental rather than, or in addition to, human implications.

But, again, in order to accomplish this reading—or, at the very least, in order to recognize the methodological potential of conflating mathematical with rhetorical improbability or of conflating the transmission with the storage of information—it is necessary to sideline not just agency, but bodies and embodiment as well. Just as in previous chapters, moving away from these concepts was not an attempt to trivialize them or the questions and problems that they raise, neither is that the purpose of doing so in this chapter. Far from marginalizing embodiment as a means of reifying the liberal humanist subject or in the hope of privileging (what has been defined as masculine) abstract thought over (what has been defined as feminine) material existence, marginalizing embodiment here is a means of demonstrating the methodological potential of doing away with all human (and nonhuman) subjects and of recognizing that the material and the physical universe consists of far more than biology, and certainly far more than human biology.

The threat at the heart of overly abstract or theoretical speech—at the basis of abandoning common sense—can indeed, once more, be found as much at the intersection of language, computation, and the environment as it can at the intersection of language, subjects, and bodies. It can be found in the frighteningly physical and viral potential of dynamic and proliferating code. And as a result, the long-standing theme of the overly theoretical feminist—as relevant throughout the twentieth and into the twenty-first centuries as it was in the nineteenth—becomes multidimensional and multifaceted in ways that it perhaps was not before. At stake are not only speakers and subjects, certainly not divisions between humans and nonhumans, but how modes of speech can be designated as improbable, regardless of their actual frequency, and can thereby pack their punch—not in the world of humans communicating meaning to other humans but in the world of information, stored, sorted, and now also transmitted. At stake is speech with temporal and spatial implications rather than speech possessed of content or meaning.

Or, put another way, just as stories of Singleton or the insane suffragists described a situation in which their speech turned any and all language about, say, rights into information-rich and message-poor noise that irrevocably altered the physical and linguistic systems in which this language operated, stories of theorizing suffragists describe a situation in which speech, designated infinitely improbable—and therefore codified into infinitely large packets of information—irrevocably saturated the systems through which this information traveled and in which it was stored. Recognizing the affinity of suffragists' speech with code in both sets of stories opens up an alternative means of thinking about the environmental rather than solely political damage that this speech might do.

In both sets of stories as well—although more in the latter than the former—this environmental damage is simultaneously spatial and temporal. Moreover, as the next chapter, on stories of suffragists' speech as a mode of dream speech, shows, this fear that suffragists' speech might collapse or expand human space and time into computational space and time was by no means limited to narratives of their excessively abstract theory. Almost more so, stories of dreaming suffragists—especially to the extent that these stories seem to take seriously the supposedly premodern belief in the prophetic rather than egoistic dream experience—rest on the idea that the speech that operates within the dreamscape, as a type of code, altered simultaneously both environmental time and environmental space.

Chapter Eleven : Dream Speech

A final set of stories that appears in both sympathetic and disparaging writing about suffragists' speech places suffragists within dreamscapes or dreamworlds and describes their linguistic activities as the inspired or delirious product of these spaces and worlds. Regardless of whether attributing to suffragists a type of dream speech was a means of emphasizing the inspiration behind their proposed reforms (as it was in the prosuffrage writing) or a means of highlighting the absurdity of these reforms (as it was in the antisuffrage writing), these stories were widespread and influential. They also, once again, lend themselves to readings from the direction of computation, machine code, and the environment as much as they do readings from the direction of human subjectivity, agency, or identity. Just as before, reading suffragists' dream speech as a type of early machine code, and the dreamscapes inhabited by speaking suffragists as a variation on the "non-Cartesian space of computer memory,"[1] opens up a way of thinking about effective or threatening speech that underscores its environmental rather than human characteristics.

Recognizing the similarities between machine code and dream speech, the environmental repercussions of these modes of speech, and the peculiarly spatial implications of dream speech as machine code, however, requires also rethinking much of the recent writing on what dreams do. Appreciating the affinity between the linguistic operation of the dream and the linguistic operation of the computer, for instance, demands first of all a return to what are ordinarily understood to be premodern methods of dream interpretation—methods that place a dream's importance in the physical world, beyond human cognition, rather than in the realm of human egos, human psyches, or human subjectivity and agency. This rereading demands a return, that is to say, to public dreams, prophetic dreams, or environmental dreams, and a move away from egoistic dreams.

At stake in this rereading's interpretation of suffragists' harmful dream speech, in other words, is not the subjective state of the dreamer, as it is in modern analyses, but the likely effects that the dream has or will have on the physical world around the dreamer, as it was in premodern analyses. Once this ostensibly earlier mode of dream interpretation is taken seriously—at least as a methodological move—it then becomes possible to reread stories of suffragists' dream speech wreaking political havoc as stories instead of suffragists' machine code wreaking environmental havoc. It likewise becomes possible to think in more sophisticated ways about the staying power of the themes of the dream, dream speech, and dreamscapes in discussions of threatening speech more broadly defined.

The first part of this chapter thus consists of a brief summary of two recent, if in many ways contrary, traditions of dream interpretation—the Freudian and the Foucauldian. Although these traditions start from different premises and, in the case of Foucault's writing on dreams, attempt explicit correctives of one another, they both suggest that dreams, fundamentally, are about human subjectivity, human identity, and human agency. As much as these methods of interpretation are useful when it comes to recognizing the human or purely political implications of attributing to suffragists a type of dream speech, therefore, they make broader, nonhuman, or systemic readings of this attribution difficult or impossible.

The second part of this chapter moves away from these more recent methods of dream interpretation, and instead consists of a—once again brief—chronology of medieval and early modern analyses of what dreams do. In this second part, it becomes clear that there is and has been a longstanding tradition of recognizing the physical or environmental aspects of dreaming and dream speech—as well as of considering the overlaps and similarities between dreamscapes and other spaces. Indeed, as the stories of dreaming suffragists in the third section of this chapter suggest, this alternative tradition of dream interpretation not only remains relevant, but is necessary to a more multidimensional understanding of threatening speech. In order to explain why suffragists' dream speech should have posed such a threat, in other words—not just to human subjects, not just to politics, but to environments, spaces, and systems—it is necessary to take this premodern mode of dream interpretation seriously.

Modern Dream Interpretation, Human Subjects, and Human Agency

An assumption that underlies many recent histories of dream interpretation is that there was a distinct eighteenth- or nineteenth-century break between premodern methods of analyzing dreams—methods commonly associated with the classical Greek scholar Artemidorus of Daldis—and the modern methods of analysis popularly attributed to Sigmund Freud among others. According to these histories, premodern dreams were understood to pack a public, physical, political, or environmental punch, whereas modern dreams were nothing more than the subjective product of an individual ego. Indeed, once the "fundamental conflict between the introspective theory of Freud and the predictive theory of Artemidorus"[2] had ostensibly been resolved in favor of Freud, premodern public or environmental dreams seemed forever relegated to the realm of historical oddity. For scholars of dream literature in Europe, Artemidorus became both the foundation and the foil for modern takes on the dreaming subject. What interested these scholars was the extent to which the public and the private had apparently shifted—the extent to which, unlike twentieth-century assumptions, the "normative assumptions widespread in Artemidorus' day" placed dreams not into "a baffling private universe but [in]to the public sphere."[3]

In other contexts—for instance, in the Ottoman Middle East—the shift from public, worldly dreaming to a dismissal of dreaming as an environmentally meaningful act likewise seemed to occur in the nineteenth century, "the classic science of dream interpretation los[ing] its prestige with the advent of modernity."[4] It is true that there are some scholars who choose to situate the break between public, environmental dreams and private, subjective dreams in the idea of a divide between East and West rather than in the idea of a divide between not-modern and modern, arguing, for instance, that unlike those in the "East," "we Westerners separate our dreams sharply from waking life, [and] we typically do not regard our dreams as significant, at least in public discourse."[5] Such analyses, however—despite the fact that they displace temporal onto geographical categories—are arguably operating within the same historiographical tradition. There is, again, a distinct break between the private and the public, or the subjective and the environmental, operation of the dream.

But this break is also part of a more complicated history than it might initially appear to be—and to accept it as a methodological starting point is to deny to stories of dream speech their full complexity. Or, put another way, as effective as it may be to describe the dream solely in terms of human subjectivity and human egos, doing so disallows alternative, environmental interpretations of what dream speech may be doing or how it might cause harm—interpretations that seem in many ways to be at the heart of writing about suffragists' dreams. It likewise makes impossible any discussion of dreamscapes mapped onto nonhuman spaces, such as the spaces of computer memory, rather than, or in addition to, dreamscapes mapped onto purely subjective or egoistic spaces. As useful as Freudian or Foucauldian takes on dream interpretation might be, their focus on the human subject or human agency at the expense of all else makes them ineffective or even damaging to any interpretation of dream *speech* that does not take the human as its starting point.

The human-centered nature of Freudian dream analysis is relatively straightforward. As Freud states in his *Interpretation of Dreams,* for instance,

> Dreams are absolutely egoistic. In cases where not my ego but only a strange person occurs in the dream-content, I may safely assume that by means of identification my ego is concealed behind that person. . . . [I] may also give my ego multiple representations in my dream, either directly or by means of identification with other people.[6]

Not only, in other words, does Freud make clear that both the starting point and the ending point for dream interpretation is the human ego, but if the dreaming subject identifies this ego with something else, it is almost without exception with another *human* being.[7] Rarely is the possibility that the dreaming subject might identify with nonhuman things or objects or spaces considered. The most effective point of reference for dream analysis or for discussions of dream speech is the human ego.

More to the point, though, is how this human-centered approach to dreaming affects Freud's descriptions of dream speech in action or operation. Without going into the detail that the complexity of Freud's discussion deserves, Freud's method of dream interpretation turns dream speech into an activity founded, even if paradoxically, on human agency. One of the key aspects of the theory of contradiction (or its absence) that he elaborates in his *Interpretation of Dreams*, for example, is that "the dream is, as it were, *centered elsewhere;* its content is arranged about elements which do not constitute the central point of the dream-thoughts."[8] As a result, it is possible to determine that not just signs, but certain arrangements of signs, represent entirely other or unexpected aspects of the dreamer's psyche. According to Freud, the dream thus "reproduces *logical connection* in the form of *simultaneity.*"[9] Likewise, "dreams are quite incapable of expressing the alternative 'either or'; it is their custom to take both members of this alternative into some context, as though they had an equal right to be there."[10] Indeed,

the attitude of dreams to the category of *antithesis* and *contradiction* is very striking. This category is simply ignored; the word "No" does not seem to exist for a dream. Dreams are particularly fond of reducing antithesis to uniformity, or representing them as one and the same thing.[11]

As a result, it is the analyst's job to insert "the *either-or* in its context in the dream-thoughts" only "after interpreting the dream."[12] One way in which an appropriate insertion of this sort might be accomplished is, for instance, to recognize that "the inability to do something in the dream is *the expression of a contradiction, a 'No'*"[13]—meaning that in fact the non-linear or chaotic dream is quite open to organization based on linearity, contradiction, antithesis, or dichotomy.

Some have criticized this move on Freud's part by questioning the validity of relentlessly ordering and organizing even the disordered realm of the dream.[14] His interest in order is indeed arguably part of a distinct (and anachronistic) nineteenth-century attitude toward scientific inquiry—far removed from the mid- to late-twentieth-century scientific interest in, say, nonlinear dynamics.[15] An additional point that might be made in reference to Freud's impetus toward linear order, however, is that by emphasizing the analyst's role in transforming the absence of contradictions into ordered dichotomies or alternatives—or by insisting that all illogical simultaneities or uniformities in the dream can and should be transformed into logical linearities via analysis—he is also positing the inexorable superiority or importance of the human subject possessed of agency over nonhuman spaces or environments. Human will and choice—explicitly the "either-or"—is suddenly introduced in Freud's discussion into a system or environment in which human choice was previously marginal or even irrelevant.

Whereas prior to analysis what occurred in the dream was an operation or execution, full of information, absent meaning, and unrelated to human identity, after analysis the dream became solely a means of transmitting messages or meaning. What had once been a nonhuman environment suddenly became a human conversation. Key to Freud's impetus toward order is thus not only a problematic nineteenth- or early twentieth-century fear of disorganization, and not only an anachronistic scientific method, but a distinct challenge to environmental or system-oriented approaches to dream interpretation. By suggesting that contradiction and choice must always exist within the dream environment, even if they do not appear to, Freud is also suggesting that systems or environments initially irrelevant to human activity must always be subordinated to human choice and agency. The vocabulary of human agency in this mode of interpretation thus does not just detract attention from the nonhuman, and potentially computational, implications of dreaming and dream speech, it actively makes impossible any discussion of these implications.

Indeed, when later writers in the Freudian tradition such as Jacques Lacan emphasize the underlying linguistic character of dreams and dream analysis[16]—transforming, as David Caudill has put it, the "the basic mechanisms that were, for Freud, responsible for the content of dreams . . . into linguistic concepts"[17]—they reinforce the subordination of system or environment to human subject, and of nonhuman speech to human speech. As much as Lacan argues that dream speech operates "independently of its meaning, since it is a senseless discourse," and that in turn its effectiveness lies precisely in dissolving the coherent human subject,[18] he nonetheless continues to stress that language is a means of transmitting messages to and from humans rather than about the alteration of a system.[19]

The fact that in Lacan's analysis these messages are without meaning and that the transmission always reaches its destination does not alter the fundamental point that at the heart of speech—and dream speech especially—is conversation and not execution. There thus remains a distinct relationship in his mode of dream interpretation among, first, agents transmitting or failing to transmit messages, second, the impossibility that dream speech might have nonhuman characteristics, or have affinities with nonhuman linguistic activities such as the operation of machine code, and third, the lack of any interest in the environmental or spatial manifestations of the dreamscape as a nonhuman space, potentially similar to the space of computer memory. Once again, the focus on agency in dreams—even dissolved or incoherent types of agency—makes impossible a focus on any nonhuman, environmental aspects of these dreams.

In essence, then, Freudian dream interpretation not only reinforces the importance of human agency in discussions of dream speech, but makes difficult or impossible any nonhuman, environmental, or for that matter computational interpretations of what dream speech might do. Foucault presents his alternative take on dream interpretation as, in many ways, a corrective to this Freudian approach, but, as will become clear, he too denies the possibility that dream speech might be capable of a distinctly nonhuman operation. Once again, without doing justice to the complexity of Foucauldian studies of dreaming,[20] it is nonetheless possible to locate in at least one essay—his 1954 introduction to Ludwig Binswanger's 1930 "Dream and Existence"—an emphasis on human identity and agency that does not greatly differ from that of Freud.

One of the key points that Foucault makes in this piece is that he is working in a tradition that does not completely throw out premodern insights into dreaming. As Forrest Williams, Binswanger's and Foucault's English translator notes, Foucault is thereby working in the same mode as Friedrich Nietzsche, who maintained an ongoing interest in dreams and dreaming,[21] and who to some extent recognized the environmental potential of the dream world—especially as something other than a system of signs leading to human or subjective truth.[22] Most recent philosophers have not maintained this Foucauldian or Nietzschean interest, however, and as Williams continues,

> the dream *itself*, as a phenomenon, has hardly been taken seriously, in its own right, in modern philosophy. On the contrary, philosophers have largely neglected their dreams. The celebrated discussion of dreaming by Descartes at the beginning of modern philosophy illustrates concisely this customary dismissal of the phenomenon of the dream.[23]

Indeed,

> in our times, dreams do not even need to be explicitly dismissed by philosophers, since they now may simply be abandoned to the dis-

cipline of psychoanalysis, where they may become intellectually interesting as symptoms or signs of something that happened in the
past.[24]

Williams, that is, describes a familiar history of dream interpretation,
that begins, first, with a break in the early modern period, when
Descartes dismissed what he initially thought to be a prophetic dream in
favor of a narrow focus on rational human subjectivity. The story then
concludes with a second break—the advent of "our times"—when
dreams were revived for, but relegated to, studies of human egos and historical pasts.

It is this history to which Foucault responds, that he in many ways
replicates, but that he also challenges in his introductory essay. Like Binswanger, who tried to "link up" with the "forgotten tradition" of premodern dream interpretation,[25] Foucault also tries to salvage some of the
wider, or public, implications of the dream experience. He thus starts
with the premodern "Hebrews," who, he argues, understood dreaming as
a "concrete form of revelation," a distinct "imaginary experience," and
therefore incapable of being "wholly reconstituted by psychological
analysis."[26] He then shifts his attention to the nineteenth and early
twentieth centuries—or to the moment at which, with the introduction
of psychoanalysis, the dream was gradually denied depth as experience,
and instead became merely sign and symbol. "Psychoanalysis," Foucault
claims, "gave the dream no status beyond that of speech, and failed to see
it in its reality as language."[27] As a result, Freud

> restored a psychological dimension to the dream, but he did not
> succeed in understanding it as a specific form of experience. . . .
> [F]reud psychologized the dream—and the privilege it thus acquired
> in the realm of psychology deprived it of any privilege as a specific
> form of experience.[28]

Here, therefore, the modern shift in thinking and writing about dreams
condemned dreaming not only to human egos and to historical pasts,
but—and more disturbing—to a single, narrow, and particular linguistic
mode. According to Foucault, the dream became in the modern period
nothing more than a sign or a message in need of context and interpretation. What Binswanger offers, Foucault thus argues, is a replacement of
this flattened dream of the modern period with the "forgotten" and com-

plete dream experience that existed in the premodern period.[29] Binswanger's interpretation also allows for, as Jerrold Siegel writes, an analysis of what dreams *did* as well as what they *said*.[30]

At the same time, however, both Binswanger (as read by Foucault) and Foucault himself remain as indebted to theories of human agency and human speech as Freud did. Binswanger's starting point, for instance, is that what differentiates the dream from other states is less that it often happens during sleep than that it implies a distinct mode of existence.[31] More specifically, Binswanger links his discussion of dreaming to Hegel's dialectic of existence and to his analysis of the fifth-century BCE philosopher Heraclitus. Returning to Hegel's argument that "'if we do not stand in relation to the whole, then we are merely dreaming,'"[32] Binswanger goes on to argue that

> for Heraclitus, genuine awakeness is, negatively put, the awakening from private opinion (*doxa*) and subjective belief. Put positively, it is life (and not just the life of thought!) that accords with the laws of the universal, whether this universal be called *logos, cosmos, sophia,* or whether it is considered as a combination of all of them in the sense of a rational insight into their unitary, lawful interrelation and in the sense of action according to this insight.[33]

As a result, Binswanger's therapeutic response to those whose existence is dreaming rather than waking is a call to human action and, familiarly, human choice:

> there come moments when a man must decide whether, in pride and defiance, to cling to his private opinion—his private theater, as one patient put it—or whether to place himself in the hands of a physician, viewed as the wise mediator between the private and the communal world, between deception and truth. He must, that is, decide whether he wishes to awaken from his dream and participate in the life of the universal, in the *koinos* [communal] *cosmos*.[34]

For Binswanger, "to dream means: I don't know what is happening to me. . . . [I]n no way," he argues, "does the individual emerge as he who makes the dream, but rather as the one for whom . . . the dream occurs."[35] And it is thus the psychiatrist's job—as it was in Freud's discussion—to open up a new environment, a new arena, in which the patient might make the (correct) choice of awake, conscious, active, universal existence over the (incorrect) choice of dreaming, unaware, passive, particular existence.

Participation in the "cosmos" therefore does not involve the recognition that the universe is something of which humans form only a small or insignificant part, but the recognition that, as a human, a sane individual might bring the universe into the service of human identity or human community. Nonhuman linguistic activity or experience is inconceivable in this analysis—as are spaces that might operate or execute via nonhuman dream speech. Indeed, what is unhealthy about dreamers who do not place themselves into the hands of a physician is that these dreamers remain unable actively to make their dreams—they become a passive part of dreams that, intransitively "occur."

As a result, such dreamers not only have no will—they also have no human existence. And this, according to Binswanger, is an undesirable state of affairs. There is a dichotomy, therefore, once again set up between seeking out or reviving agency on the one hand and recognizing the activity or value of the nonhuman environment—in this case a dreamscape, dream space, or dream environment quite capable of operating or executing without human intervention, and in the absence of the human dreamer—on the other. Once the physician finds human agency, the dream environment ceases to be of any importance. And as long as the dream environment continues to execute or "occur," there can be no human choice, decision, agency, or existence—things, in a distinctly, nonhuman, and arguably computational way, simply happen. They go into operation.

When Foucault takes up Binswanger's discussion of dream as existence, he leaves behind, for the most part, the normative, therapeutic solution that went along with it. While agreeing that the dream can very effectively be interpreted via reference to the Hegelian tradition, he does not agree that the proper decision for any sane patient is to awaken. Nor does he insist that the physician must, at all costs, replace the dream environment with human agency. Indeed, if there is a running theme throughout Foucault's introduction to the Binswanger piece, it is that the dream is a mode of existence just as valid as any other.[36] The therapeutic drive that characterized Binswanger's writing disappears. Nonetheless, Foucault's discussion remains focused on human agency and human subjectivity, and thus implicitly denies the possibility that dream speech and dream existence might operate in a nonhuman mode to alter or transform nonhuman space. Despite the fact that Foucault allows the environment, especially in its spatial manifestations, a much greater role in dream interpretation than Freud did, he still disallows any interpretation of dream speech as a type of code operating—rather than merely "doing," as in Siegel's analysis—on systems or networks.

Although Foucault, unlike Freud, makes a point, for example, of recognizing that "the things and the animals, even the empty space, even objects distant and strange which populate the phantasmagoria" are as much subjects in a dream as the dreamer or the other humans who inhabit it, he still argues that at heart the dream is about *being* a subject, or, more to the point, being an "I."[37] "To dream," he argues, "is not another way of experiencing another world. It is for the dreaming subject the radical way of experiencing its own world."[38] As much as this move shifts Foucault's writing away from the relentless focus on human activity and human projection that characterized Freud's work,[39] therefore, it still remains indebted to theories of human identity. By displacing not the human subject with the dream environment, but the dream environment with the human subject—with the "I"—he, like Freud, makes any analysis of speech as an environmental rather than human phenomenon quite difficult.[40]

Likewise, although Foucault does not automatically dismiss, as Freud does, the validity of a universe in which there are no contradictions, no dichotomies, and no "either-or's," he takes these aspects of the dreamscape not as a framework for thinking about the unique, potentially nonhuman operations of the dream environment, but as a framework for thinking about human ethics and human activity. Whereas Freud simply does not accept the absence of dichotomies and "logical constructs"—be they temporal (in the dream's problematic "simultaneity") or spatial (in the dream's refusal to dichotomize)—because such constructs were so "indispensable to the natural sciences" as they were conceived of in the late nineteenth and early twentieth centuries[41]—Foucault takes this absence seriously.

Foucault's recognition of a world in which dichotomies between subject and object,[42] between near and far, between now and before, or between space and thing leads, however, not to a discussion of dream speech operating dream spaces or dream environments, but to a discussion of human "freedom," "responsibility,"[43] "alienation."[44] It leads, in brief, to a reconfiguration or redefinition of the human agency and human identity for which these spaces and environments provide nothing more than a context.[45] The environment, in other words, is once more nothing but a backdrop for the play of agency—and Foucault's focus on agency turns nonhuman linguistic activity and nonhuman worlds into things that cannot, in and of themselves, be relevant to the philosophy of dreaming. As much as Foucault, then, if not Freud, sought to maintain links with premodern modes of dream interpretation, in at least one respect his writing on dreams departs from these earlier traditions in much the same way that Freud's did. Foucault does not take seriously, as many premodern scholars of dreaming did, the possibility that dreaming might indeed have more to do with the physical world that dreamers may or may not inhabit—with spaces or environments only tangentially relevant to these dreamers—than with these human dreamers themselves.

This is not to say that all premodern scholars of dreaming focused on how dream speech operated on both dreamt and nondreamt environments rather than on what dream speech might signify about the dreaming human subject. There remained an ongoing debate, in a variety of contexts, about whether dreaming was something solely to do with the private universe of the dreamer or whether it might be relevant to public, broadly physical worlds.[46] But the idea that the latter of these two approaches might be more appropriate remained a valid option. It was entirely possible, that is to say, to read dream speech as something less about signification, less about the subjective state of the human dreamer, and more about operation, more about the alteration of dreamscapes as environments and nonhuman spaces. In short, what has been described as the premodern mode of dream interpretation allows a discussion of dreaming that does not focus solely on human agency, and does not thereby block the potentially nonhuman operation of dream speech or dream existence.

Premodern Dream Interpretation, Code, and
the Environment

The idea that there might be some continuity between premodern dream interpretation or dreamscapes and the spaces of computer memory is even more anachronistic than the idea that there might be some continuity between suffragists' speech and machine code. Nonetheless, at the basis of this chapter's rereading of stories of dreaming suffragists are the assertions, first, that recognizing such continuities is not only possible, but methodologically necessary, and second, that only once these continuities have been recognized can stories of suffragists' dream speech take

on more multidimensional qualities. Only when nonlinear interpretations of time are taken seriously, that is to say—only when anachronism
ceases to be the obstacle to these histories that it might initially appear
to be—can the threat posed by suffragists' dream speech be recognized in
its full potential.

Or, put another way, by ignoring how dream speech relates to the human ego and instead emphasizing how dream speech might execute
miraculous or prophetic operations in the physical world, premodern
methods of dream interpretation make possible both a distinctly computational understanding of the linguistic activities that occur during a
dream and a distinctly nonhuman understanding of dreamscapes themselves—an understanding that does indeed map these pre-eighteenth-
century spaces onto twentieth-century computer memory. More to the
point as far as the suffrage narrative goes, these premodern modes of interpretation arguably did not, as has been suggested, disappear with Freud
or the Enlightenment individual. Stories of dreaming suffragists wreaking
havoc on the world of which they form a part indeed demonstrate that
the nonhuman implications or aspects of dreaming remained part of narratives of dream speech even as its egoistic aspects gained prominence.

What, though, does it mean for a dreamscape to reflect computer
memory? Once again, one way of describing the space of computer memory is, as Hayles puts it, that it is non-Cartesian—that within it, "all addresses are equidistant (within near and far memory, respectively), so all
lexias are equally quick to respond to the click of the mouse."[47] As a result, Hayles continues, "our usual sense that time is passing as we watch"
is reversed, and instead, "time becomes a river that always already exists
in its entirety, and we create sequence and chronology by choosing which
portions of the river to sample."[48] It is true that this interpretation of the
space of computer memory is to a large extent indebted to theories of human agency. The fact that all addresses are spatially and temporally
equidistant implies, according to the passage above, that human choices
and decisions are even more important than they might be otherwise—
"choosing which portions of the river to sample" being the only means of
creating a meaningful "sequence" or "chronology" out of an infinitely
condensed or expanded space.

If, however, the choice or decision of the human user is ignored for
the moment, the computer memory that Hayles describes can likewise be
defined as a space that operates via language or code on, or as, the physical world. The relationship between the click of the mouse and the tem-

poral and spatial reconfiguration of memory, for instance, suggests a distinct overlap between the physical world and the computational world. The space that is computer memory changes, but it changes only given simultaneous changes in the physical world. More to the point, the space that is the physical world also changes—any and all addresses suddenly becoming available—but, once more, these changes occur only given ongoing, simultaneous alterations to computer memory. The two spaces—computational and physical—are thus irreversibly intertwined and reliant upon one another. Each operates within the other. Or, more provocatively, each operates as the other.[49]

Again, though, this interconnectedness becomes clear only when choice or decision leaves the picture—when, against Freud, times and spaces remain simultaneous and nondichotomous, when language remains nonlinear, and when all three remain beyond any therapeutic reach. The space of computer memory, that is to say, operates as the physical world precisely to the extent that speech is executed at all times and spaces at once. Whereas human speech in this situation requires deciding which portion of the temporal river that is computer memory to sample—turning this memory into a sequence or line—machine code in this same situation rests on the recognition that, as Hayles states, the river always exists in its spatial and temporal entirety. The space of computer memory thus does indeed operate as the physical world, but only when speech operates as a type of code.

And it is in this way that the space of computer memory reflects dreamscapes as they were conceived by many premodern theories of dream interpretation. Like computer memory, dreamscapes, according to these analyses, not only overlapped with the physical world but, under the proper linguistic conditions, operated *as* the physical world. Similarly, like computer memory, these dreamt spaces operated in such a way only to the extent that speech occurred at all times and spaces at once. Although various medieval Christian concerns about whether an individual might commit a sin during a dream indicate an overriding interest in human ethics, will, and agency,[50] for example, the way in which this concern was articulated likewise suggests, above all, a theory of dream space mapped linguistically onto physical space.

When Augustine, for instance, becomes "worried that a genital erection and emission might be public evidence of an unchaste dream episode,"[51] this worry is at least in part predicated on a fear that the dreamscape might colonize the physical space that is his body and, once there, do work within this space. The problem here, in other words, is not that the human, as a subject, might be deprived of agency in the realm of the dream. It is that the physical world that is the body might, as a simultaneous dream world, go into operation—and, once in operation, become an unavoidable, public, linguistic event (i.e., testimony of an unchaste episode). Far from worrying that a nonlinguistic or nonrational body might betray his linguistic or rational self, that is to say, Augustine is instead worried about a hyperlinguistic body-as-space being brought into execution. He is worried that his body and the dreamscape will become intertwined, and that language will in turn happen in the dream world, in the physical or bodily world, and in the public, political, or religious world all at once. Put another way, Augustine fears both the collapse of the dreamscape into physical space and the collapse of linear human language into nonlinear executable code.

In a similar way, the medieval European fear that the dreams of ordinary people, if not necessarily those "of saints and Christian kings," might be "devilish illusion"[52] indicates both an interest in what dream speech might do to the dreamer and *also* an interest in how dream worlds might become the physical world or vice versa. As Lisa Bitel notes in her discussion of the Christianization of pagan Germanic dream culture, conversion to Christianity did not mean simply that what was once a fuzzy line between the two spaces suddenly became clearly demarcated. It did not mean that whereas battles fought in, say, Beowulf's dreams had direct environmental repercussions,[53] conversations that occurred in the dreams of Christians had no effect on the waking universe. Nor was there simply a "transition from the pleasurable doubts of pagan dreams to the anxiety of Christian dream-visions"[54]—although in part such transitions did occur.[55]

More than that, Bitel argues, medieval Christian dream culture kept the question of any actual connection among the dream world, the physical world, and the spiritual world open. Like the medieval Muslim dream theory that posited not just an overlap among these three spheres, but the possibility that "things imagined or dreamt, at least by people with developed spiritual faculties . . . could become incarnated as reality,"[56] medieval Christian dream theory also allowed for the direct working of dream speech on the physical world. Proof of truly spiritual dreams, for instance, often appeared in the form of physical "souvenirs" left behind in the waking world by visiting saints,[57] while communities remained convinced that the only way to remain safe—in the dream world, the physical world, *or* the spiritual world—was to dream "in the company of other Christians."[58] In short, therefore, whereas it is true that a major concern in discussions of medieval Christian dreaming was whether a human subject might be capable of differentiating a true dream from a devilish illusion, such differentiation was based in turn on how and when dreamscapes might and might not operate as the physical environment. The state of the dreamer was in this way an issue almost always subordinated to how and when dream spaces might simultaneously be physical space.

In addition to dream space operating as physical space in these early modes of dream interpretation, though, language, too, collapsed into a nonlinear, executable form—a type of machine code—happening at all times and spaces at once. Indeed, these spatial and linguistic aspects of dreaming were directly reliant upon one another, with the execution of alternative, nonlinear languages responsible for mapping dream spaces onto the rest of the world. As Carolyn Carty argues in her essay "The Role of Gunzo's Dream in the Building of Cluny III," the story of Gunzo and the church can be read *both* as a familiar linear narrative *and* as a less familiar nonlinear narrative. Or, put another way, the story of Gunzo's dream and the church lends itself both to sequential human language and to fractal computational language.

On the one hand, for example, Carty notes that the relationship between the dream and the actual building of the church follows what appears to be a rational progression: "like their classical predecessors," Carty states, "the Fathers and other religious writers viewed revelatory dreams as divine messages often brought to man through such intermediaries as angels or saints."[59] On the other hand, however, once the story—of Gunzo, the paralyzed monk, his dream, his building project, and the lifting of his paralysis once the church had been completed—became a text in the form of an illuminated manuscript, this linearity disappeared:

> for the reader, the textual message given to the paralyzed monk (in the left-hand column) is simultaneous to the pictorial representation of Gunzo's future compliance and miraculous recovery (seen in the right-hand column). In effect, the reader has a vision or, in the Macrobian classification, a *visio* of the event as well as its miraculous consequences long before he actually reads about it; he thereby becomes a vicarious dreamer.[60]

Here, in other words, the dream does not merely suggest to the monk that he ought to do something upon waking up, after which he takes action. This is not a story in which Gunzo has a dream, and then, as a result, takes it into his head to advise the abbot to build the new church. Instead, the dream is simultaneous with the building of the new church and the monk's bodily cure. The dreamscape, that is to say, operates inexorably as physical space—both architectural and bodily. And, more to the point, the dreamscape and physical space operate in this way *only* because linear human language has collapsed into a variation on nonlinear machine code—only because of the saturation of all space and time by executable or operational speech.

But these medieval interpretations of the dreamscape as physical world and dream speech as, effectively, code ceased to hold sway, so it is argued, with the advent of Cartesian reason, Enlightenment rationality, or modern empiricism and positivism. Once the self-contained and self-conscious individual subject appeared, such interpretations of dreams became an epistemological impossibility.

Perhaps, though, this transition was not as stark as it might appear to be. Indeed, as will become clear over the rest of this chapter, variations on these apparently premodern themes continued to appear even into the late twentieth century, albeit in unexpected places and altered forms. In narratives of the dreaming suffragist, for instance, the basic premise that dream spaces might operate as physical space—or, alternatively, that dream spaces might play the same environmental role as computer memory—remains intact. The primary difference in these more recent takes on dreamscapes as memory or dream speech as code is simply that the changes that occur in the physical world are increasingly presented as *damage* to the physical world—and more particularly damage to the environment. When suffragists dream, they pose a distinct linguistic and spatial threat to the natural world.

Dreaming, Speaking Suffragists

Stories of dreaming suffragists played on both the idea that suffragists' speech operated or executed as a sort of premodern dream speech and the idea that, as a result, this speech worked on the physical world as dreamscape. In each of these variations on the theme, the fundamental message was that suffragists' speech posed the same threat to the emergent concept of the environment that medieval dreaming would have, should it have appeared in the nineteenth or twentieth centuries. Citing especially the tendency for suffragists' dream speech to eschew linearity in favor of execution at all times and spaces at once—citing, that is, the extent to which all addresses were equidistant and all space equally alterable when suffragists spoke—these stories of threatening dream speech rested squarely on two assumptions. First, dreamscapes could and did map onto the physical world under the proper linguistic circumstances. And, second, this mapping caused distinct environmental harm.

In a statement to the House of Representatives in 1913, for instance, antisuffrage advocate Ella Dorsey compared the ballot desired by suffragists to the "glittering object" that launches a subject into a hypnotic dream. Noting, first, that focusing on such an object is the "first step in hypnotism," Dorsey goes on to argue that regardless of the object's intrinsic value, "the mind" very quickly becomes "oblivious to everything but that object." Suffragists, therefore, "have held up before their eyes the ballot, which has induced visions and dreams, but the dreams have no reality and the visions are vain. We cannot say that what they see is even a mirage, because a mirage is simply a false picture, an inverted image of a real truth, but these ladies have something before them that is not." Finally, as a result of operating in this dreamlike state, suffragists "turn a deaf ear" to "reason," to "experience," and "to even the voice of nature."[61]

A number of years earlier, in 1882, the *Boston Globe* ran a more jocular article entitled "Emotional Legislation," in which it took a poem that Julia Noyes Stickney "compelled" the state legislative committee on women's suffrage to hear as "suggestive of what might be the result of placing women on equal political footing with men." Among the likely outcomes of this move, according to the article, were women legislators supporting a proposed bill on improved sewers in Boston by reciting "a sonnet to the Cloaca Maxima, adapted from Horace," while others opposed it "in a vigorous decalet on Dishwater," or "a discussion on proposed amendments of the divorce law" prompting a performance of "'Antony and Cleopatra,' a wild, weird, fleshly thing, yet very tender, very yearning, very precious." The article concludes, first, with the prediction that in order to understand or follow legal arguments, "the members of the House [will have to] cling passionately to one another and think of faint lilies" and, second, with the hope that "the day is not far distant when the rugged path of the legislator will be strewn with the flowers of poesy and the statute books be filled with the choicest fruits of the imagination."[62]

Each of these passages in a different way begins to tell a story of suffragists' speech as dream speech—the first by invoking the hypnotic state of the dreamer and the second by describing the poetry, fantasy, and whimsy of the dream itself. Each likewise hints at the spatial and temporal collapse or expansion on which this speech rests. By condemning dreaming suffragists for condensing any and all issues into the unreal and glittering, but physical, object that is the ballot, for instance, the first passage makes clear that one quality of suffragists' dream speech is its potential to concentrate the narrative world around it into a single, material focal point—to collapse, in this case, the linear, well-spaced human narrative of electoral politics into the nonlinear, if nonetheless physical, nonspace of the object (or code).

Likewise, by repeatedly emphasizing the tangential and metaphorical quality of the poetic suffragist's speech (in implicit contrast to the straightforward and, again, linear quality of masculine speech), the second passage takes the problematic spatial effects of this speech in the opposite direction. Noting that any and every irrelevant, far-flung metaphor or "address" would be equally accessible—or equidistant—to women engaged in legislative debate, the passage makes clear that the moment poetic, dreaming suffragists begin to speak, so too law will cease to be bounded, finite, or sequential. Like poetry (or code), law expressed by dreaming suffragists will instead become fractal—spatially infinite or at least potentially so. In both takes on the activities of dreaming suffragists, therefore, it is above all the computational, or proto-computational, potential of their speech that poses the most distinct threat.

That their speech poses this threat specifically to something called the *environment*, however, is also at least insinuated in these passages. As Dorsey argues in her discussion of hypnotized suffragists, the problem, again, with reducing the world to a focal point in the form of a glittering object is not just that this object may not have any true value. Nor is it that this focus produces a mirage—an image that Dorsey describes as simply an inversion of the truth. More than that, the problem with condensing both the narrative and the environment in which this narrative occurs into the single point of nonspace represented by a physical object is that it brings about a collision between the world of dreams and the physical world. It produces *not* mirages, but visions and dreams, and makes differentiating between space and nonspace or between dream and physicality impossible. The nonlinear dream speech of the hypnotized suffragist thus operates precisely in such a way that dreamscape and physical world—all times and spaces—become one. Or, as Dorsey concludes, the dream speech associated with this hypnotized state operates by conjuring up what "is not" in place of what is. It maps the natural observable environment onto the nonexistent, nonspace, or nothing, that is the dream.

Likewise, as much as the *Boston Globe* article on "Emotional Legislation" is intended as a mockery rather than as a serious statement about the harms of suffragists' speech, it points to a fear not far removed from Dorsey's. "Emotional Legislation" is a cause for concern, again, not because it might lead lawmakers to make irrational decisions based on little or no empirical evidence. It is a cause for concern because a particular and unique form of speech might alter the existing world, defined simultaneously by law and by the physicality of, say, the Boston sewage system, alongside the dream world of poetry, imagination, and fantasy. The fear here is not that women as women will upset social or political hierarchies. It is not that the divide between public and private will disintegrate alongside the disintegration of conventional gender roles. It is that suffragists' executable speech might make good on its threat to map an existing legal and physical environment onto the "wild, weird, and fleshly, yet very tender, very yearning, very precious" space of the dream. It is that this nonlinear mode of speech might indeed operate effectively within the environmental havoc that is non-Cartesian legal and physical space.

Once again, though, the peculiarly environmental harm inherent in this speech becomes most apparent in the writing that describes explicitly and in detail the dreamscapes in which it operates. In a 1916 article called "Suffragist Songs But No Talk in Park," for instance, on the difficulties suffragists in New York faced in getting permits for their demonstrations in Central Park, the *New York Times* noted that "technicalities of the law" would lend to the protest "a kaleidoscopic effect. It may even have a now-you-see-it and now-you-don't aspect." In order to remain in keeping with the law, indeed, the suffragist program "will now 'move on' like Little Joe from spot to spot."[63]

On the one hand, therefore, it is the suffragists' *human* or *political* speech[64] that is presented as dangerous in this article—so dangerous, in fact, that it must be replaced by, or turned into, song. On the other hand, though, as the article and, by implication, the suffragists themselves recognized, the *content* of their speech was less of a potential threat than its songlike mode of operation or execution. Indeed, it is precisely suffragists' speech in the form of the song that will turn the park into a kaleidoscopic dreamscape—operating in a way that rational legal or political argumentation, evaluated according to its content, never could.

Whereas human speech, presented in one place, bounded spatial and temporally, and following accepted rules of logic, would reinforce the rational structure of the park as natural environment, songs that move around, that have little to do with logic, that start and stop at random, that operate in a now-you-see-it-now-you-don't nonsequence, and that, fundamentally, assume all space and time to be equidistant and equally accessible, will turn this physical environment into a fantastic dream world, into a kaleidoscope, or into quintessential non-Cartesian space. Like the non-Cartesian world of the parrhesiastes, the non-Cartesian computational space of the dream is the only possible spatial outcome for this physical, nonhuman mode of speech.

Suffragists' speech thus interacts with law and politics in this early twentieth-century *New York Times* article in precisely the way that the author of "Emotional Legislation" feared it would in the mid-nineteenth century. Expressed as they are in the language of the dreaming, poetic suffragist, legal "technicalities" operate here not to define and delimit a rational world of citizens and their political identities, but instead to map a surreal, proto-computational dreamscape onto the deliberately created natural environment that is Central Park. Dream speech, that is to say, operates, according to this narrative, on a politically meaningful, human-centered environment precisely as if it were a physically executable, object-centered nonspace—eliminating in the process any line between the physical and the nonphysical, or among dream, memory, and natural world.

Indeed, as much as each of these stories of dreaming suffragists differs from the others, each is also united to these others by the same three assumptions: first, that physical spaces can be transformed alongside the dream spaces; second, that this spatial overlap owes its existence to the peculiarly computational quality of suffragists' dream speech—to its fractal rather than linear quality; and finally, third, that the spatial transformations that occur as dream speech is executed are distinctly harmful—that they threaten not just politics and the self, but more so, and above all, the environment.

Conclusion

Dreams and dream speech appear with frequency in modern political discourse—indeed, with more frequency than one might expect given the problematic or irrational logic that underlies the usual dream narrative. Regardless of whether dreaming operates as the optimistic rhetorical basis for a policy proposal—in the "I had a dream" mode—or as a means of hinting that seemingly sound political language might be nothing more than the dreamlike vaporings of a delirious mind, the dream is alive and well in nineteenth-, twentieth-, and twenty-first-century political speech. It is less frequently invoked in environmental speech[65] or, more pointedly, in machine code.

Nonetheless, at the foundation of this chapter is the idea that the dream might serve as a point of intersection among all three of these modes of speech—political, environmental, and computational—or, at least, that the rhetorical appropriation of the dream either to support or denigrate some policy decision is more complicated than it initially appears to be. Not only does politically mobilizing dreams introduce optimism or ridicule into policy discussions, after all, doing so also issues a uniquely powerful or threatening linguistic challenge to these policies and to the structures they support. Dream speech, that is to say, is a linguistic activity with the potential to transform or alter both political or legal worlds *and* (or *as*) natural environments, physical spaces, and the nonspaces of computer memory. Analyzing political speech as a type of dream speech, therefore, allows an alternative investigation of the links among electoral politics, the workings of nature, and the operations of machines, as much as it allows Freudian or Foucauldian investigations of the state, citizen, agent, or subject.

Indeed, to the extent that these environmental approaches to dreaming persisted in stories about women's suffrage, there clearly remained an ongoing fear not that dreamers as subjects might make irrational or incorrect political decisions, but that dream speech might transform, and damage, physical worlds and environments. More to the point, the influential modern theories of dreaming that take identities and agency rather than environments as their starting point for analysis have arguably blocked any recognition of this aspect of dream speech. The fixation on human egos and human identity to the exclusion of all else in, for instance, Freudian dream analysis makes any discussion of the environmental, computational, or natural worlds in this context impossible. It shuts down not only, as Foucault argued, discussions of dreaming as a mode of existence, but also discussions of dream speech as something that acts on and within the world.

As a result, these theories can account for neither the continuing rhetorical force of the dream in modern politics nor the role that stories of dreaming suffragists have played in these politics. These theories cannot explain why it is, for example, that dream speech—appropriated as it has been by politicians and political thinkers of every conceivable background—also remained a type of speech associated with the harmful linguistic activity of nineteenth- and early twentieth-century suffragists. Nor can these theories account for the peculiar spatial and temporal manifestations attributed to this linguistic activity. In order to get at these alternative readings of the story of dreaming suffragists, and of dream speech more broadly, it is necessary to move away from Freudian subjectivity, choice, and agency, and away from the modern insistence that prophetic or public dreaming is a thing of the past. In order to recognize the full potential of dream speech, one must embrace the anachronism of suffragists' speech as machine code—operating in both nonspace and infinite space—and of premodern dreamscapes executing as the proto-spaces of contemporary computer memory.

Conclusion to Part Two: Depopulating Environments

Francis Parkman has made a number of appearances in the previous chapters, but his relevance to the preceding stories of suffragists' threatening speech might still seem somewhat limited or tangential. A case can be made, however, that writers like Parkman—concurrently political philosophers, antisuffrage advocates, and, above all, naturalists or nascent environmentalists—represent an additional entry point into the rereadings of the suffrage narrative that these chapters have proposed. Indeed, many scholars have already discussed at length the underlying connection between Parkman's concern about the environment and his politics. Some have noted, for instance, how his fantasy of the Indian as part of nature or part of the wilderness helped in the production of an imperial self.[1] Others have focused on this same fantasy in order to demonstrate a broader shift from "an Enlightenment belief in a universal human species" to a theory of race that might work "as part of the 'Brahmin caste's' response to dangerous (volcanic, feverish, as it were) working-class, immigrant behavior."[2] And even those who have tried to dissociate Parkman's "environmentalism" from his political and historical views have nonetheless recognized that he very much "fused his talents as a naturalist-horticulturalist with his literary work."[3]

Proto-environmentalist work such as Parkman's, however, need not necessarily be read solely as work about self and other,[4] about how defining certain spaces as "wildernesses" leads to the definition of certain (human) identities as "wild,"[5] or, more fundamentally, as an assault, via the rhetoric of nature, on agency. In addition, as the previous seven chapters have suggested, environmentalism of the sort advocated by Parkman might also result from a distinct attitude toward *speech*—and more specifically nonhuman speech—and it might thus have less to do with the problems that nonhuman systems like nature pose to human politics and more to do with the irrelevance of humans and their politics to nature and the world writ large. One goal of the seven stories retold in these chapters has been to explore what it might mean for human politics to be eliminated by, or, more precisely, incorporated into, a nonhuman linguistic world.

In retelling what appears to be a hyperbolically human story of human politics—the story of women's suffrage—from the vantage point of nonhuman speech, and in the language of machine code, that is to say, these chapters have tried to show how central to political narratives nonhuman things might be, and likewise how marginal, except as things among other things, humans and human-related phenomena are. In turn, these chapters have also made the implicit case that what humans do—creating a discourse of the environment alongside a problematic politics of nature, say, or agitating for or against suffrage—is perhaps of less methodological importance than it might initially appear to be. Marginal as they are, humans as political beings are perhaps not worth criticizing *or* praising to the extent that writers like Parkman have been.

Put differently, whereas scholarship resting on agency and identity might read Parkman as an environmentalist who, inappropriately, did not understand his own existence as a thing or space—or, alternatively, as a political thinker who played fast and loose with nature and wilderness to make his dehumanizing points—these chapters read Parkman as someone whose political speech on behalf of humans and things was largely beside the point. Parkman's politics—or anyone's politics, for that matter—need not, given this alternative reading, be censured or praised for their ignorant, oppressive, or progressive content. In addition to opening up new lines of inquiry and posing new historical and political questions, therefore, the methodological move that underlies these chapters also posits a route around the scholarship of accusation and resentment[6] that has characterized so much recent, and recently anthropocentric, writing. In addition to demonstrating the broadly defined things that speech might do, that is to say, these chapters have also demonstrated the things that speech need not be assumed to do.

Instead of looking for friends, enemies, or advocates in speech that ostensibly supports or attacks secularism, for example, it becomes possible via this alternative methodology to look instead for what this speech might accomplish—for how it might operate against, alongside, or on top of other, sometimes even human, modes of speech. Rather than reading antisecularists (or secularists, for that matter) as themselves threats to a humanist project, for example, it becomes possible to consider the possibility that the point of antisecular speech is not to alter social or political worlds to the detriment of certain human groups, but to offer up additional, complementary modes of linguistic activity—modes beyond question and answer, call and response, blame and pain, or cause and effect. In turn, it becomes possible to rethink legal and political responses, like those of the U.S. Supreme Court, to secularist or antisecularist activity— and to rethink these responses without immediate recourse to preexisting parties or camps.

Similarly, rather than holding up the monster, the repetitive hysteric, or the insane psychopath as both empowering challenges to the liberal, humanist subject and as cautionary tales about the horrific results of linguistic and, or as, physical incoherence—as so much recent critical writing (awkwardly) has—it becomes possible with this new methodology to avoid either position. The monster ceases to be simply a cipher for the blurring of the lines between subject and object or between human and nature, it ceases to be simply the crisis that humans must both love and fear for the threat it poses to coherent, self-conscious embodied existence, and instead it becomes one of many nodes through which monstrous speech is executed. Far from demonstrating to humans what it means to be (and not to be) human, monstrous speech can now demonstrate that the human uses of language—as nothing more than a means of representing, describing, or transmitting messages or meaning to other humans—are insufficient in the contemporary world. It can demonstrate that language in its purely human manifestations is not (yet) physical or environmental enough, and that the monster, like the machine running code, has not (yet) taken its properly normative place.

The repetitive parrhesiastes and the insane psychopath are, in the same way, released from their constricting roles as both people to valorize for their destabilizing effects and people to pity or to cure for the same reason. And stories of both figures are released from reflexive readings based solely in indignation or the desire to repair or mend. Just as the parrhesiastes—as repetitive and overwhelming as a machine running code—is far more effective than any modern human speaker when it comes to executing, altering, or for that matter engulfing or devastating, networks, systems, or environments, so too the figure running insane or psychotic speech can be the norm in a world in which it is the physicality, rather than content, of language that is key. The speech activities of neither the parrhesiastes nor the hysteric or psychopath need be compared and found wanting against linear, coherent, human speech if this new methodology is the starting point of analysis—if speech is evaluated according to its capacity to work on, or to overwhelm, the physical world, its capacity to sort or store ever increasing amounts of data, and its capacity, essentially, to go viral.

Indeed, when speech exists to perpetuate a sea of meaningless information out of which infinite alternative environments might emerge— rather than to persuade or convince humans, via dialogue, of some argument or talking point—parrhesia and insane speech have the advantage. As a result, the scholarship of accusation and redress becomes irrelevant to these activities—as do the various progressive political positions that grudgingly permit the continuation of such speech activities in the name of human tolerance. The speech activities of the parrhesiastes or psychopath, that is to say, become valid according to these alternative readings not because we humans must be forbearing and open-minded but because human speech is no longer a benchmark or reference point for linguistic effectiveness.

Finally, witch's speech, theorists' speech, and dream speech all avoid appropriation by those out to accuse or to cure when the stories of each are retold in the absence of agency and in the language of machine code. When the consent of the witch is defined as a computational mode of consent—predicated on the alteration of physical or environmental systems rather than on forming (or not forming) witches into subjects or citizens—neither accusations of politically or legally undermining consent nor curative extensions of consent to those who are ostensibly without it can be valid, or for that matter viable, moves. Mobilizing consent as a means of attack or a means of protection, and thereby using it to reinforce narrow categories of political belonging,[7] are not possible when consent is a computational rather than human characteristic.

The invocations of (supposedly masculine) common sense against (supposedly feminine) abstraction or theory—along with criticisms of such invocations—likewise take on new, and less aggressive, connotations when they are addressed by means of this alternative methodology. Rather than denigrating theory (or for that matter common sense) as the defining characteristic of some radical (or conservative) political oppo-nent, it becomes possible to read each as a necessary and, again, normal part of the physical world—no longer operating in political or social op-position to one another. Moreover, if the threat posed by theory or ab-straction is a physical, spatial, or temporal threat—and if the reason that it is frightening is that it involves the production and proliferation of im-probable information that alters or overwhelms physical, spatial, or tem-poral networks—then it is unnecessary to attack theorists for their sup-posed human, political shortcomings. By doing spatial and temporal, instead of social and political work, theory becomes an integral part of the world writ large rather than the distinguishing feature of some unde-sirable political or intellectual community. And, in turn, theoretical at-tacks on common sense lose their resonance as the opposition between the two disintegrates.

The advantages of reading speech as a physical—and, more specifically, spatial and temporal—phenomenon become most pro-nounced, however, in the retelling of stories of dream speech. By recog-nizing the environmental and computational, rather than human or ego-istic, qualities of dream speech—qualities that resonate far more effectively with public or prophetic interpretive models than with sub-jective or psychoanalytical models—the full potential of the dream as a rhetorical motif suddenly becomes apparent. Calling on dreams becomes as much a physical as a political move. And the statement "I had a dream" becomes as much a means of mapping physical spaces onto the fractal, nonlinear, nonhierarchical dreamscapes that in turn resemble the spaces of computer memory as it is a means of invoking ideal human or social relationships.

Or, put another way, rather than a force that is mobilized in order to rearrange social relationships, the dream is, according to this alternative methodology, an operation that works within the infinitely accessible space and time of the world as computer memory. Unlike the dream as a purely human or political phenomenon, therefore, the dream as a com-putational phenomenon not only rearranges relationships or destabilizes hierarchies, it makes these hierarchies impossible. If space and time are either infinitely accessible or collapsed into a single point of nonspace and nontime, equality becomes not a human goal linked, once more, to a condescending human tolerance, but an empirical, physical reality. Like the speech of witches and theorists, dream speech, according to these rereadings, operates beyond any possible scholarship of accusation, or politics of remedy and cure.

Although the purpose of the past seven chapters has been to retell stories of *threatening* or *harmful* speech—or to explain in a more multidimensional way why certain speech activities, such as those of the suffragists, have posed threats or caused harm—speech of this sort need not necessarily be described in such a way. Even when it is overwhelming systems, altering physical worlds, and destroying environments, such speech might also, after all, be simply *effective*. Like code, it need not operate according to human ethical standards—even if, on occasion, it *can* operate according to these standards. And indeed, suffrage advocates like Catt arguably recognized this dual potential of speech-as-code and, for the sake of their own human goals, did mobilize it rather than simply letting it go into operation.

It is thus not just a methodological problem, but also a political problem, that scholarship on writing like Joaquin Miller's 1884 article in the *Boston Globe* ignores the fact that he described both the human *and* the nonhuman aspects of suffragists' speech—that as much as his writing is an act of discursive violence against human subjects, this is not all it is. What this scholarship has not accomplished—and what, with its relentless focus on agency and identity, on indignation and redress, it has prevented from happening—is a discussion of what it might mean if speech does not start and end with human subjectivity. It has prevented an alternative scholarship that asks: if speech need not work in this way, is it possible that the implications of writing like Miller's might have different ethical implications?

Is it possible that what is at stake in such writing is not what happens to humans when their speech is discounted as nonhuman—not whether it is or is not an act of oppression to define certain humans as "nature" or the "environment," or to exclude these humans from the purely human linguistic sphere—but rather what happens to the physical world, to systems, to networks, and indeed to nature, when nonhuman speech goes into effect? Posing and addressing such questions is arguably a worthwhile methodological project—leading to a multidimensional exploration of speech's potential, an exploration that brings together seemingly disparate narratives of witches, monsters, and theorists, of dreams and antisecularists, or of psychopaths and classical Greek parrhesiastes, in alternative, complex, and useful ways.

PART THREE : A Set of New Questions

Although suffragists' speech serves in this book more as one of many examples of speech that might benefit from being recast as machine code than it does as a topic of discussion in and of itself, the fact that the women's suffrage movement is so rhetorically central to the argument here begs a number of questions. Most pressing, it leaves open the question of what the operation of machine code—on the physical world, on nature, on systems, and on something called the environment—has to do (or not to do) with voting. More pointedly, it leaves unanswered the question of whether there might be some connection between the environmental threats posed by suffragists' speech as code and broader theories of—or a retheorization of—electoral politics. The conclusion to this book is devoted to proposing some open-ended answers to these open-ended questions.

It proposes these answers, however, in an oblique way, by posing two narrower questions of more recent or contemporary interest and by addressing two challenges—one recent and one older—to liberal democratic theory. The first of these questions is why the increasing babble, the excessive talk, and the surplus of information frequently associated with the Internet have been a source of concern to political commentators.[1] The second is why, at the same time, there continues to be an interest in informed citizenship—with politicians, especially, who admit to not following the news being censured or met with disapproval.[2] The first of the *challenges* is that posed by Gayatri Spivak to the notion that early feminist speech in Europe and the United States was a source of empowerment to "women" writ large. The second of the challenges is that posed by Carl Schmitt to the idea that voting is an effective means of articulating a popular general will. These two questions and two challenges may seem irrelevant to one another—and likewise irrelevant to the interaction of machine code, electoral politics, and the physical world. But there is arguably a point of intersection among them, and it is at this intersection that the additional relevance of the previous seven stories of suffragists' speech might be found.

Indeed, at least one answer to these questions and one effective response to these challenges can be found in the realm of computational speech and in a theory of electoral politics based on such speech. One reason for the concern and horror with excessive information on the one hand, for example, and the absence of, or lack of interest in, information, on the other, is that each makes clear what information *as* information can do. Each makes clear that there is as much space in the political realm for the production, proliferation, sorting, and storing of information, for the linguistic saturation of political as well as physical systems, as there is room for speech acts that form community among humans or citizens. The fears of the babble that is the Internet, of the political candidate uninterested in the news, of the speaking suffragist, and of the machine running code, in other words, are in many ways the same. They are a fear of speech that operates, executes, and proliferates rather than transmitting content—and they are a fear that more often than not gets situated in the speech of public women.

But, at the same time, this ostensibly harmful or threatening computational speech is likewise a mode of speech that, perhaps paradoxically, meets the challenges to liberal democratic theory posed by scholars like Spivak and Schmitt. Although such speech addresses these challenges in a distinctly nonliberal, and indeed nonhuman, way—evading dialogue, for instance, altogether—it holds out the possibility of an electoral system that is effective in ways that Schmitt did not consider, and that is open to early feminist speech of precisely the sort that Spivak condemned. Although machine code is harmful and threatening, therefore, it can also be effective or useful when it is distilled into a theory of electoral politics—or at least into a history of the franchise and voting. If nothing else, it explains the staying power of electoral systems in the face of constant criticism, the effectiveness of archaic activities like voting in twenty-first-century posthuman contexts, and the value as well as danger inherent in the speech activities of feminists like the suffragists.

The purpose of addressing these challenges to traditional feminism and to traditional theories of electoral politics from the direction of machine code, therefore, is not (inconsistently) to privilege, or return to, human interests and concerns. Nor is it to reinstate the false distinction between human and nonhuman speech that has been dismantled over the past chapters. Instead it is more modest than that. It is to throw into sharper relief the *methodological* benefits of taking machine code as a starting point for analyses of speech. It is to show that even discussions of, and scholarship on, the most seemingly human-centered issues—electoral politics and conventional feminism—can profit from the computational shift initiated in the previous seven stories.

As a result, it is likewise to show that designating certain things (in this case speech) "human" and certain other things "nonhuman" is a methodologically meaningless (human) act, given the scholarly implications of *all* speech being code. Indeed, lurking behind the arguments that constitute this final section of the book is an additional conclusion drawn from the stories retold here: although the gender dynamics that underlie liberal political identity represent *one* set of power relations that suddenly look quite different when speech is code, they are by no means the only topic open to a computational retelling. Once women's suffrage has met machine code, any number of other historical, political, or sociological problems become open to the same nonhuman turn. Once women's suffrage has met machine code, that is to say, at stake is not who speaks as a human and who does not, not how speech might benefit some humans and how it might not, but how speech in general might operate, regardless of such human versus nonhuman categorizations.

The conclusion to this book is thus divided into two short chapters. The first, on anachronistic computation, explores a number of implications of the idea that the potential for computational speech, or for the operation of machine code, existed before the twentieth-century[3] invention of computers or computer language. It makes the case that suffragists' speech was indeed a variation on code, and that reading it as such upsets in valuable or constructive ways assumptions not just about what speech can do but also about what feminist theory does. More particularly, it mobilizes this idea in response to Spivak's challenge to early feminist speech writ large. As a result, this chapter allows for the incorporation of stories of, for instance, uninformed women politicians into the alternative narrative of women's suffrage, and also into the computational narrative of threatening speech proposed throughout the book.

The second chapter sketches, in light of these arguments and in light of the alternative methodology that framed the previous section, the beginnings of a theory of electoral politics. This chapter takes as its starting point Schmitt's challenge to electoral or parliamentary politics and posits that when speech is a means of saturating electoral systems *as* physical systems—rather than a means of describing or representing the desires, ideas, or ideals of states and citizens—this challenge becomes a far less pressing one. This chapter thereby incorporates recent stories of electronic or computational babble and cacophony—stories that serve more often than not as cautionary tales about the end of human choice, agency, or identity—into the history told here. In doing so, it makes the case that meaningless mechanical babble might have optimistic as well as pessimistic connotations—and that going viral might be a distinctly feminist event.

Chapter Twelve : Anachronistic Computation

One issue that has posed a difficulty throughout the book is the anachronism of positing nineteenth-century speech activities as a variation on the twentieth- or twenty-first-century linguistic mode that is machine code. Although the seven stories of suffragists' speech that made up the previous section hinted at the virtues, as well as the difficulties, of embracing anachronism, therefore, dealing head on with its prominent role as a framing device for these stories is also worthwhile. Indeed, this anachronistic take on threatening speech, its antecedents, and its legacy is fundamental to the rereadings undertaken in this book not just for methodological reasons, but for historical reasons as well.

As James Martel has argued in his cogent reading of Walter Benjamin's "trans-temporal conspiracies" and temporal "constellations," "for Benjamin, time is not a continuity but a series of moments inter-related 'through events that may be separated from [one another] by thousands of years.'" Moreover Benjamin, Martel continues, "looks for these 'constellations' for the purpose of doing battle. By resorting to [the] kinds of transtemporal connections described above, Benjamin is attempting to circumvent our own compromise, our own participation in a sense of time and inevitability that is inherently self-defeating."[1] In addition to its methodological and historical benefits, in other words, challenging temporal linearity holds out possibilities for an affirmative *politics* as well.

With that in mind, the methodological reasons for embracing anachronism in this context are, once again, relatively straightforward. In proposing a nonlinear, fractal, or chaotic interpretation of a nonlinear, fractal, or chaotic mode of speech, it would be inconsistent to insist then on a linear, syllogistic historical time line reliant on singular cause-and-effect relationships. In order for the spatial, temporal, environmental, *and* political implications of suffragists' speech as code to become clear, it is necessary to abandon the dependence on methods or vocabularies (such as the vocabulary of agency) that make effective discussion of such speech impossible or inconceivable. Linear historical methods make these discussions impossible.

In addition, however, an *alternative* linear time line does also become possible when this new, anachronistic methodology is brought into play—a time line that places the potential for computational speech before the existence of computers, and that in turn traces the implications of this speech's operation or execution within nineteenth-, twentieth-, and twenty-first-century systems. This alternative time line is the subject of this chapter. When speech acts as machine code, regardless of whether actual machines exist, or do not yet exist, to run this code, it necessarily leads to the reimagination of a number of historical and political as well as physical and environmental relationships.

One such relationship is that among feminists, feminist theory, and the world. A key assumption in much of the historical as well as political writing that has taken agency rather than code as its starting point, for example, is that to the extent that there is a complexity to many, especially nineteenth-century, feminist positions, this complexity is founded on—and limited to—how these feminists have been complicit in oppressive discursive and political structures. When early feminists like the suffragists are criticized, that is to say, they are criticized almost without exception for their human shortcomings.[2]

By proposing a time line that describes early feminist speech as non-human and computational, however, the implications of this speech become quite different—and an alternative, arguably less accusational, history becomes not only possible, but necessary. According to such a history, early feminists would neither embrace, in a politically suspect manner, the Cartesian split between mind and body, nor would they challenge this split by valorizing the politics of embodiment or the situated subject. Instead, these feminists would operate as nodes on a linguistic network that destabilized the *physical and environmental* foundations of both Cartesian subjectivity and the challenges to this subjectivity. Whereas histories that avoid anachronism—assuming that if there ever was a computational speech, it cannot have existed prior to the twentieth century—demand historical actors who either supported or fought these mind-versus-body or language-versus-materiality opposi-tions,[3] that is to say, a history that embraces anachronism describes a mode of speech that, from its initiation, undermined, or better yet, ig-nored, such oppositions.

At the heart of this alternative history of early feminist speech, there-fore, would not be a universe that pits mind and language on the one hand against body and materiality on the other, but one that assumes language and materiality operate apart from—and occasionally even against—mind *and* body. Similarly, at the heart of this alternative history of speech would be an arena in which the linguistic representation of physical (and political) actors that accompanies such splits is largely beside the point—and where language's physical operation in the absence of *any* actors is key. As a result, not only would human embodiment and the linguistic representation of human bodies become less pressing historical issues, but the historiographical impetus toward condemning early feminists for their inappropriate attitudes toward bodies and representation would lose mo-mentum. If early feminist speech operates like code, that is to say, then it is difficult to write a history of feminists who do violence to the bodies of others via linguistic or discursive misrepresentation.

To provide an example of this resituated historiography, when Gaya-tri Spivak, for instance, based her challenge to "American feminists" for their complicity in the "production . . . of the colonial object"[4] in part on the idea that, "strictly speaking, since we are questioning the human be-ing's control over the production of knowledge, the figure that will serve us better is writing, for there the absence of the producer and receiver is taken for granted,"[5] she both presented a prototypical and influential cri-tique of early feminist speech as human speech and also demonstrated the poverty of analyses that take human speech *alone* as their starting point. On the one hand, according to Spivak's argument, early feminists achieve sovereign subject positions by producing colonial objects through discourse. But on the other hand, there is no such thing as au-thoritative control over the production of knowledge—there are no sov-ereign producers of knowledge—because forms like writing are always apart from, and before, these human speakers and their speech.

The result of such analyses is a situation in which speech thus re-mains the oppressive act of a solely human subject while writing becomes the crisis of this subject. Like Derrida's "woman," who works as the meta-physical crisis of masculine logocentrism,[6] writing here works to subvert the human speaker. Even though it is explicitly defined as something apart from producer or receiver, therefore, writing is nonetheless as an-thropocentric a phenomenon in this context as speech. Speech and writ-ing simultaneously reify and destabilize human, and *only* human, exis-tence. Or, more pointedly, speech and writing together both produce the oppressive early feminist subject *and* dissolve this subject.

Indeed, one of the simpler conclusions to be drawn from theories re-liant on speech as a human activity that operates within a linear histori-cal time line is that early feminists did not in fact exist. Or, in an even simpler format, if the category "feminist" overlapped completely with the category "producer of knowledge," and if there were no producers of knowledge, then there were no early feminists. And this was a frequent historiographical move made in 1990s writing on the topic: as much as they tried, early feminists never could successfully achieve sovereign sub-jectivity, and certainly not feminist subjectivity, because their linguistic activity was in the end destructive—it annihilated any coherent category of "citizen," "subject," or "feminist."[7]

But again, these conclusions become self-evident only if early femi-nist speech is understood to be human speech, if writing is understood to work apart from, or before, this speech, and if the harm or effectiveness of both is that each reinforces as well as undermines the subjectivity of (human) speakers. Or, put another way, when speech is solely a human activity, and when knowledge, language, and subjectivity remain inextri-cably intertwined, the only possible end point to Spivak's theoretical and historiographical challenge is the elimination of, or end to, the figure of the early feminist. If instead, however, Spivak's challenge is taken up from the anachronistic vantage point of nineteenth-century computa-tional speech, alternative conclusions present themselves.

Early feminists, for instance, can quite easily exist as nonexistent producers of knowledge if, first, the lines among speech, writing, knowl-edge, information, and noise evaporate; second, the work of this speech is physical rather than representational; and third, as a result, the Carte-sian assumptions that underlie both valorizations and critiques of em-bodiment or representation become irrelevant.[8] If speech is no longer confined to the human realm, and if language is connected instead to physical and informational systems, early feminism once again becomes possible. Indeed, given an anachronistic, rather than strictly chronologi-cal, historical time line, early feminists become key figures once more—in a computational, however, rather than humanistic theory of (in the case of the suffragists, electoral) politics.

Put differently, when speech is informational rather than representational, when it acts instead of describing, it need not—and indeed cannot—be condemned for its human foibles. The threat inherent in such
speech is not that others might be silenced via representation, but that
everyone and every*thing* might speak too much and evade silencing altogether. It is the threat posed by noise rather than knowledge, by material
and physical, rather than intellectual, linguistic activity, and by alternative modes of speech that cannot be condemned *by* humans, *for* humans.[9]

The sidelining of mind, body, knowledge, and representation in favor of physicality, materiality, information, and language that accompany
this book's embrace of anachronism, therefore, initiate a quite distinct
historiographical revision—in this case in the study of feminist speech.
Instead of arguing simply that early feminist speech was central to nine-
teenth-, twentieth-, and twenty-first-century politics because it was complicit in oppressive human discursive structures (although clearly it was),
historical narratives can now also focus on its foundational role in systemic, computational, and natural systems and networks.

Embracing anachronism, that is to say, helps to demonstrate the
staying power of additional and affirmative—even if sometimes harmful
or threatening—nonhuman modes of speech that incorporate and neu-
tralize the violent human speech criticized by so many late twentieth-
century scholars. These additional modes of speech operate not in favor
of certain humans and against others, but through the linguistic activity
of humans and nonhumans together. In this way they rescue early feminists from their role as pantomime villains and resituate them in a new,
computational story of electoral politics—demonstrating that the questions of whether it is oppressive to be objectified, whether it is undesirable to be defined as part of nature or the environment, and whether it is
possible to be the coherent victim or perpetrator of epistemic violence,[10]
are not only unnecessarily anthropocentric, but, once again, very much
beside the nonhuman point.

Chapter Thirteen : Toward the Beginnings of a Theory of Electoral Politics

How, though, might this alternative story of electoral politics proceed? One effective starting point for it is the challenge to liberalism and parliamentary democracy posed by Carl Schmitt—a challenge similar in many ways to that posed by Spivak to early feminist speech. Like Spivak's, Schmitt's challenge rests fundamentally—and convincingly—on the notion that parliamentary democracy, like early feminist speech in Spivak's analysis, cannot, on its own terms, exist. Schmitt provides a number of examples—from the enforcement of rights rhetoric to the empty formalities of political debate[1]—to demonstrate that liberalism disintegrates as a coherent phenomenon in the face of the various discourses that it has put into play. One of the most effective of these examples, however, is the absurdity of imagining the vote or general suffrage to be a manifestation of a democratic general will.[2]

Like Spivak's critique of feminist speech, therefore, Schmitt's critique of parliamentary democracy and, more narrowly, of voting has prompted much soul searching, a number of reactions, and a great many attempts to rescue electoral politics from their discursive contradictions. Also like Spivak's critique of feminist speech, Schmitt's critique of the vote has arguably remained effective, if not necessarily fashionable. From the perspective of human speech and human linguistic activity, it is difficult to deny that Schmitt, like Spivak, has a point.

From the perspective of machine code, however—and from the perspective of information rather than knowledge, of linguistic execution rather than linguistic description or representation—Schmitt's argument becomes less imperative. If nothing else, the points that he raises begin to seem less significant. Like Spivak, for instance, Schmitt situates his critique squarely within a discussion of representation and, implicitly, embodiment. For instance, "If the franchise is given to an increasing number of people in an ever-broader extension," he argues, "then that is a symptom of the endeavor to realize the identity between state and people; at its basis there is a particular conception about the preconditions on which one accepts this identity as real."[3] After describing a number of examples of this identity,[4] he continues,

> All of these identities are not palpable reality, but rest on a recognition of the identity. It is not a matter of something actually equal legally, politically, or sociologically, but rather of identifications. Extension of the suffrage, the reduction of electoral terms of office, the introduction and extension of referenda and initiatives—in short, everything that one identifies as an institution of direct democracy or a tendency toward it and all those things which, as has just been mentioned, are governed by the notion of an identity—are in consequence democratic. But they can never reach an absolute, direct identity that is actually present at every moment. A distance always remains between real equality and the results of identification.[5]

At the basis of Schmitt's criticism of voting as a mechanism of democracy, in other words, is the assumption that extending suffrage to an ever increasing amalgam of individual citizens or bodies is an attempt to produce some elusive equality that might rest on the total representation of these citizens and bodies. He assumes that electoral procedures are in fact about representing individual citizens—or worse, about representing the specific and discrete beliefs, thoughts, and views of these citizens.

Like Spivak, that is to say, Schmitt works according to the notion that speech is a solely human activity—and that the speech activity that is the vote is likewise a solely human act. The futility of voting or the extension of suffrage thus results, according to his analysis, from the fact that complete representation is in the end impossible—or at best, once again, a form of epistemic violence. What he fails to consider is the possibility that speech, especially when it is manifested in voting, may not have anything to do with representation, with human equality, with citizens and their bodies, or for that matter, and in a distinctly liberal vein, with dialogue or the exchange of beliefs, thoughts, and views. By insisting that electoral systems are confined to such matters, Schmitt, like Spivak, ignores their nonhuman potential. He ignores both the threat and the promise held out by linguistic activities that operate beyond narrow human interests, and he misses the point of what speech, and in this case voting, might do.

He misses, that is, what suffragists like Catt understood—or, at least, what the linguistic behavior of these suffragists suggested—that giving the vote to an "increasing number of people in an ever broader extension" is as much a systemic event as it is a liberal, parliamentary, or humanistic initiative. It is as much an expansion of systems and networks, and a proliferation of information as noise, as it is a tool for elevating human choice or, to use Schmitt's term, decision—be it the decision of the sovereign or the decision of some ineffectively represented collective.

Extending the franchise is not, as Schmitt imagines, necessarily an attempt to bring more humans into politics. More so, it is, or has become, an escape from the narrowly human aspects of politics altogether. It results from the noise of the Internet or the silence and babble of the uninformed public woman—from the elaboration of political systems that are as operational within natural worlds as they are sociologically meaningful within human worlds. Extending the franchise is in this way part of an alternative, nonhuman electoral politics that becomes intelligible only when speech is understood to operate in a computational, nonhuman mode.

The theory of electoral politics sketched throughout this book is thus far more descriptive or explanatory than it is normative. Its purpose is not to argue that democracy in general should be more attuned to nonhuman activities, or that political systems should incorporate computational modes of speech into their operation, but that understanding the speech that is voting, and the speech that surrounds the vote, as varieties of machine code can *explain* a number of trends in electoral politics that other theories do not. In particular, doing so can help to explain the increasing virulence of the babble or cacophony that has ostensibly replaced responsible political discussion and debate.

Or, to end on a *slightly* normative note, this nonhuman, computational theory of electoral politics provides a template for describing threatening or harmful speech—speech that is *not* dialogue—from a positive vantage point. It provides a template for an *affirmative* history of threatening speech. And within that history, it provides an additional template for stories of feminist speech, of information and noise, of the

uninformed and the hyperinformed, of statistics, polls, or numbers without meaning, of political landscapes as fractal as dreamscapes, and, in
short, of the many figures, things, and spaces that continue to populate
the electoral realm. It charts, in other words, not only a way around the
anthropocentric challenges posed by scholars such as Schmitt and Spivak, but the plots of multiple new historiographical and political, as well
as computational and physical, arenas.

Conclusion to Part Three: Telegraph Girls

The questions and challenges with which this concluding section began do undeniably relate to one another. What does the operation of machine code have to do with voting? Taking machine code as the model for speech introduces a possible solution to the problems of electoral politics discussed by scholars like Schmitt. What connection might there be between the environmental threats posed by suffragists' speech as code and this retheorization of electoral politics? Interpreting suffragists' speech as an environmental, physical, or computational activity—rather than as an oppressive representational activity—introduces a possible solution to the problems of feminist speech discussed by scholars like Spivak. Doing so indeed situates examples of feminist speech like the suffragists' at the center of this alternative electoral theory.

Each of these moves also helps to explain, historically, the increasingly prominent—and arguably effective—political roles played by electronic babble and by the uninformed public woman. Retelling stories of suffragists' threatening speech from the direction of nonhuman code, in other words, is a useful exercise at this point if for no other reason than that these stories serve as a historical foundation for contemporary voting behavior and for contemporary behavior surrounding the vote.[1] These stories likewise offer up a historical context for what is all too frequently understood to be a sudden and unexpected linguistic and political turn—the ostensible decline of political discourse in the face of unprecedented technological change. By setting such a foundation and providing such a context, these stories indeed demonstrate that the speech activities ordinarily interpreted as by-products of something called the "information age" have always been active and executing. It is simply that narratives of these activities have been overshadowed by narratives of human speech, human dialogue, and human (or nonhuman) agency.

Most important, though, retelling these stories of suffragists' speech is a means of opening up a space for thinking broadly about the physicality of language and about the various ways in which this language can go into operation—about what precisely it means to environments and to physical worlds when speech becomes monstrous, magical, dangerously theoretical, damaging to secularism, overwhelmingly repetitive, an assault on sanity, or nothing more than a dream. Although these concluding chapters have been devoted to the gender and political implications of recasting speech as code, in other words, electoral politics and gender relations are only two of *many* aspects of the physical or environmental reach of the argument presented here. Indeed, the purpose of abandoning agency as an analytical framework throughout this book has been to avoid the tendency to distill all talk of speech into talk of politics, or for that matter, into talk of gender oppression. Speech here, once again, is a physical operation that works on the world as a natural system. Absent agency, it is largely accidental. But at the heart of the narrative surrounding it is the idea that perhaps accidents—the overwhelming of systems with infinite information, the chaotic proliferation of insane networks, and the collapsing of environments into single points of nonspace—might be taken more seriously as historical phenomena.

Or, more narrowly, this narrative gestures toward the possibility that Warren Weaver's mid-twentieth-century telegraph girl might have something in common with other telegraph girls—for instance, the girl whom Henry James described in 1898, at the height of the women's suffrage movement. Unlike Weaver's telegraph girl, the girl whose story James tells in *In the Cage*[2] is anything but discreet and proper. Far from ignoring the content or meaning of the messages that move through her, she not only attends to them, but memorizes them, and develops from them intense relationships with the men and women who send them. In this sense, James tells a humanizing story of an affective individual who could have been—but is not—overwhelmed by the modern informational network of which she forms a part.

At the same time, however, like Weaver's telegraph girl, James's girl has no name. And it is at this point that the two start to meld into one another. Although the implicit threat posed by James's telegraph girl, for example, is that she knows people's secrets, whereas the implicit threat posed by Weaver's girl is that, pure node, she does not, the stories of each lead to the same conclusion. In both, language situated in informational networks becomes irrelevant to—or in some cases works against—the language spoken by "men" transmitting messages. In both, speech ceases to have anything to do with humans—the point of James's novella precisely that, despite all of her efforts, the girl's affective human capacities change nothing—and instead has to do with systems. And in both, fundamentally, the "message" to be taken away from the narrative is that privileging information or noise over knowledge or representation may no longer be a human choice—may no longer be something a man or a girl may decide to do or not to do—but instead may increasingly be the only speech activity that is possible.

Notes

INTRODUCTION TO PART ONE

1. Warren Weaver, "Recent Contributions to the Mathematical Theory of Communication," September 1949 (http://grace.evergreen.edu/~arunc/texts/cybernetics/weaver.pdf): 15–16.

2. I am deliberately referring to this speech as a type of *machine* code. Unlike, for instance, programming code—that is, what programmers write, and what is eventually translated by operating systems into machine language—machine code is what the computer does when it changes the ones and zeros on the bit. It is spoken *as* it physically changes the bit, or broadly, the system.

3. The use of the terms "human" and "nonhuman" throughout the book is not an attempt to set up a dichotomy or opposition between the two, but to make a more nuanced case that the human is a small (and arguably insignificant) part of wider nonhuman systems and environment. Referring to these systems and environments as nonhuman, in other words, is not a means of denying their human elements, but of making a methodological point about the role that human concerns should or should not play in histories of speech. Equally valid terms might be "posthuman," "post/human," or any of a number of other descriptions of scholarship that does not take the human as a starting point of analysis.

4. Donna Haraway, *Simians, Cyborgs, and Women: The Reinvention of Nature* (London: Routledge, 1990).

5. N. Katherine Hayles, *My Mother Was a Computer: Digital Subjects and Literary Texts* (Chicago: University of Chicago Press, 2005): 1.

6. N. Katherine Hayles, *How We Became Posthuman: Virtual Bodies in Cybernetics, Literature, and Informatics* (Chicago: University of Chicago Press, 1999): xii.

7. Ibid., xiii.

8. Hayles, *My Mother*, 2.

9. Hayles, *How We Became Posthuman*, 161. For Hayles's in-depth discussion of this theme, see pp. 161–78.

10. As Latour states, speech may "no longer [be] a specifically human property." Bruno Latour, *Politics of Nature: How to Bring the Sciences into Democracy*, trans. Catherine Porter (Cambridge: Harvard University Press, 2004): 65.

11. Or, as Matthew L. Jones has argued, the story of Descartes' invention of the modern subject has become "a comforting fable" in which "knowledge and truth" were assumed to "rest upon the individual subject and that subject's

knowledge of his or her own capacities." Matthew L. Jones, "Descartes' Geometry as Spiritual Exercise," *Critical Inquiry* 28 (1) (2001): 40–71, 40–41.

12. For an excellent discussion of these various positions, see Rosi Braidotti, *Nomadic Subjects: Embodiment and Sexual Difference in Contemporary Feminist Theory* (New York: Columbia University Press, 1994): especially 77.

13. See, for instance, Gayatri Spivak, "Can the Subaltern Speak?" in Cary Nelson and Lawrence Grossberg, eds., *Marxism and the Interpretation of Culture* (Urbana: University of Illinois Press, 1988): 271–313, 289.

14. Described, for instance, in Carole Pateman, *The Disorder of Women: Democracy, Feminism, and Political Theory* (Stanford: Stanford University Press, 1989): 18.

15. Louise Michele Newman, *White Women's Rights: The Racial Origins of Feminism in the United States* (New York: Oxford University Press, 1999).

CHAPTER ONE

1. Thomas Dumm, *Democracy and Punishment: The Disciplinary Origins of the United States* (Madison: University of Wisconsin Press, 1987): 17.

2. Michel Foucault, *"Society Must be Defended": Lectures at the Collège de France, 1975–1976*, trans. David Macey (New York: Picador, 2003): 92.

3. "For all words, are subject to ambiguity; and therefore multiplications of words in the body of law, is multiplication of ambiguity; besides it seems to imply, by too much diligence, that whosoever can evade the words, is without the compass of the law." Thomas Hobbes, *Leviathan* (New York: Simon and Schuster, 1962): 271.

4. "And this proceeding of popular, and ambitious men, is plain rebellion; and may be resembled to the effects of witchcraft." Ibid., 259.

5. "The way by which a man either simply renounceth, or transformeth his right, is a declaration, or signification, by some voluntary and sufficient sign, or signs, that he doth so renounce, or transfer; or hath so renounced, or transferred the same, to him that accepteth it. And these signs are either words only, or actions only; or, as it happeneth most often, both words, and actions. And the same are the BONDS, by which men are bound, and obliged; bonds that have their strength, not from their own nature, for nothing is more easily broken than a man's word, but from fear of some evil consequence upon the rupture." Ibid., 99.

6. Sovereignty being the authority to represent, linguistically, all others. This is the defining characteristic of sovereignty in Jean Bodin's more or less contemporary work as well. Indeed, according to Bodin's analysis, it is precisely the inescapable validity and authority of the sovereign's voice that demonstrates him to be sovereign: "but there is no need for money and an oath to oblige a sovereign ruler if the subjects to whom he has given his promise have an interest in the law being kept. For the word of the prince should be like an oracle, and his dignity suffers when one has so low an opinion of him that he is not believed unless he swears, or is not [expected to be] faithful to his promises unless one gives him money." Jean Bodin, *On Sovereignty: Four Chapters from The Six Books of the Commonwealth*, trans. Julian H. Franklin (Cambridge: Cambridge University Press, 1992): 14.

7. "It is true, that a sovereign monarch, or the greater part of a sovereign assembly, may ordain the doing of many things in pursuit of their passions, contrary to their own consciences, which is a breach of trust, and of the law of nature; but this is not enough to authorize any subject, either to make war upon, or so much as to accuse of injustice, or in any way to speak evil of their sovereign; because they have authorized all his actions, and in the sovereign power, made them their own." Hobbes, *Leviathan*, 193.

8. Ibid., 163.

9. Samantha Frost, "Hobbes and the Matter of Self-Consciousness," *Political Theory* 33 (4) (2005): 495–517, 497.

10. Bruno Latour, *We Have Never Been Modern*, trans. Catherine Porter (Cambridge: Harvard University Press, 1993): 19.

11. To put it differently, whereas theorists like Frost convincingly argue that Hobbes's materialism is more complicated than it initially appears because it allows for a nuanced take on embodied human subjectivity (a take that, say, Cartesian dualism does not allow), I argue that his materialism is complicated in its potential, but nonetheless still material, marginalization of human bodies. Instead of overcoming the temptation "to read [his] machine metaphor as evidence that Hobbes's materialist rejection of Descartes's philosophy entails that subjects be little more than machines" (Frost, "Hobbes," 501), I ask what it means for humans to be anything less than part of a mechanical network. Indeed, Frost's emphasis on "memory," and particularly on memory and "vital responses" (503), as the basis for Hobbes's materialist or physical self-consciousness seems to lend itself as well to this nonhuman computational reading of his work as it does to her own human-centered reading.

12. I should note that one of Cook's purposes in the book is to emphasize the diversity of interpretations of the duty—activist and quietist, verbal, physical, and mental, individual, collective, and bureaucratic, etc. Keeping this diversity in mind, I will nonetheless be drawing on only a few of these interpretations, and only to the extent that they are relevant to my discussion.

13. Michael Cook, *Commanding Right and Forbidding Wrong in Islamic Thought* (Cambridge: Cambridge University Press, 2000): 6, 155.

14. "[Ibn Taymiyya] seems to see the duty as one to be performed first and foremost (though not exclusively) by what the Koran calls 'those in authority' (*ulu 'l-amr*). In one passage he states that the performance of the duty is obligatory for 'those in authority,' whom he specifies as the scholars . . . the political and military grandees . . . and the elders . . . of every community; it is their duty to carry out the duty vis-à-vis the common people subject to their authority." Ibid., 155.

15. Ibid., 34.

16. Some arguing, for example, that it must by definition be a verbal activity alone, even if "it was a conventional legal usage," speak of it as a physical and mental one as well. For instance, an Imami scholar in 1621 "suggested in passing that it did not really make sense to speak of 'commanding' or 'forbidding' except with reference to some kinds of verbal performance, but he accepted that it was a conventional legal usage to do so." Ibid., 285.

17. Ibid., 317–18.

18. Ibid., 71.

19. Ibid., 5.

20. Carl Schmitt, *Political Theology: Four Chapters on the Concept of Sovereignty*, trans. George Schwab (Chicago: University of Chicago Press, 2005): 9. See also p. 13.

21. "The essence of liberalism is negotiation, a cautious half measure, in the hope that the definitive dispute, the decisive bloody battle, can be transformed into a parliamentary debate and permit the decision to be suspended forever in an everlasting discussion." Ibid., 63.

22. Invoking Hobbes as "the classical representative of the decisionist type," for instance, Schmitt argues that this "type" "discovered the classical formulation of the antithesis: *autoritas, non veritas, facit legem.*" A few pages later, he continues: "the form that [Hobbes] sought lies in the concrete decision, one that emanates from a particular authority. . . . [W]hat matters for the reality of legal life is who decides." Engaging in a materialist reading of Hobbes, therefore, Schmitt removes effective or threatening speech from the realm of message, content, meaning, truth, or falsehood, and defines it instead as a physical articulation of sovereign authority—as something that operates only through the material existence of the sovereign. Ibid., 33, 34–35.

23. Carl Schmitt, *Concept of the Political*, trans. George Schwab (Chicago: University of Chicago Press, 1996): 47.

24. "Liberalism . . . has attempted to transform the enemy from the viewpoint of economics into a competitor and from the intellectual point into a debating adversary." Ibid., 28.

25. "Instead of a clear distinction between the two states, that of war and that of peace, there appears the dynamic of perpetual competition and perpetual discussion." Schmitt, *Concept of the Political*, 71–72. See also *Political Theology*, 63.

26. Once again, in a partial echo of Hobbes's discussion of how words might assault law: "for all words, are subject to ambiguity; and therefore multiplications of words in the body of law, is multiplication of ambiguity." Hobbes, *Leviathan*, 271.

27. "What I learn from reading Andrea's book and listening to her tonight is that what Barton Joseph defends as his free speech is premised on what Linda describes as her life." Catharine A. MacKinnon, *Feminism Unmodified: Discourses on Life and Law* (Cambridge: Harvard University Press, 1987): 129.

28. Ibid., 129–30.

29. Ibid., 156.

30. Ibid., 210.

31. Ibid., 146.

32. Ibid., 209.

33. Wendy Brown, "Freedom's Silences," in *Edgework: Critical Essays on Knowledge and Politics* (Princeton: Princeton University Press, 2005): 91.

34. Ibid., 93.

35. It should be noted that there has been a growing critique in recent years of the idea that recognition is, or should be, at the heart of linguistic activity or exchange. For examples of this work, see Lois McNay, *Against Recognition* (Cambridge: Polity Press, 2008), Patchen Markell, *Bound by Recognition* (Princeton: Princeton University Press, 2003), and many others.

36. Brown, *Edgework*, 85.

CHAPTER TWO

1. N. Katherine Hayles, *Chaos Bound: Orderly Disorder in Contemporary Literature and Science* (Ithaca: Cornell University Press, 1990): 2. As she writes with specific reference to Saussure: "Saussure initiated semiotics by proposing that the proper study for linguistics was *la langue* rather than *la parole*, the system of language rather than words, and by showing that relations within *la langue* could be specified only as a series of differences. The analogous movement within science came with Shannon's theory of information. Saussure's theory separated sign from referent; Shannon's theory separated information from meaning. In Shannon's equations, the informational probability of an element can be calculated only with reference to the ensemble from which it is drawn, that is, not absolutely but through a series of differences. This move allows the information content of a message to be quantified *regardless of its context or meaning*. The inward-turning structures of Saussurean linguistics and information theory are not arbitrary theoretical choices. In the absence of external reference, these theories could be defined *only* internally." Ibid., 178.

2. As Kristin Asdal has noted in her analysis of Latour's more general (that is, not purely speech-related) theories: "the works of both [Haraway and Latour] . . . attempt to break away from established dichotomies between nature and culture, science and politics, and the way these dichotomies have influenced the telling of histories. . . . [B]oth Haraway and Latour argue that we have never been fully modern in the sense that nature and culture, people and things, human and nonhuman, and science and politics have each been kept in their own spheres. It is only our theories that tell us this; in practice, we do not know how our nature-cultures are or should be composed." Kristin Asdal, "The Problematic Nature of Nature: The Post-Constructivist Challenge to Environmental History," *History and Theory* 42 (4) (2003): 60–74, 66.

3. See, among other works, Jean Baudrillard, *The System of Objects*, trans. James Benedict (New York: Verso, 1996).

4. Latour, *Politics of Nature*, 65.

5. Ibid., 86.

6. Latour also spends some time describing the ethical significance of these examples—the extent to which some of them (the nonhuman speaker) advance useful dialogue, and the extent to which some of them (the "speaking fact") obstruct useful dialogue. For instance, "we find ourselves in a situation where a speech impediment is preferable to an analytical clarity that would slice off mute things from speaking humans in a single stroke." Ibid., 67. I do not take up these ethical issues in this book.

7. Ibid., 68.

8. Ibid., 67.

9. Ibid.

10. Ibid.

11. Ibid., 70.

12. Ibid.

13. At the same time, Latour remains interested in the traditional question of how this speech might affect, or threaten, bodies, subjectivities, and identities as well. Ibid., 68.

14. Hayles, *My Mother*, 50.

15. See, for instance, Hayles's discussion of the competition between the Shannon-Wiener theory of information divorced from meaning and the MacKay theory of information that attempted to take meaning into consideration. Hayles, *How We Became Posthuman*, 56.

16. This theory of information is related, but not identical, to the information that became popularized in the mid-twentieth-century rhetoric of the "Age of Information": "although the rise to dominance of information in the biological and computer sciences has received increasing attention in recent years, less sustained interest has been paid to a third important stage of the morphogenesis of 'information.' The site of emergence for this stage was in the social sciences, especially economics and sociology. Beginning in the 1950s, a number of economists and social theorists began to isolate and focus on the increasing importance to the U.S. economy of the 'information sector,' that is, the sector that produced and distributed knowledge, rather than, for example, agricultural or manufactured goods. . . . [Marshall] McLuhan [1964] proclaimed that we were living in a 'new electric Age of Information,' and developed several striking claims about information itself, claiming, for example, that 'the electric light is pure information,' because it is 'a medium without a message.' Although McLuhan's book was dismissed by some as not appropriately rigorous in its analysis and argumentation, his claims have proven to have continuing impact and significance (especially in the 1990s, as a generation who came to age with computers and the World Wide Web (WWW) have now found added meaning in his catch phrases, design, and aphoristic analyses)." Robert Mitchell and Phillip Thurtle, "Data Made Flesh: The Material Poiesis of Informatics," in Robert Mitchell and Phillip Thurtle, eds., *Data Made Flesh: Embodying Information* (London: Routledge, 2004): 1–26, 8.

17. On occasion, discussions of this physicality has become almost hyperbolic. For instance, "many people would argue that natural languages are much more broadly based than programming languages, a stance that relegates code to the relatively small niche of artificial languages intended for intelligent machines. Recently, however, strong claims have been made for digital algorithms as the language of nature itself. If, as Stephen Wolfram, Edward Fredkin, and Harold Morowitz maintain, the universe is fundamentally computational, code is elevated to the lingua franca not only of computers but of all physical reality." Hayles, *My Mother*, 15.

18. As Thacker puts it: "information, while not an object or a thing, is nevertheless the constantly varying, quantitative value of a message or content at a given point within either the cybernetic system or the line of communication." Eugene Thacker, "Data Made Flesh: Biotechnology and the Discourse of the Posthuman," *Cultural Critique* 53 (Winter 2003): 72–97, 83.

19. Hayles, *Chaos Bound*, 6.

20. Ibid.

21. While also noting that such a separation was by no means a given as information theory developed. Hayles, *How We Became Posthuman*, 56.

22. Hayles, *Chaos Bound*, 6.

23. Ibid.

24. He precedes this passage as follows: "in fact, two messages, one of which

is heavily loaded with meaning and the other of which is pure nonsense, can be exactly equivalent, from the present viewpoint, as regards information. It is this, undoubtedly, that Shannon means when he says that 'the semantic aspects of communication are irrelevant to the engineering aspects.' But this does not mean that the engineering aspects are necessarily irrelevant to the semantic aspects. To be sure, this word information in communication theory relates not so much to what you *do* say, as to what you *could* say. That is, information is a measure of one's freedom of choice when one selects a message. If one is confronted with a very elementary situation where he has to choose one of two alternative messages, then it is arbitrarily said that the information, associated with this situation, is unity. Note that it is misleading (although often convenient) to say that one or the other message, conveys unit information." Weaver, "Recent Contributions," 5.

25. Hayles is to some extent making this point in the following passages: "although code originates with human writers and readers, once entered into the machine it has as its primary reader the machine itself." Hayles, *My Mother*, 50. And, "rectifying voltage fluctuations could be compared to Saussure's 'rectification' of actual sounds into idealized sound images. Importantly, however, rectification with code happens in the electronics rather than in the (idealized) system created by a human theorist. Thus it is a physical operation rather than a mental one, and it happens while the code is running rather than retrospectively in a theoretical model. These differences again illustrate that code is more intrinsically bound to materiality than Saussure's conception of *la langue*" (44).

26. Hayles, *How We Became Posthuman*, 275.

27. Thacker, "Data Made Flesh," 72.

28. Ibid., 87.

29. For instance, Mitchell and Thurtle, "Data Made Flesh," 1.

30. Or, as Hayles states in commenting on Thacker's article: "'change the code,' Thacker observes, 'and you change the body.' Information here does not exclude materiality, as it tends to do with researchers who specialize in computer simulations; rather, materiality is seen as the site at which information patterns exert control over form and function. Concentrating on regenerative medicine, including tissue engineering, stem cell research, and therapeutic cloning, he sees this research as part of a larger paradigm he calls 'biomedia' in which information produces the body purified of errors. In this purification, the body is not only regenerated but actually redesigned by its informatting with informational codes. The term 'biomedia' brilliantly captures the tension between the body's materiality, and the idea that materiality is essentially a substrate for information." N. Katherine Hayles, "Afterword: The Human," *Cultural Critique* 53 (Winter 2003): 136.

31. Indeed, another way of methodologically sidelining, if not ignoring, human bodies and agency is to read, for instance, the writing on the harm that computer language might cause to human identities and human bodies as simply a subset of the writing that warns of what computer language might do to the environment. Rather than resituating or reifying the liberal humanist fear and fantasy of minds divorced from bodies, in other words, these discussions might instead be emphasizing the more recent fear that computer language might

threaten the environment. To the extent that everything becomes system, net-work, context, or environment when computers speak, it indeed would make very little sense if human bodies, identity, and agency were somehow unaltered by this linguistic activity. To the extent that these bodies, identities, and agen-cies are altered, however, it is not because of their human qualities but because of their existence within environmental networks. Yes, in other words, computer language is relevant to humans. But to assume that it is uniquely relevant to hu-mans is arguably not only a mistake, but an obstacle to understanding what pre-cisely computer language does. In order to get at any alternative interpretation of the harm that this language might do, therefore, it is necessary to move away from this approach and to keep its environmental qualities in mind. The point here is not simply that humans should not stand above or apart from the envi-ronment—or that humans should recognize themselves as part of a field. It is that humans are analytically and methodologically insignificant (at least in this con-text) in relation to the environment or system. Asdal gestures toward the same idea in her discussion of Haraway and Latour: "Thus humans do not stand above nature, as implied by contrasting humanity and the biosphere, but in relation with nature. Haraway and Latour use different concepts to build from this per-spective: articulation and partial connections on Haraway's part, and attach-ment—which replaces his earlier, most well-known actor-network concept—on the part of Latour." Asdal, "Problematic Nature of Nature," 70.

32. Hayles, My Mother, 227.

33. Nigel Thrift and Shaun French, "The Automatic Production of Space," Transactions of the Institute of British Geographers 27 (3) (2002): 309–35, 330.

34. Elaine Graham, Representations of the Post/Human: Monsters, Aliens, and Others in Popular Culture (Manchester: Manchester University Press, 2002): 5.

35. Ibid., 5.

36. Hayles, My Mother, 19–20.

37. Hayles notes that she is uninterested in evaluating the accuracy of Wol-fram's claims—choosing instead to "explore the implications of what it means to be situated at a cultural moment when . . . computation as means and as metaphor are inextricably entwined as a generative cultural dynamic." Ibid.

38. For a further discussion (and defense) of using the terms "nature" and "the environment" interchangeably, see the conclusion to part 1.

39. "This is the world of 'local intelligence' in which everyday spaces be-come saturated with computational capacities, thereby transforming more and more spaces into computationally active environments able to communicate within and with each other. This change is taking place as a result of two main developments. The first of these is the move to 'ubiquitous,' 'everywhere' or 'per-vasive' computing, computational systems which are distributed through the en-vironment in a whole range of devices, 'a physical world invisibly interwoven with sensors, actuators, displays and computational elements, embedded seam-lessly in the everyday objects of our lives and connected through a continuous network'." Thrift and French, "Automatic Production of Space," 315 (citation omitted).

40. Ibid., 309.

41. Ibid.

42. "Increasingly, spaces like cities—where most software is gathered and

has its effects—are being run by mechanical writing, are being beckoned into existence by code." Ibid., 311.

43. Ibid., 329.

44. See the conclusion to part 2 for an extended discussion of the role that "wilderness" plays in the stories that constitute this book.

45. Whereas the "concept of ecology originated in the second half of the 1800s, and was intended to cover the study of the supposed equilibrium between organisms and the external world." Asdal, "Problematic Nature of Nature," 63.

46. Hayles, *Chaos Bound*, 5.

47. Hayles, *How We Became Posthuman*, 36–37.

48. For instance, "taken as a group, these essays demonstrate that just as the posthuman is increasingly necessary to understand what counts as human, so understanding the posthuman requires taking the human into account. We do not leave our history behind but rather, like snails, carry it around with us in the sedimented and enculturated instantiations of our pasts we call our bodies." Hayles, "Afterword: The Human," 137. In addition, "while biotech research raises many of the issues common to both the extropian and critical posthumanist discourses, it also elucidates unique relationships between human and machine, flesh and data, genetic and computer 'codes.' Both threads offer valuable insights into the ways in which notions of 'the human' diversify, self-transform, and mutate as rapidly as do new technologies." Thacker, "Data Made Flesh," 73.

49. For instance, "at the core of this critique is the problematic of the humanist subject with its traditional repercussions on questions of agency, identity, power, and resistance. Notwithstanding the technoscientific developments that inform much of what counts as posthumanist thought, the question of what it means to be human has been a source of contentious debate in the humanities for the last two decades. The revolutionary Enlightenment narratives that challenged an oppressive feudal order and reenvisioned 'man' as rational, autonomous, unique, and free have been in turn challenged and deconstructed. The emancipatory impulse of liberal humanism has come to be understood as being unwittingly complicit in colonialist, patriarchal, and capitalist structures. As Heffernan (in this issue) writes, 'Understood as local, fluid, contingent, and as contesting and rending the hierarchies of nature/culture, self/other, male/female, human/nonhuman, this postmodern subject is by now a familiar alternative to the conception of the self as fixed, autonomous, authentic, coherent, and universal.' The postmodern subject is an unstable, impure mixture without discernable origins; a hybrid, a cyborg." Bart Simon, "Toward a Critique of Posthuman Futures," *Cultural Critique* 53 (Winter 2003): 1–9, 3–4.

50. David Holmes, *Virtual Politics: Identity and Community in Cyberspace* (London: Sage, 1998).

51. "This is a book about what it means to be human. Or, more precisely, it is an examination of the impact of twenty-first-century technologies—digital, cybernetic and biomedical—upon our very understanding of what it means to be human. I will argue that some of the most definitive and authoritative representations of human identity in a digital and biotechnological age are to be found with two key discourses: Western technoscience (such as the Human Genome Project) and popular culture (such as science fiction)." Graham, *Representations of the Post/Human*, 1.

52. Hayles, *How We Became Posthuman*, 4–5.
53. Ibid.
54. Ibid.
55. For instance, "reacting against the VR rhetoric of disembodiment, they critique this rhetoric as deriving from 'an essentially uninterrogated Cartesian value system, which privileges the abstract and disembodied over the embodied and concrete.' They propose, by contrast, to building 'an unencumbering [sic] sensing system which modeled the entire body of the user.'" N. Katherine Hayles, "Reconfiguring the Mindbody," in Mitchell and Thurtle, *Data Made Flesh*, 229–48, 235.
56. For instance, "this modern notion of information—most notably in the extropian concept of uploading—does not exclude the body or the biological/material domain from mind or consciousness, but rather takes the material world as information. This powerful ideology not only informs research in cognitive science but in the life sciences as well. Hayles's critical point is that informatics is a selective process, and those things that are filtered or transformed in that process—such as a notion of the phenomenological, experiential body, or 'embodiment'—simply become by-products of an informatic economy." Thacker, "Data Made Flesh," 80. See also: "Bartlett and Byers's close reading of this film teases out the tension of the human and the posthuman alluded to by Badmington and calls attention to the humanist pretension latent in the desire to dissolve the material body. Indeed, Bartlett and Byers remain wary of the popular posthuman subject and note the surface correlation between the deconstructive model of postmodern subjectivity and the fluid, flexible, and fragmented subjects of The Matrix." Simon, "Critique of Posthuman Futures," 5.
57. Hayles, *How We Became Posthuman*, 243–44.
58. Once again, this criticism of disembodiment has appeared in the work of a number of other posthumanist writers as well. For instance, Thacker, "Data Made Flesh," 81–82, 85. And also Simon, "Critique of Posthuman Futures," 6.
59. Hayles, *How We Became Posthuman*, 12.
60. Moreover, "the body's dematerialization," she continues, "depends in complex and highly specific ways on the *embodied* circumstances that an ideology of dematerialization would obscure. Excavating these connections requires a way of talking about the body responsive to its construction as discourse/information and yet not trapped within it." Ibid., 193.
61. Noting, for instance, that "as new and more sophisticated versions of the posthuman have evolved, this stark contrast between embodiment and disembodiment has fractured into more complex and varied formations." Hayles, *My Mother*, 2.
62. For instance, "in light of these complex intermediations, let me advance a proposition: to count as a person, an entity must be able to exercise agency. Agency enables the subject to make choices, express intentions, perform actions. Scratch the surface of a person, and you find an agent; find an agent, and you are well on your way toward constituting a subject . . ." Ibid., 172.
63. Ibid., 2.
64. N. Katherine Hayles, "Limiting Metaphors and Enabling Constraints in Dawkins and Deleuze/Guattari," *SubStance* 30 (1–2) (2001): 144–59, 158.
65. Or, as Thacker has argued, the "blind spot" of arguments that divorce

human subjects from technology is "that the ways in which technologies are themselves actively involved in shaping the world are not considered"—that there is no "due consideration to the ways in which 'nonhumans' and 'actants' are also actively involved in the transformation of the world." Thacker, "Data Made Flesh," 76.

66. More specifically: "the actor-network theory with which Latour has been primarily associated was a strategy to reveal how humans and nonhumans are connected to one another through a network where they develop together. Science, society, and technology are thought of as a field for human and nonhuman agency. The human subject is no longer in the center with its power to create worlds. The nonhumans are also drawn in as co-producers." Asdal, "Problematic Nature of Nature," 72.

CHAPTER THREE

1. Laura M. Ahearn has effectively described much of the tension, as well as the variety, that exists in writing about agency. For instance, "Jean and John Comaroff have called agency 'that abstraction greatly underspecified, often misused, much fetishized these days by social scientists.' While this assessment may be a bit harsh, it is true that scholars often fail to recognize that the particular ways in which they conceive of agency have implications for the understanding of personhood, causality, action, and intention. Agency therefore deserves 'deeper consideration and more extensive theoretical elaboration.' Let me propose, then, a provisional definition of the concept: Agency refers to the socioculturally mediated capacity to act. According to this bare bones definition, all action is socioculturally mediated, both in its production and in its interpretation. Although this definition provides us with a starting point, it leaves many details unspecified. The following are some questions to ponder—questions that may be answered in different ways by different scholars. Must all agency be human? Can nonhuman primates, machines, technologies, spirits, or signs exercise agency? Must agency be individual, leading to charges of unwarranted assumptions regarding Western atomic individualism? Or can agency also be supraindividual—the property, perhaps, of families, faculties, or labor unions? Conversely, can agency be subindividual—the property of 'dividuals,' as when someone feels torn within herself or himself? What does it mean to be an agent of someone else? Must agency be conscious, intentional, or effective? What does it mean for an act to be conscious, intentional, or effective?" Laura M. Ahearn, "Language and Agency," *Annual Review of Anthropology* 30 (2001): 109–37, 112–13 (citations omitted).

2. As it was further developed by John Searle, *Speech Acts: An Essay in the Philosophy of Language* (Cambridge: Cambridge University Press, 1969): 54–72.

3. J. L. Austin, *How to Do Things With Words* (Cambridge: Harvard University Press, 1975): 109–14.

4. He notes, for instance, the danger of arguing that, say, the act of marriage, betting, judicial sentencing, etc. are "only words": "but probably the real reason why such remarks sound dangerous lies in another obvious fact, which is this. The uttering of the words is, indeed, usually a, or even *the*, leading incident

in the performance of the act (of betting or whatnot), the performance of which is also the object of the utterance, but it is far from being usually, even if it is ever, the *sole* thing necessary if the act is to be deemed to have been performed." Ibid., 8.

5. Ibid., 133–40.

6. "In this sense, an 'act' is not a momentary happening, but a certain nexus of temporal horizons, the condensation of an iterability that exceeds the moment it occasions." Judith Butler, *Excitable Speech: A Politics of the Performative* (New York: Routledge, 1997): 14.

7. As Austin argues, one of the important characteristics of the illocutionary act is that it is a "conventional" act. Austin, *How to Do Things*, 120–21. Or, as Butler puts it, "how does one go about delimiting the kind of 'convention' that illocutionary utterances presume? Such utterances do what they say on the occasion of the saying; they are not only conventional, but in Austin's words, 'ritual or ceremonial.' As utterances, they work to the extent that they are given in the form of a ritual, that is, repeated in time, and hence, maintain a sphere of operation that is not restricted to the moment of the utterance itself." *Excitable Speech*, 3.

8. Butler, *Excitable Speech*, 150–51.

9. For instance, "pornography hides and distorts truth while at the same time enforcing itself, imprinting itself on the world, making itself real. That's another way in which pornography *is* a kind of fact." MacKinnon, *Feminism Unmodified*, 136. Or, "the Seventh Circuit allowed the fact that pornography has a theory to obscure the fact that it is a practice, the fact that it is a metaphor to obscure the fact that it is also a means" (212).

10. "The legal effort to curb injurious speech tends to isolate the 'speaker' as the culpable agent, as if the speaker were at the origin of such speech. The responsibility of the speaker is thus misconstrued. The speaker assumes responsibility precisely through the citational character of speech. The speaker renews the linguistic tokens of a community, reissuing and reinvigorating such speech. Responsibility is thus linked with speech as repetition, not as origination." Butler, *Excitable Speech*, 39. "The constraints of legal language emerge to put an end to this particular historical anxiety, for the law requires that we resituate power in the language of injury, that we accord injury the status of an act and trace that act to the specific conduct of a subject. Thus, the law requires and facilitates a conceptualization of injury in relation to a culpable subject, resurrecting 'the subject' . . . in response to the demand to seek accountability for injury" (78).

11. Despite this critique, MacKinnon herself cautions against linear reasoning of this sort in other contexts: "but on a group basis, as women, the selection process is absolutely selective and systematic. Its causality is essentially collective and totalistic and contextual. To reassert atomistic linear causality as a sine qua non of injury—you cannot be harmed unless you are harmed through this etiology—is to refuse to respond to the true nature of this special kind of harm." MacKinnon, *Feminism Unmodified*, 157.

12. Butler, *Excitable Speech*, 78.

13. "When we claim to have been injured by language, what kind of claim do we make? We ascribe an agency to language, a power to injure, and position ourselves as the objects of its injurious trajectory. We claim that language acts,

and acts against us, and the claim we make is a further instance of language, one which seeks to arrest the force of the prior instance. Thus, we exercise the force of language even as we seek to counter its force, caught up in a bind that no act of censorship can undo." Ibid., 1.

14. And "how what it [the subject] creates is also what it derives from elsewhere. " Ibid., 15.

15. Ibid., 26–27.

16. Ibid.

17. Ibid., 4.

18. Ibid., 5.

19. Ibid., 159.

20. Or, as Barad notes, "perhaps the most crucial limitation of Butler's theory of materiality is that it is limited to an account of the materialization of human bodies, or more accurately, to the construction of the surface of the human body (which most certainly is not all there is to human bodies). . . . [I]n contrast to Butler's more singular focus on the human body, the framework of agential realism does not limit its reassessment of the matter of bodies to the realm of the human." Karen Barad, "Getting Real: Technoscientific Practices and the Materialization of Reality," *differences* 10 (2) (1998): 87–128, 107.

21. Butler, *Excitable Speech*, 15. Butler makes a similar point in *The Psychic Life of Power:* "in its resignifications, the law itself is transmuted into that which opposes and exceeds its original purposes. In this sense, disciplinary discourse does not unilaterally constitute a subject in Foucault, or rather, if it does, it *simultaneously* constitutes the condition for the subject's de-constitution. . . . [A] subject only remains a subject through a reiteration or rearticulation of itself as a subject, and this dependency of the subject on repetition for coherence may constitute the subject's incoherence, its incomplete character. This repetition or, better, iterability thus becomes the non-place of subversion, the possibility of a re-embodying of the subjectivating norm that can redirect its normativity." Judith Butler, *The Psychic Life of Power: Theories in Subjection* (Stanford: Stanford University Press, 1997): 99.

22. As Austin argues (by way of scare quotes), "the illocutionary act 'takes effect' in certain ways, as distinguished from producing consequences in the sense of bringing about states of affairs in the 'normal' way, i.e. changes in the natural course of events. . . . [S]o here are three ways, securing uptake, taking effect, and inviting a response, in which illocutionary acts are bound up with effects; and these are all distinct from the producing of effects which is characteristic of the perlocutionary act." Austin, *How to Do Things*, 117–18.

23. "That linguistic domain over which the subject has no control is exercised by the speaking subject. Autonomy in speech, to the extent that it exists, is conditioned by a radical and originary dependency on language whose historicity exceeds in all directions the history of the speaking subject. And this excessive historicity and structure makes possible the subject's linguistic survival as well as, potentially, that subject's linguistic death." Butler, *Excitable Speech*, 28.

24. Ibid., 52.

25. Austin highlights the fragility of the response in the illocutionary situation when he notes that it is "by convention" that "many illocutionary acts invite . . . a response or sequel," but that the line between convention and lack of

convention is difficult to define, and that the responses themselves blur the distinction between illocutionary and perlocutionary speech. Austin, *How to Do Things*, 117–18.

26. Butler, *Excitable Speech*, 52.

27. Ibid., 136.

28. "Acting one's place in language continues the subject's viability, where that viability is held in place by a threat both produced and defended against, the threat of a certain dissolution of the subject. If the subject speaks impossibly, speaks in ways that cannot be regarded as speech or as the speech of a subject, then that speech is discounted and the viability of the subject called into question. The consequences of such an irruption of the unspeakable may range from a sense that one is 'falling apart' to the intervention of the state to secure criminal or psychiatric incarceration." Ibid., 136.

29. Hayles, *Chaos Bound*, 9.

30. Ibid., 11.

31. For instance, "central to this scenario is performative language. [Neal] Stephenson [in *Snow Crash*] takes his inspiration not from J. L. Austin or Judith Butler but from computational theory." Hayles, *How We Became Posthuman*, 274. And, a page later, "computational theory treats computer languages as if they were, in Austin's terms, performative utterances." Ibid., 275.

32. Ibid., 274.

33. She concludes this passage with the statement I noted before: "although code originates with human writers and readers, once entered into the machine it has as its primary reader the machine itself." Hayles, *My Mother*, 50.

34. Although I should note that Hayles complicates, and begins to bring this analysis back around to human speakers later on in the book: "in natural languages, performative utterances operate in a symbolic realm, where they can make things happen because they refer to actions that are themselves symbolic constructions, actions such as getting married, opening meetings, or as Butler has argued, acquiring gender. Computational theory treats computer languages as if they were, in Austin's terms, performative utterances. Although material changes do take place when computers process code (magnetic polarities are changed on a disk), it is the act of attaching significance to these physical changes that constitutes computation as such. . . . [M]achine language is coextensive with enaction, but it is extremely difficult for humans to read machine language, and it is almost impossible for them to process machine language intuitively." Hayles, *How We Became Posthuman*, 274–75.

35. Hayles, *My Mother*, 177.

36. Ibid., 172.

37. Ibid., 192.

38. Recall, for instance, her point that "we are never only conscious subjects, for distributed cognition take place throughout the body as well as without; we are never only texts, for we exist as embodied entities in physical contexts too complex to be reduced to semiotic codes; and we never act with complete agency, just as we are never completely without agency. In a word, we are the kind of posthuman I would want this word to mean." Hayles, "Limiting Metaphors," 158.

39. She also critiques Richard Dawkins's displacement of agency. Hayles, "Limiting Metaphors," 149.

40. Hayles, *My Mother*, 173–74.

41. "Like the selfish gene, the biomorph proves to be a stalking horse for the reinscription of the liberal humanist subject. Who really has agency in these performances is not so much the entity in itself (gene or biomorph) as the human narrator who constructs them as agents through metaphors operating without the productive push-pull effect of balancing constraints. The willful erasure of constraints functions to recuperate agency for the human speaker. It is not the actors within the story who exercise final agency, but the human narrator who crafts the story so as to solidify his own agency even as he supposedly gives it away." Hayles, "Limiting Metaphors," 152.

42. Ibid., 157.

43. Ibid.

44. Ibid., 158.

45. Extending agency to nonhuman actors or actants has a long history. For one convincing articulation of the benefits of doing so, see Barad: "if agency is understood as an enactment and not something someone has, then it seems not only appropriate but important to consider nonhuman and cyborgian forms of agency as well as human ones. This is perhaps most evident in consideration of fields such as science, where the 'subject' matter is often 'nonhuman.'" Barad, "Getting Real," 112. For one example of the methodological pitfalls of this move, see also Jane Bennett's discussion in *Vibrant Matter: A Political Ecology of Things* (Durham: Duke University Press, 2010). In order to extend agency to nonhuman things, networks, or grids—all in the name of a less anthropocentric politics—Bennett dissociates language from agency altogether. "Speech," for instance, is repeatedly placed alongside "human" in her book, even as human versus nonhuman dichotomies are challenged. And rather than "speech," nonhumans have "variable capacities" (108). Moreover, earlier on in the book, Bennett states that "instead of focusing on collectives conceived primarily as conglomerates of *human* designs and practices ('discourse'), I will highlight the active role of *nonhuman* materials in public life" (1–2). By understanding discourse and language to be fundamentally human properties in order to rescue agency for nonhuman actants, however, Bennett arguably emphasizes the *exceptional* quality (if not necessarily the centrality) of humans as the only "things" that speak. Her recourse to agency thus seems to reify precisely the anthropocentric politics from which she seeks to distance herself.

46. Annette Burfoot also criticizes these attempts to develop alternative theories of (nonhuman) agency—although for reasons very much opposed to my own—in her article, "Human Remains: Identity Politics in the Face of Biotechnology," *Cultural Critique* 53 (Winter 2003): 47–71: "[Karen] Barad, following a trend in technoscience as well as in some science and technology studies, seeks to extend agency to the objects of science (typically nonhuman bodies) as well as to the means science and technology use to view and formulate the world around them. She is inspired both by the physicist Neils Bohr and his theoretical considerations of the nature of materiality and by Butler's materialization (which we have already seen as an extension of Foucauldian and Lacanian

logic). Barad introduces her own term, 'agential realism,' to represent a marriage of Bohr's rejection of Newtonian realism (akin to the Cartesian subject) and Butler's release of the body from material binds" (57). For a more extensive critique of the methodological problems with extending agency to objects, see the previous note on Bennett's *Vibrant Matter*.

47. Burfoot, "Human Remains," 47, 48.

48. Ibid., 68.

49. "Finally, providing agency to scientific bodies may be intellectually stimulating, but it also carries political risks. Assigning agency to scientific apparatuses (even though Barad's aim to dismantle observation-independent bodies is a good one) contributes to the atomization of human bodies as a 'natural' act, thus obscuring the political motivations for doing so and further denying the body as a significant aspect of cognition." Ibid., 69.

50. Or, as Lawrence Grossberg has argued, "I do not mean to reject the concept of identity or its importance in certain political struggles; but I do reject the subsumption of identity within a logic of difference and the assumption that such structures of identity necessarily belong to particular subject groups. And I believe it is important to ask whether every struggle over power can or should be organized around issues of identity. At the very least, it may be necessary to rearticulate the category of identity and its place in cultural studies and politics." Lawrence Grossberg, "Cultural Studies and/in New Worlds," *Critical Studies in Mass Communication* 10 (1993): 1–21, 12.

51. Dennis W. Allen, "Viral Activism and the Meaning of 'Post-Identity,'" *Journal of the Midwest Modern Language Association* 36 (1) (2003): 6–24, 18.

52. Ibid.

53. Ibid., 14.

54. Ibid., 20. Or, as he notes earlier, "And, although [the viral activist group] Rtmark could be read as celebrating the plasticity of postmodern identity or the potential for self-fashioning as a political strategy, when you take their political interventions as a whole, those interpretations don't finally seem adequate explanations of the assumptions underlying Rtmark's anarcho-activism. To put it another way, I suspect that they see Madonna's endless permutations as somewhat beside the point" (17).

CHAPTER FOUR

1. Sarah Barringer Gordon, "The Liberty of Self-Degradation: Polygamy, Woman Suffrage, and Consent in the Nineteenth Century America," *Journal of American History* 83 (3) (1996): 815–47, 816–17.

2. Ibid., 833.

3. "Like other political structures in a democracy, marriage was a creation of the exercise of the sovereignty that ultimately rested in the whole people, rather than in individual husbands and wives. Exit, unlike entrance, was a matter for which the will of the spouses was necessary but not sufficient. . . . [A] separate political identity for women, according to anti-suffragists, was tantamount to 'discontent with marriage and . . . legislation to facilitate divorce.'" Ibid., 836, 841. For a variation on this idea, see, for instance: "women's citizenship thus be-

came a touchstone to justify less than participatory citizenship, and in this connection, marriage was central . . . [H]aving or supporting dependents was *evidence* of independence. Thus marriage as well as property empowered a man in civic status showing his capacity for citizenship by making him head of a household. . . . [I]n corollary, marriage made women into dependents. There was no middle ground here: either one was independent and had the capacity to have dependents or one was dependent on someone else." Nancy F. Cott, "Marriage and Women's Citizenship in the United States, 1830–1934," *American Historical Review* 103 (5) (1998): 1440–74, 1451–52.

    4. Sarah Barringer Gordon, *The Mormon Question: Polygamy and Constitutional Conflict in Nineteenth-Century America* (Chapel Hill: University of North Carolina Press, 2002).

    5. Gabrielson is also careful to situate Austin's discussion of sovereignty within a meaningful historical context, however: "[Austin's] essay advances a unique argument for women's full participation in political life, one that departs from both of the standard scripts used in the women's movement of the period— the equal rights approach and the virtue-based gender difference argument." Teena Gabrielson, "Woman-Thought, Social Capital, and the Generative State: Mary Austin and the Integrative Civic Ideal in Progressive Thought," *American Journal of Political Science* 50 (3) (2006): 650–63, 651, 653.

    6. "This new perspective began to emerge in radical suffragist argument in the 1880s, and it based claims to citizenship on the labor of women, operating also on a broad understanding of labor thought that included every kind of women's work, in reproductive and sexual labor as well as the work place, in unpaid as well as paid labor." Sandra Stanley Holton, "'To Educate Women in the Rebellion': Elizabeth Cady Stanton and the Creation of a Transatlantic Network of Radical Suffragists," *American Historical Review* 99 (8) (1994): 1112–36, 1133. "While it is not surprising to find anti-suffrage women invoking a maternalist vision of women's sex-specific social obligations, it is noteworthy to find such views in the writings of leading socialist feminists and Labor party women." Seth Kovan and Sonya Michel, "Womanly Duties: Maternalist Politics and the Origins of Welfare States in France, Germany, Great Britain, and the United States, 1880–1920," *American Historical Review* 95 (4) (1990): 1086–1108, 1087.

    7. For an additional discussion of suffrage and democratization theory, consider Teri L. Caraway's work, in which she argues that "by confining the study of democratization to the incorporation of (white) men, not only is an important historical event overlooked but the picture of the politics of democratization is skewed. . . . [D]emocratization is also a story of the extension of formal political citizenship to new categories of individuals and of the continual exclusion of others." Teri L. Caraway, "Indonesia and Democratization: Class, Gender, Race, and the Extension of Suffrage," *Comparative Politics* 36 (4) (2004): 443–60, 443.

    8. "On the one hand, if women adapt to male norms by asserting their equality and sameness with men, they do so at the cost of negating the reproductive and nurturing roles disproportionately associated with women, thereby destroying their specificity as women. On the other hand, if women assert their difference from men, their very specificity as women categorizes them as deviant from the universalistic formulation of the liberal principle that all individuals are equal, in the sense of being the same. Thus, as [Kate] Nash notes, 'most contem-

porary feminist political theorists see liberalism as unequivocally incompatible with feminism . . .'. [T]his study finds, however, that sameness and difference need not be mutually exclusive approaches. . . . [W]omen's political citizenship, rather than requiring an either/or choice between individual equality and women's group difference, advance on the paradoxical combination of both." Eileen McDonagh, "Political Citizenship and Democratization: The Gender Paradox," *American Political Science Review* 96 (3) (2002): 535–52, 548.

9. McDonagh is also careful, like Gabrielson, not to lose sight of the historical context in which this take on citizenship developed. She continues, "from an historical institutionalist perspective, the American case reveals the paradoxical foundation of women's political citizenship." Ibid., 536.

10. Sandra F. VanBurkleo, *"Belonging to the World": Women's Rights and American Constitutional Culture* (New York: Oxford University Press, 2001).

11. For examples of recent discussions that question the necessarily empowering potential of speaking out, see the work of Brown and Marianne Constable: "both sides nonetheless subscribe to an *expressive* and *repressive* notion of speech, agreeing on its capacity to express the truth of an individual's desire or condition, or to repress that truth. Both equate freedom with voice and visibility, both assume recognition to be unproblematic when we tell our own story, and both assume that such recognition is the material of power as well as pleasure. Neither confronts the regulatory potential in speaking ourselves, its capacity to bind rather than emancipate us." Brown, *Edgework*, 86. And, "the silences of law are many. They gesture not only toward the justice to be found in laying claim to voice and to the power to be had in speech, but also toward the possibilities of justice that lie in silence." Marianne Constable, *Just Silences: The Limits and Possibilities of Modern Law* (Princeton: Princeton University Press, 2005): 8. And, "this turn to silence runs against much contemporary work that talks of both law and language as the powerful resources of society in a technical age. . . . [T]he silences in the texts of law today are far from empty. They speak not only of limits, but also of possibilities, of justice in the contemporary law associated with actual empirical and social reality." Constable, *Just Silences*, 11.

12. VanBurkleo, *Belonging to the World*.

13. The question of the relative effectiveness of the Nineteenth Amendment to do more than grant the right to vote appears in a variety of contexts. For instance: "why suffrage failed to transform women's citizenship remains a puzzle. . . . [Reva Siegel] sees the Nineteenth Amendment as a 'missed constitutional opportunity' that was afforded little significance beyond the franchise. In explaining this, Siegel focuses on contemporary accounts of gender relations and differences as 'natural' rather than historical." Gretchen Ritter, "Jury Service and Women's Citizenship Before and After the Nineteenth Amendment," *Law and History Review* 20 (3) (2002): 479–515, 481. Ritter continues, "what the jury service campaign reveals is that the judicial failure of suffrage to provide equal citizenship was due to the existence of a constitutional structure that devalued political rights like voting. That structure was developed partly in reaction to the effects of earlier rights advocates to claim full citizenship . . . under the Reconstruction Amendments" (483).

14. "The struggle for women's legal rights has continued almost unabated through the decades since the suffrage victory, but rarely, if ever, has the monu-

mental achievement of the Nineteenth Amendment been cited as a constitutional support for women's claim to full equality. The goal of this note is to resurrect the broader purpose of the heroic suffrage campaign by arguing that the Nineteenth Amendment can and should be recognized as an affirmation of women's constitutional equality." Jennifer K. Brown, "The Nineteenth Amendment and Women's Equality," *Yale Law Journal* 102 (8) (1993): 2175–2204, 2175.

15. Sara Hunter Graham, *Woman Suffrage and the New Democracy* (New Haven: Yale University Press, 1996). For an additional argument, from the sociological perspective, that later twentieth-century women's movements in the United States drew on tactics developed by suffragists, see Steven M. Buechler, *Women's Movements in the United States: Woman Suffrage, Equal Rights, and Beyond* (New Brunswick: Rutgers University Press, 1990).

16. Aileen Kraditor, *The Ideas of the Woman Suffrage Movement, 1870–1920* (New York: Columbia University Press, 1967).

17. "The counter movement's solution to the tactical dilemmas was to conduct a quiet campaign defined as educational rather than political, thus legitimating its activism within the traditional female realm of moral reform. . . . [A]t fairs, [antisuffragists] distributed literature, provided rest areas for weary women and children, and devised 'silent speeches' printed on cloth and mounted on rollers for public review." Susan E. Marshall, "Ladies Against Women, Mobilization Dilemmas of Anti-feminist Movements," *Social Problems* 32 (4) (1985): 348–62, 352. And, more to the point, "the field [of women's history] has generated a great body of work with a significant void—studies of women who opposed or were indifferent to woman suffrage, those who fought against the integration of schools, and those who clung tenaciously to their separate sphere rather than abandon its confines. This essay is part of a growing body of literature on conservative women and female anti-feminism." Elna Green, "From Antisuffragism to Anti-communism: The Conservative Career of Ida M. Derden," *Journal of Southern History* 65 (2) (1999): 287–316, 287.

18. Martin Pugh, *The March of the Women: A Revisionist Analysis of the Campaign for Women's Suffrage 1866–1914* (New York: Oxford University Press, 2000).

19. And the intersection among feminist activism, war, and embodiment more generally is certainly not unique to English movements. "War" was a repeated trope in writing in the United States on suffrage (see, for instance, Linda G. Ford, *Iron-Jawed Angels: The Suffrage Militancy of the National Women's Party, 1912–1920* [Lanham, MD: University Press of America, 1991]), and in France many women in fact *repudiated* any right to vote on the logic that they, like soldiers, should make this sacrifice in order "better to serve their country": "gardienne de l'unité de la société, les femmes doivent renoncer au droit de vote, exactemente comme les militaries qui acceptant cette mutilation de leur citoyenneté pour mieux server leur patrie. . . . [L]e désordre de l'étranger où votent les femmes deviant alors l'utime argument des partisans du status quo." Odille Rudelle, "Le vote des femmes et la fin de 'L'exception Française," *Vingtième Siècle Revue d'histoire* 42 (April–June 1994): 52–65, 60.

20. Barbara Green, *Spectacular Confessions: Autobiography, Performative Activism, and the Sites of Suffrage, 1905–1938* (New York: St. Martin's Press, 1997).

21. Laura E. Nym Mayhall, "Defining Militancy: Radical Protest, the Constitutional Idiom, and Women's Suffrage in Britain, 1908–1909," *Journal of British Studies* 39 (3) (2000): 340–71, 371.

22. Ibid., 341–42. See also, "shifting our gaze away from the bodies of WSPU members in prison . . . to the idioms they deployed in articulating their grievances should draw our attention from the transgressive power of violence . . . about which we know a great deal, to the transgressive power of diverse forms of nonviolent protest, about which we know little in this context" (370–71).

23. "Once the Liberal government introduced forcible feeding as an antidote to the suffragette hunger strike, militants created a visual activism, dependent upon the exhibition of women's tortured bodies as spectacle. . . . [T]he image of the tortured suffragette figures prominently in the canonical histories and autobiographies of the women's suffrage movement written by participants. . . . [S]uffragette militancy enacted the radical ideal that citizens had the right to resist tyrannical authority; militancy's implementation became a contest over the uses and utility of physical force in negotiations with the state." Ibid., 341–42, 344.

24. Laura E. Nym Mayhall, *The Militant Suffrage Movement: Citizenship and Resistance in Britain, 1860–1930* (New York: Oxford University Press, 2003).

25. Ellen Carol DuBois, *Feminism and Suffrage: The Emergence of an Independent Women's Movement in America* (Ithaca: Cornell University Press, 1978).

26. "As scholars have noted, where the discourse of difference initially universalized the experience of motherhood as a means of uniting women, it also drove a wedge between middle-class and working-class women. The emphasis on virtue was used by middle-class white women to distinguish their own (superior) claims to citizenship from those of working women, immigrants, and women of color." Gabrielson, "Woman-Thought," 654.

27. Graham, *Woman Suffrage*.

28. See especially the chapter "Classes and Races" in Buechler, *Women's Movements*.

29. Rosalyn Terborg-Penn, *African American Women in the Struggle for the Vote, 1850–1920* (Bloomington: Indiana University Press, 1998).

30. Newman, *White Women's Rights*.

31. Vron Ware, *Beyond the Pale: White Women, Racism, and History* (New York: Verso, 1992).

CONCLUSION TO PART ONE

1. Or, as Colin Nazhone Milburn puts it, "Western metaphysics sees writing as fallen but also dangerous, because it corrupts natural language. Writing is a dangerous supplement. But its status as a supplement outside of language paradoxically reveals that writing was never outside of language, for something that was indeed outside could not corrupt the inside, and thus, as Derrida concludes, language is writing. The preface functions in this same supplementary way: both outside of the text and part of the text, the preface comes to replace the text, until 'there is nothing but text, there is nothing but extratext, in sum an "unceasing preface" that undoes the philosophical representation of a text, the received

opposition between text and what exceeds it.'" Colin Nazhone Milburn, "Monsters in Eden: Darwin and Derrida," *MLN* 118 (3) (2003): 603–21, 613.

2. As Hayles writes, "until now, Derrida says, Western thought has persisted in believing in a Logos capable of revealing immediate truth. Speech is privileged because it is the embodiment of Logos, the word that is also presence. Writing, by contrast, is belated, a fall from presence into absence, the signifier of a signifier, inferior because twice mediated. These assumptions are inverted in *Of Grammatology*, which proclaims the beginning of a 'grammatological' epoch in which writing is privileged over speech. . . . [F]or Derrida, writing includes not only marks on the page but its deeper traces within the psyche. Residing at a deeper level than words can reach, the Derridean trace remains inaccessible to direct verbalization. It is 'always already' present, the elusive and ineffable difference from which all subsequent inscription derives. In this sense writing, as the mark of difference, not only precedes speech but actually brings it into being." Hayles, *Chaos Bound*, 178.

3. Hayles, *My Mother*, 40.

4. For more on the intersection of natural systems and linguistic systems (and, by extension, computational systems), consider not only the overlap of Latour's writing on nature's speech and Hayles's writing on code, but Milburn's take on what he calls "Darwin's textualization of the world": "But Darwin's textualization of the world releases nature from its imprisonment within the dominating concept of the book, for Darwinian textuality, like Derridean textuality, is about transformation, dispersion, and play. The signs of Darwinian nature are written in an always 'changing dialect'—the Darwinian book of nature is never closed, never complete, never locked between two covers. It continues to write itself, spilling beyond the page, enfolding its own surface, effacing its own history, signifying the absence of some stories and resurfacing others. The Darwinian book of nature is not a book: it is a text. Text nested within text, preface within preface, the Darwinian and Derridean texts graft with the text of nature, and thus we say: 'There is nothing outside of the text.'" Milburn, "Monsters in Eden," 615.

5. Hayles, *My Mother*, 48.

INTRODUCTION TO PART TWO

1. As in Butler, *Excitable Speech*, 136.

2. Joaquin Miller, "Woman Suffrage Advocates at the Capitol," *Boston Daily Globe* (March 17, 1884): 6.

3. Ibid.

4. Ibid.

5. Ibid.

6. Ibid.

7. For instance, as Asdal writes in summarizing this scholarly position in the work of Haraway and Latour: "in her historical study of the development of primatology and the way women scientists' primate studies have been represented to the public, she makes a point of how women are often assumed to be closer to nature, or more natural, than men. On the one hand, women have been elevated as Nature in the form of Mother Earth. At the same time, women have

been reduced to their sex, to their biology. Women have been the Other, the passive nature, the object of others' critical gaze. Haraway's point is that that which has historically been defined as nature has very often turned out to be 'someone' else. What we have perceived as nature or as merely passive objects have turned out to be of a highly social nature. Or as Latour puts it, 'Feminists have shown how the process of identifying women with nature played a key role in creating a context that legitimized their lack of political rights.'" Asdal, "Problematic Nature of Nature," 67. See also: "in this way, Haraway's concern with gender is expanded to include studies of nature in general. Defining something as 'nature' is highly problematic because in doing so we risk not capturing our co-actor's power of agency. This dismissal of agency is reinforced by the way these stories raise the question of the role of science and expertise. If we define something as nature, we simultaneously also create a space for the expert, the spokesperson, who can speak on nature's behalf. We thereby obstruct others as subjects with agency. Thus a great deal is at stake in historical studies of nature: What are we doing when we define something as nature? Who speaks on behalf of nature, exotic ecosystems, or threatened species?" (69).

CHAPTER FIVE

1. As they were described by Goldwin Smith, cited in Pugh, March of the Women, 124, and in John Elliot Cairnes, Collected Works, ed. Thomas A. Boylan and Tadh Foley, vol. 1 (London: Routledge, 2004): 51.

2. Frederick A. Maxse (Vice-Admiral), Reasons for Opposing Woman Suffrage (London: W. Ridgway, 1884): 17.

3. "Trouble When Women Voted," New York Times (May 6, 1894): 16.

4. Graham, Representations of the Post/Human, 232.

5. "Throughout the book I will be concerned to explore the implicit motifs of religion and the sacred that run throughout representations of the post/human. If the post/human destabilizes the ontological hygiene of Western modernity, then one crucial index of that is the secularism of modernity. Religion and the sacred resurface in unexpected ways within the post/human condition, such as the analogies between forms of technophilia and the world-views of hermetism and Gnosticism, discussed in Chapters four and seven. I characterize this as the re-emergence of a discourse of the re-enchantment of contemporary culture via reappropriation of ancient world-views whereby the material, immanent physical world is deemed to be but a corrupt reflection of a higher, more spiritual realm in which the face of the divine is more clearly apprehended." Ibid., 16.

6. "Aspirations toward a digitalized post-biological humanity often reflect the desire for a spiritualized, non-corporeal body as the fulfillment of a disdain for the mortality of the flesh. Technophobia, ostensibly, seems to be driven by denial of progress, fear of change, loss of control; but the evidence suggests that so-called technophilic attitudes are subtended by similar projections, valorizing technologies as protections against fears of vulnerability, contingency, impurity and mortality." Ibid., 230.

7. This notion has been both summarized and critiqued, for instance, by Graham: "yes the frontier between humanity and divinity is, arguably, as much a

product of modernity as the problematic objectification of nature, and the reification of gender difference . . . so why not the religious symbolic of modernity? Above all, the birth of modernity, and especially humanism, is premised on the creation of *alterity* in the guise of nonhumans, God and 'nature', those things which have to be excluded from the coherent master category of secular humanism. In elevating human reason and human agency, modernity thus rests on what Bruno Latour calls the 'crossed out God, relegated to the sidelines.' The secular evacuation of religion in the name of purification, the separation of the natural and supernatural and the elevation to the heavens of a transcendent, immutable God are necessary parts of the logic of purification and translation. The invisible guarantor of predictable laws, discernible in the ordered patterns of creation, but distanced from intervening in the universe (as for example in Deism) poses no serious threat to scientific freedom." Ibid., 217.

8. Talal Asad, *Formations of the Secular: Christianity, Islam, Modernity* (Stanford: Stanford University Press, 2003): 67.

9. Ibid., 71.

10. Ibid., 74.

11. Ibid., 68.

12. Ibid., 74.

13. Ibid., 94.

14. Ibid., 95.

15. Ibid., 75.

16. Horace Bushnell, *Women's Suffrage: The Reform Against Nature* (New York: Charles Scribner, 1869): 182.

17. Ibid.

18. Ibid.

19. Bushnell is also responding here to what he understands J. S. Mill's argument in *Subjection of Women* to be. He states later on that he has not actually had the chance to read Mill's work.

20. As, for instance, Michiyo Morita in part understands Bushnell's argument: "he believed that women's authority should have a softer element developed in a more sheltered way of life, making it different and much more complete than male authority. He further argued that if a woman went after male or political authority 'hoping to win it by the sublime rage of a candidacy, she would come out *minus*, even in her victory, to be no authority at all.'" Michiyo Morita, *Horace Bushnell on Women in Nineteenth-Century America* (Lanham, MD: University Press of America, 2004): 99.

21. The "grace" argument appeared in prosuffrage writing as well: "let us, then, hope for increased grace and knowledge; and, just so far as they are able to make wise interpretations of Scripture, following the spirit rather than the letter of apostolic teaching, and entering fully into the mind of Christ in these matters, they will come to an increase of power and to the realization of that old promise." Mother, "Two Letters on Woman Suffrage," *Putnam's Magazine, Original Papers on Literature, Science, Art* 2 (12) (1868): 701–12, 711.

22. Lee J. Makowski, *Horace Bushnell of Christian Character Development* (Boston: University Press of America, 1999): 115.

23. "Bushnell used the words grace and inspiration synonymously. . . . Bushnell did not conceive of grace as some *thing* separate from God which, as it were,

God gives to the creature in preparation for the divine indwelling. For Bushnell grace is not an intermediary between God and the human person. . . . For Bushnell, grace always refers to the presence of God. And, most specifically, in order to highlight the relational intentionality of the word, grace is the presence of God to the human person in Christ. As such, grace is the ever-present personal act of favor on the part of God toward the human person. We have no claim on it. 'God comes into men . . . in the communication of himself.'" Ibid.

24. "As such, grace is what God is for us, even in view of our sinful rejection of God. That is to say, sin does not cause God ever to withdraw the divine invitation. . . . Secondly, the acceptance of grace in faith leads to a change in the status of the creature. . . . the real change which occurs in the creature upon the acceptance of the divine invitation is a *theopoesis*." Ibid., 122.

25. "The struggle which faith always entails is not the same as the uneasiness of belief understood as the acceptance of something in spite of the lack of evidence. He maintained that faith is reasonable, although he insisted that the object of faith could never be deduced by the exercise of reason alone. The object of faith is something given to faith. Yet the fact that faith has its object given to it, an object that can never be mastered or controlled, did not imply for him a lack of intelligence in the act of faith." Ibid., 52.

26. Or, as Hayles writes in a different context, with regard to "literary theorists," "Chaos theorists, by contrast, value chaos as the engine that drives a system toward a more complex kind of order. They like chaos because it makes order possible." Hayles, *Chaos Bound*, 22–23.

27. Frederick Maxse was the father of Leo Maxse, who edited the conservative-right *National Review*.

28. Maxse, *Opposing Woman Suffrage*, 17.

29. Ibid., 17–18.

30. As they are described, for instance, in J. E. Cairnes, "Woman Suffrage: A Reply to Goldwin Smith," *Every Saturday: A Journal of Choice Reading* (October 10, 1874): 395–440, 396.

31. Graham, *Representations of the Post/Human*, 230.

32. Asad argues that bodies that do not die might be described as possessing agency but not subjectivity. I would argue that in these situations, agency is so altered as to become something else entirely: "agents need not necessarily coincide with individual biological bodies and the consciousness that is said to go with them. Corporations are both liable under the law and have the power to carry out particular tasks. . . . [B]ecause 'corporations never die' they can be described as agents but not as having subjectivity." Asad, *Formations of the Secular*, 74.

33. "Trouble When Women Voted," *New York Times* (May 6, 1894): 16.

34. Ibid.

35. Statement of Mr. Charles L. Underhill, Representing Men's Antisuffrage League of Massachusetts, House Committee on Woman Suffrage, *Resolution Establishing a Committee on Woman Suffrage: Hearing before the Committee on Rules*, 63rd Cong., 2d sess., Dec. 3–5, 1913, 60–61.

36. "By the simple device of using 'information' and 'entropy' as if they were interchangeable terms, [Claude] Shannon's choice gave rise to decades of interpretive commentary that sought to explain why information should be identified with disorder rather than order. For the alliance between entropy and

information to be effective, information first had to be divorced from meaning . . . and had to be associated instead with novelty. . . . [O]nce randomness was understood as maximum information, it was possible to envision chaos (as Robert Shaw does) as the source of all that is new in the world." Hayles, *Chaos Bound*, 51.

37. "The Ladies Take Their Turn," *New York Times* (February 14, 1885): 3, 3.

38. John Weiss, "Woman Suffrage," *The Radical* (June 1869): 1–18, 1.

39. Ibid., 17.

40. J. M. Buckley, "The Wrongs and Perils of Woman Suffrage," *Century Illustrated Magazine* 48 (4) (1894): 613–23, 614.

41. The extent to which this redefinition of electoral politics is not simply an echo or repetition of the usual "statistical" take on mass democracy might be found in Warren Weaver's discussion of "choice" in the realm of information theory. Rather than positing choice as a cause that leads to some political or ethical effect, he posits choice as the measure of information. The more choice, in this scenario, the more randomness, and the less certainty, in turn, of what choice has been made: "it is generally true that when there is noise, the received signal exhibits greater information—or better, the received signal is selected out of a more varied set than is the transmitted signal. This is a situation which beautifully illustrates the semantic trap into which one can fall if he does not remember that 'information' is used here with a special meaning that measures freedom of choice and hence uncertainty as to what choice has been made. It is therefore possible for the word information to have either good or bad connotations. Uncertainty which arises by virtue of freedom of choice on the part of the sender is desirable uncertainty. Uncertainty which arises because of errors or because of the influence of noise is undesirable uncertainty." Weaver, "Recent Contributions," 11.

42. For an additional variation on the idea that suffragists' speech is "unanswerable," see Francis Parkman's article on "The Woman Question Again," which concludes with the well-traveled idea that women's speech allows for no response: "we have replied to our critics, but must decline further debate. We do not like to be on terms of adverse discussion with women . . . and we willingly leave them the last word if they want it. Whatever we may have to say on the subject in the future will not be said in the way of controversy." Francis Parkman, "The Woman Question Again," *North American Review* 130 (278) (1879): 16–30, 30.

43. Again, this type of speech "causes changes in machine behavior and, through networked ports and other interfaces, may initiate other changes, all implemented through transmission and execution of code." Hayles, *My Mother*, 50.

44. Justices Stevens and Ginsburg in their dissenting opinions particularly emphasized the monument's potential to produce identity-based divisiveness or hatred, using this idea as a touchstone for their broader theory of antisecular speech. For instance, "recognizing the diversity of religious and secular beliefs held by Texans and by all Americans, it seems beyond peradventure that allowing the seat of government to serve as a stage for the propagation of an unmistakably Judeo-Christian message of piety would have the tendency to make non-monotheists and nonbelievers feel like [outsiders] in matters of faith, and

[strangers] in the political community. *Pinette*, 515 U. S., at 799 (STEVENS, J., dissenting). Displays of this kind inevitably have a greater tendency to emphasize sincere and deeply felt differences among individuals than to achieve an ecumenical goal. *Allegheny County*, 492 U. S., at 651 (STEVENS, J., concurring in part and dissenting in part)." Stevens and Ginsburg dissenting in *Thomas Van Orden, Petitioner v. Rick Perry* 545 U.S. 677 (2005) 3, p. 15.

45. Justice Thomas, concurring in *Van Orden v. Perry*, 3–4.
46. Ibid.

CHAPTER SIX

1. Graham, *Representations of the Post/Human*, 12.
2. Hayles, *My Mother*, 163–64.
3. Milburn, "Monsters in Eden," 603.
4. "How can such a protean entity mean anything at all? Cultural critics have swelled the chorus: 'nature' is not only unclear; it is dangerous. Almost every ideology seeks to sign up nature for its cause, to bolster its shaky political credentials with nature's authority. Just because that authority has been so widely commandeered, critics imagine nature as a kind of blank screen or mirror on which the most diverse human fantasies may be projected. Paradoxically, the most obdurate authority—nature's necessity—has been joined in these accounts to the most malleable of cultural constructs—nature as anything you care to make it." Lorraine Daston and Fernando Vidal, "Introduction: Doing What Comes Naturally," in Lorraine Daston and Fernando Vidal, eds., *The Moral Authority of Nature* (Chicago: University of Chicago Press, 2004): 1–20, 11.
5. Latour, *Politics of Nature*, 74.
6. Michel Foucault, *Abnormal: Lectures at the Collège de France, 1974–1975*, trans. Graham Burchell (New York: Picador, 2005): 56.
7. Ibid.
8. Ibid., 64.
9. See, for instance, Mary Louise Pratt, *Imperial Eyes: Travel Writing and Transculturation* (New York: Routledge, 1992): 12.
10. For instance, as Milburn reading Darwin and Derrida rather than Foucault, puts it: "together, Darwin and Derrida enact a critique of artifactual constructions of nature that disrespects boundaries and emphasizes the deviances, the perversions, the mutations, and the monstrosities of the world. Monsters disrupt totalizing conceptions of nature and destroy taxonomic logics, at once defining and challenging the limits of the natural." Milburn, "Monsters in Eden," 604.
11. "Bushnell on Woman Suffrage," *New York Observer and Chronicle* (June 17, 1869): 190, 190. As Bushnell himself wrote, "this harnessing of men and women together, and calling it government, is making, in fact, a conjunction against nature, which has the doom of failure on it beforehand. . . . [I] would say, instead, that government is to govern, and that women are not; and therefore, that when government makes conjunction with women, it must take up ideas that cannot be sufficiently excluded." Bushnell, *Women's Suffrage*, 130.
12. "Woman Suffrage: . . . Miss Anthony's Age Ascertained," *New York Times* (February 6, 1870): 8, 8.

13. "The Pacific Coast: Hot Weather—An Insane Advocate of Woman Suffrage," *New York Times* (June 22, 1872): 1, 1.

14. "Take Me Home to Mama: Placarded Boys Forced to Speak on Woman's Suffrage," *Boston Globe* (December 8, 1894): 12, 12.

15. MCA, "A Woman's Letters from Washington," *The Independent . . . Devoted to the Considerations of Politics, Social, and Economic . . .* (Feb. 4, 1869): 1, 1.

16. "New Woman a Freak, Says Bishop Doane: One Who Strives for Man's Work 'a Horrible, Misshapen Monster,' He Declares: Sees Suffragists' Doom," *New York Times* (June 9, 1909): 7, 7.

17. Ibid.

18. "Woman suffrage is a chimera. It is based, like most things feminine, on illusion and caprice. Equal political rights, indeed! What would be the outcome? . . . I have ransacked the deluge of letters from feminists in THE TIMES, but fail to find any clear, substantial argument sustaining the right of women to vote. There was no paucity of assertion that woman was the equal of man, and of other up-to-date inept and ridiculous hyperbole. Many of the statements looked plausible enough on first view, but on analysis they fell like a house of cards. I could not help thinking that that would be the well-merited fate of the issue next November." T.E.W., "All Illusion and Caprice," *New York Times* (February 21, 1915): XX2, XX2.

19. W. W. Gregg, "The Third Sex," *New York Times* (September 15, 1918): X3, X3.

20. Ibid.

21. "Suffragists Win [NY State] Senate Test Vote," *New York Times* (April 6, 1916): 1, 1.

22. Henry A. Wise Wood, "Government a Man's Job: The War Teaches a Believer in Woman Suffrage to Oppose the Extension of the Right to Vote," *New York Times* (May 3, 1917): 14, 14.

23. Mary G. Kilbreth in "Antis See Danger in Woman Autocracy," *New York Times* (January 12, 1918): 12, 12.

24. Butler, *Psychic Life of Power*, 99.

25. For a nuanced discussion of this point, see John T. Parry, *Understanding Torture: Law, Violence, and Political Identity* (Ann Arbor: University of Michigan Press, 2010): 211–12.

26. "The present phase of graft hybrid investigation dates from a paper by Hans Winkler, published in 1907. Although the results of this first paper were somewhat disappointing, they deserve mention, because they opened up a new method of investigation. A scion of *Solanum nigrum* was grafted on *S. Lycopersicum*, and after growth had been resumed, a transverse cut was made in such a way to sever both stock and scion, it being hoped that adventives shoots would grow from the cut surface along the line of contact of stock and scion. Such adventives shoots actually appeared, and in one case the new shoot involved tissues of both stock and scion. However, the new form was not a graft hybrid, for clearly one side of the shoot was *Solanum nigrum* and the other *S. Lycospersicum*; to this peculiar structure Winkler gave the suggestive name *chimera*." "Current Literature," *Botanical Gazette* 51 (January–June, 1911): 147.

27. "Long before Aristotle called not only human beings, but also bees, po-

litical creatures, these social insects had already assumed a firm place in the Greek lexicon of poetic moralizations. Hesiod, in his didactic *Works and Days*, exhorts his brother to industry by contrasting the laboring bee to the drone . . . [I]ndeed, Hesiod elsewhere uses the bee/drone dichotomy to poeticize the human division of labor along gender lines." Danielle Allen, "Burning *The Fable of the Bees*: The Incendiary Authority of Nature," in Daston and Vidal, *Moral Authority of Nature*, 74–99, 74.

28. "The symbol of the bee as a model for the citizen, laborer, and monarch seems almost too trite—too consistent a poetic invocation of nature and too obvious in its implications—to be worth taking seriously in an examination of how various conceptions of nature, different as to time and place, contributed to the construction of moral authority in each." Ibid., 76.

29. Ibid., 89.

30. Hayles, *How We Became Posthuman*, 33.

31. Hayles draws explicitly on psychoanalytic theory to make this argument. I instead take her argument as a jumping-off point for a less psychoanalytic discussion.

CHAPTER SEVEN

1. Michel Foucault, *Fearless Speech*, ed. Joseph Pearson (Los Angeles: Semiotext(e), 2001): 12–13. See also Michel Foucault, *The Government of Self and Others: Lectures at the Collège de France, 1982–1983*, trans. Graham Burchell (New York: Palgrave-Macmillan, 2010).

2. Foucault, *Fearless Speech*, 12.

3. In *The Government of Self and Others*, Foucault explicitly states in reference to the distinction between human speech and divine speech that "*parresia* [sic] is a human practice, a human right, and a human risk" (154). Nonetheless, a case can be made that as similar as computational speech might be to divine speech, in this case it shows up the nonhuman potential of this ostensibly purely human activity. For instance, soon after making the point that parrhesia is a peculiarly *individual* human activity (304), Foucault goes on to highlight its "operational" character: "philosophy will present itself as having the monopoly of *parresia* [sic] inasmuch as it presents itself as operating on souls, as a psychagogy. Rather than being a power of persuasion which would convince souls of anything and everything, philosophy presents itself as an operation which will enable souls to distinguish properly between true and false, and which, through the philosophical *paideia*, will provide the instruments needed to carry out this distinction" (305).

4. In differentiating parrhesia from the performative utterance, for instance, Foucault states that whereas the latter is predicated on the speaking subject's position or status, parrhesia involves a "retroaction—such that the event of the utterance affects the subject's mode of being." Ibid., 68.

5. This overlap becomes particularly clear, for instance, when Foucault notes that parrhesia "has no other form than to be, in its simplicity and spontaneity, as close as possible to the reality to which it refers. It is a discourse which does not owe its strength (its *dunamis*) to the fact that it persuades. It is a dis-

course which owes its *dunamis* to the fact that it springs from the very being which speaks through it." Ibid., 327.

6. Although it is perhaps most obvious in parrhesia's specifically biological, rather than broadly physical, qualities.

7. Foucault, *Fearless Speech*, 17.

8. Ibid.

9. For instance, "we can say that *parresia* [*sic*] is a way of telling the truth, but what defines it is not the content of the truth as such. *Parresia* [*sic*] is a particular way of telling the truth." Foucault, *Government of Self*, 52.

10. Foucault, *Fearless Speech*, 13.

11. Ibid., 63.

12. As, for instance, Hayles summarizing Weaver puts it: "reasoning that if a message is perfectly ordered, the receiver will be able to guess what it will say, [Warren] Weaver suggests that a 'noisy' message will be more surprising and hence will convey more information. He is now in a quandary, for by this reasoning, gibberish should convey the maximum possible information. To close off this possibility, Weaver introduces a distinction between desirable and useless information. True, gibberish is maximum information. But since it is not desired, it does not really count as information. Hence the maximum amount of information is conveyed by a message that is partly surprising and partly anticipated." Hayles, *Chaos Bound*, 55.

13. This nonbiological as well as biological physicality of parrhesia becomes apparent in Foucault's interpretation when he notes, for instance, that "philosophical *parresia* [*sic*] does not necessarily or exclusively go through *logos*, through the great ritual of language in which one addresses the group or even an individual. After all, *parresia* [*sic*] may appear in the things themselves, it may appear in ways of doing things, it may appear in ways of being." Foucault, *Government of Self*, 320.

14. There is a discrepancy between Foucault's analysis of parrhesia and Cartesian speech in his *Fearless Speech* lectures and his analysis of the same relationship in his lectures in *The Government of Self and Others*. In the first, he argues that parrhesia is not possible in a post-Cartesian epistemological framework. In the second, however, he states nearly the opposite—that "if we want to look upon philosophy's emergence in the sixteenth century as criticism of these [Christian] pastoral practices, then I think we can consider that it was as *parresia* [*sic*] that it actually asserted itself anew. After all, if Descartes' *Meditations* are in fact an enterprise to found a scientific discourse in truth [they are] also an enterprise of *parresia* [*sic*] in the sense that it is actually the philosopher as such who speaks in saying 'I,' and in affirming his *parresia* [*sic*] in that precisely scientifically founded form of evidence, and he does this in order first of all to play a particular role in relation to the structures of power of ecclesiastical, scientific, and political authority in the name of which he will be able to conduct men's conduct." Foucault, *Government of Self*, 349. Although I am responding more to Foucault's take on parrhesia and modern discourse in *Fearless Speech* than I am in *The Government of Self and Others*, it is worth pointing out that this shift in his thinking supports my point that parrhesia can manifest itself in modern and contemporary environments far more than it undermines this point.

15. Foucault, *Fearless Speech*, 14.

16. For a more extensive discussion of non-Cartesian *space* in relation to suffragists' speech as code, see below, chapter 13, on dream speech and dream environments.

17. Foucault, *Fearless Speech*, 14.

18. "Compulsory Voting," *The Independent* (March 3, 1881): 17, 17. For additional examples of the compelled speech genre, see, for example, "But there is no doubt whatever that a large majority of the pledged members [of the House of Commons in favor of suffrage] are at heart stoutly opposed to woman suffrage, and rejoice that they were not compelled to vote for it last Friday." "One Man Who Had the Courage to Say 'No' to a Woman," *New York Times* (March 24, 1907): SM8. "If women are given the suffrage, it will be their undoubted duty, whatever their repugnance, to vote. Is it fair to lay upon their shoulders a burden which the majority are unwilling to bear? . . . I therefore think I voice the opinion of many of my sisters in demanding that they shall not be allowed to cram suffrage down our throats." A Spinster and a Taxpayer, "The Demand for Votes: Woman Suffragists Should not Force Suffrage Where Not Wanted," *New York Times* (September 20, 1909): 6, 6. For another variation on the connection between speech about women's suffrage and compelled speech: "No intelligent woman can afford to treat the subject of woman suffrage with indifference. She must face the question whether she will or no." "The Home: An Important Decision," *Outlook* (March 10, 1894): 451, 451.

19. "History of Woman Suffrage," *New York Evangelist* (June 23, 1884): 1. For a variation on this theme, see: "another fact is that no new speakers make their appearance. The same individuals do all the talking that have done it since the meetings began. . . . Mr. Poole used the word government twenty-nine times. Mrs. Blake then flew off at a tangent from the resolution." "Woman Suffrage: . . . Miss Anthony's Age Ascertained," 8.

20. "Woman's Suffrage," *New York Evangelist* (June 24, 1869): 1, 1.

21. "The Woman Question," *New York Times* (February 25, 1865): 2, 2.

22. J. S. Eichelberger, "Analysis of Woman Vote in 1916 Upsets Theories," *New York Times* (January 21, 1917): SM5.

23. Everett P. Wheeler, "In Reply to Mrs. Harper: A Woman's Influence Is Better Than Her Vote for the Lawmakers," *New York Times* (September 19, 1915): 14, 14.

24. Louise de la Ramée (Ouida), *Views and Opinions* (London: Methuen, 1896): 309. For a variation on the evils and despotic potential of women's fanaticism about law, see also: "the number of unenforceable laws would be multiplied; hence increasing disregard for law and increased opportunity for the arbitrary exercise of public authority on the one side and favoritism and graft on the other. The form of government would become more and more paternalistic, ending inevitably in bureaucracy, which is the meanest form of despotism existing anywhere." A letter from Joseph G. Pyle, read at House Committee on Woman Suffrage, 63rd Cong., 2d sess., 1913, 93.

25. A Man, "'A Man' Explains: He Didn't Ask for a 'Hysteria of Documents' on Suffrage," *New York Times* (February 21, 1910): 8, 8.

26. Terry Croy and Carrie Chapman Catt, "The Crisis: A Complete Critical Edition of Carrie Chapman Catt's 1916 Presidential Address to the National

American Woman Suffrage Association," *Rhetoric Society Quarterly* 28 (3) (1998): 49–73, 51–52, 62.

27. One, more traditional, articulation of this fear can be found in M. G. Kilbreth (Temporary President New York State Association Opposed to Woman Suffrage), "For a Suffrage Repeal: Position of the Women Who Demand Reconsideration of State Amendment," *New York Times* (January 14, 1918), 10.

28. For more on the man's (or the human's) inability to deal with this increasing information, see Hayles: "one view, which set human intelligence and will against entropy, became irrelevant; another, which pitted information and machines against entropy, had emerged. From now on, control was increasingly seen not in terms of human will fighting universal dissipation but as information exchanges processed through machines. As the world vaulted into the information age, the limiting factor became the inability of human intelligence to absorb the information that machines could produce." Hayles, *Chaos Bound*, 46.

29. Ibid., 47.

30. "The more chaotic a system is, the more information it produces. This perception is at the heart of the transvaluation of chaos, for it enables chaos to be conceived as an inexhaustible ocean of information rather than as a void signifying absence." Ibid., 7–8.

31. This was a premodern aspect of medical practice that, he argued, reappeared in modern psychiatric practice.

32. Michel Foucault, *Psychiatric Power: Lectures at the Collège de France, 1973–1974*, trans. Graham Burchell (New York: Palgrave-Macmillan, 2006): 236–37, 243, 252, 254.

33. Or, to make this point in a different, updated context: whereas it is possible to focus on the individuals who participate in, say, the "viral activism" that Dennis Allen associates with postindustrial capitalism—and many people do try to read these activists as replicas of the mid-nineteenth to mid-twentieth-century protesters whose message inhered in their bodies, wills, and beliefs—focusing on the activist rather than on the network ignores the fact that it is "the sheer insignificance of individual identity [that] opens strategic possibilities for attacking the system itself." As Allen writes, "Rtmark recognizes that the best response to a faceless corporation is to use faceless activists, that the sheer insignificance of individual identity opens strategic possibilities for attacking the system itself. And it is here, I think, that the metaphor behind the concept of 'viral activism' is additionally apt, especially if one considers the specific example of retroviruses, which incorporate themselves into, become part of, the DNA of the host cell. Very much in the manner of a retrovirus, the activist insinuates himself into the system by fooling the system into believing he is part of it and then changes the flow of information (the genetic code; the assertion that Italians are lazy) in a way that alters the system (the production of more viruses; critical reflection, political debate, media coverage, and, probably, increased security measures). In a sense, then, Rtmark could be seen as a sort of disease within the body of postindustrial capitalism." Allen, "Viral Activism," 13. Catt's activism, that is to say, *can* be read as a liberal-humanist form of protest, but it need not be read in this way.

34. William Croswell Doane, Bishop of Albany, "Some Later Aspects of Woman Suffrage," *North American Review* 163 (480) (1896): 537–48, 537.

35. Parkman, "Woman Question Again," 24.

36. "Wise Words About Women," *New York Times* (September 23, 1879): 4, 4.

37. Ibid.

38. "Right for Women to Vote: Suffrage Must be Theirs Declares Senator Palmer," *New York Times* (April 20, 1894): 2, 2. For an antisuffrage take on this idea, linked to the notion that the speaking woman creates a world of compelled speech, see M. E. Simkins, "Suffrage and Anti-Suffrage," *Living Age* (February 6, 1909): 323–29, 324.

39. "At first glance this move seems to have much in common with recent trends within cognitive science and evolutionary biology that stress interactions between organism and environment. In Andy Clark's 'extended mind' model, for example, organisms develop adaptive behaviors by incorporating the environment into their extended cognitive systems. In a different way, Edwin Hutchins discusses such artifactual environments as the navigation room on a ship as a cognitive system that includes both human and nonhuman actors. Pressures affect the system as a whole, causing it to self-organize in ways that no single actor may fully grasp, much less control. Each actor reacts to specific local conditions, much like a stadium full of people who are holding up their individual cards without necessarily seeing the pattern as a whole. In yet another way, Lynn Margulis has undercut the secure boundaries of an organism by showing that primeval oxygen-using bacteria invaded the cell and stayed on as mitochondria, thus blurring clear distinctions between inside and outside. As Mark Hansen points out in his brilliant analysis of Deleuze and Guattari's biophilosophy, all these models emphasize the role of specific constraints and local interactions to structure the fit between organism and environment so that adaptive behaviors occur." See Hayles, "Limiting Metaphors," 153.

40. Arguably, "speaking truth to power" is likewise a difficult move in the modern, liberal context where, as Foucault has suggested in his other work, truth and power are by no means in any obvious tension with one another.

CHAPTER EIGHT

1. Foucault, *Abnormal*, 209–10.

2. Ibid., 211–12.

3. Ibid.

4. Ibid.

5. The notion that each of these variations on consent might be equally fundamental to modern political structures is not a new idea. The repetitive mode of consent—the consent of the possessed—for example, has not only been described as the basis for social contract theory, but Rousseau's theory of participatory democracy, for instance, "rests on his ideas of consent and membership: on his conception of consent as being constantly re-affirmed through the continuous participation of the members, and not that of any body of officials or representatives, that consent gives rise to." E. D. Watt, "Rousseau Réchaufée—Being Obliged, Consenting, Participating, and Obeying Only Oneself," *Journal of Politics* 43 (4) (1981): 707–19, 707. Also consider Slavoj Žižek's discussion of those who refuse

the social contract: "the 'madman' (the psychotic) is the subject who has refused to walk into the trap of the forced choice and to accept that he has 'always already chosen'; he took the choice 'seriously' and chose the impossible opposite of the Name of the Father, i.e., of the symbolic identification which confers us a place in the intersubjective space." Slavoj Žižek, *Enjoy Your Symptom! Jacques Lacan in Hollywood and Out* (New York: Routledge, 1992): 76–77.

6. Buckley, "Wrongs and Perils," 617.

7. Helen Kendrick Johnson, *Woman and the Republic*, rev. ed. (New York: Guidon Club Opposed to Woman Suffrage, 1913): 48.

8. Ibid., 50–51.

9. Excerpt from Gail Hamilton in "Editors' Table," *Godey's Lady's Book* 77 (July 1868): 82, 82.

10. Ibid., 84.

11. Elihu Burritt, "Woman Suffrage and Its Liabilities," *The Independent* (October 5, 1871): 11, 11.

12. Mrs. Arthur M. Dodge in "Says Suffrage Idea is Only Sex Fad: Mrs. Arthur M. Dodge Insists Woman's Appeal for Ballot is Based on Sex Alone," *New York Times* (May 12, 1913): 2, 2.

13. Ibid.

14. Ibid.

15. Although obviously consent is, and has become, far more complex than this idealized liberal image would suggest. For more on the complexity of consent in these contexts, see Ruth A. Miller, *The Limits of Bodily Integrity: Abortion, Adultery, and Rape Legislation in Comparative Perspective* (Aldershot: Ashgate Press, 2007).

CHAPTER NINE

1. "Although the digital subject has depth, the structures governing the relation of surface to interior differ dramatically from the analog subject. The digital subject . . . instantiates hierarchical coding levels that operate through a dynamic of fragmentation and recombination. Unlike analog subjectivity, where morphological resemblance imposes constraints on how much the relevant units can be broken up, the digital subject allows for and indeed demands more drastic fragmentation. This difference can be seen easily in the greater fragmentation of digital technologies compared to print. In traditional typesetting before the advent of computers, each letter in the alphabet was treated as a distinct unit; in speech, the corresponding phoneme also acts as an intact unit. In contrast are digital sampling techniques, where sound waves may be sampled some forty thousand times a second, digitally manipulated, and then recombined to produce the perception of smooth analog speech." Hayles, *My Mother*, 203.

2. As I am interpreting her reference here to "hierarchical coding levels": "to summarize: the analog subject implies a depth model of interiority, relations of resemblance between the interior and the surface that guarantee the meaning of what is deep inside, and the kind of mind/soul correspondence instantiated by and envisioned within the analog technologies of print culture. The digital subject implies an emergent complexity that is related through hierarchical coding

levels to simple underlying rules, a dynamic of fragmentation and recombination that gives rise to emergent properties, and a disjunction between surface and interior that is instantiated by and envisioned with the digital technologies of computational culture." Hayles, *My Mother*, 203.

3. As it was termed by Judge Heaney in his dissent in *Singleton v. Norris*, 319 F.3d 1018 (8th Cir. 2003): 1034.

4. *Singleton v. Norris*, 1026.

5. Or, as Foucault has put it, "if we take the argument a little further, or to the point where it becomes paradoxical, it means that in terms of his relationship with the sovereign, the subject is, by rights, neither dead nor alive." Foucault, *Society Must Be Defended*, 240.

6. See, for instance, "A new insanity defence," *The Economist* (March 1, 2003).

7. Aristotle, *The Politics*, trans. Ernest Barker (Oxford: Oxford University Press, 1995): 10–11, 1253(a)7. "man alone of the animals is furnished with the faculty of language. . . . [L]anguage serves to declare what is advantageous and what is the reverse, and it is the peculiarity of man . . . that he alone possesses a perception of good and evil, of the just and unjust, and other similar qualities."

8. Jacques Rancière, *Disagreement: Politics and Philosophy*, trans. Julie Rose (Minneapolis: University of Minnesota Press, 1999): 17.

9. Michel Foucault, *History of Sexuality: An Introduction*, trans. Robert Hurley (New York: Vintage, 1990): 143; Giorgio Agamben, *Homo Sacer: Sovereign Power and Bare Life*, trans. Daniel Heller-Roazen (Stanford: Stanford University Press, 1998): 7.

10. Agamben, *Homo Sacer*, 181–82, 187.

11. Or, as Asdal has noted, "that language is an important difference between humans and animals is true enough, and these forms of criticism have played an important role. But the flip side of this coin is that nature was left to the natural sciences and conceptualized in a dichotomous way: nature as positive given on the one side—culture with its capacity for active agency on the other." Asdal, "Problematic Nature of Nature," 61.

12. This being who possesses rational speech but does not recognize it is to some extent described by Rancière in the following passage: "so the simple opposition between logical animals and phonic animals is in no way the given on which politics is then based. It is, on the contrary, one of the stakes of the very dispute that institutes politics. At the heart of politics lies a double wrong, a fundamental conflict, never conducted as such, over the relationship between the capacity of the speaking being who is without qualification and political capacity. For Plato, the mob of anonymous speaking beings who call themselves the people does wrong to any organized distribution of bodies in community." I would argue, however, that there is a more specific system that might engage in this speech—something more simply "the mob of anonymous speaking beings who call themselves the people." This is a system that is, as Rancière argues, multiple, but that is not necessarily multiple in a *human* way. It is a physical, environmental system that produces speech even as it itself is altered or transformed. Rancière, *Disagreement*, 22.

13. Latour, *Politics of Nature*, 67.

14. "His [Edwin Hutchins's] study allows him to give an excellent response to John Searle's famous 'Chinese room.' By imagining a situation in which communication in Chinese can take place without the actors knowing what their actions mean, Searle challenged the idea that machines can think. . . . [A]lthough his Chinese interlocutors take these strings to be clever responses to their inquiries, Searle has not the least idea of the meaning of the texts he has produced. Therefore, it would be a mistake to say that machines can think, he argues, for like him, they produce comprehensible results without comprehending anything themselves." Hayles, *How We Became Posthuman*, 288–89.

15. "In Hutchins's neat interpretation, Searle's argument is valuable precisely because it makes clear that it is not Searle but the entire room that knows Chinese. In this distributed cognitive system, the Chinese room knows more than do any of its components, including Searle. . . . [M]odern humans are capable of more sophisticated cognition than cavemen not because moderns are smarter, Hutchins concludes, but because they have constructed smarter environments in which to work." Ibid.

16. David Hammer, "Mentally Ill Inmate Has Clemency Hearing," Associated Press State and Local Wire (December 12, 2003): State and Regional.

17. Ibid.

18. Marcus Warren, "Arkansas to Execute a Schizophrenic. Marcus Warren in New York Reports on the Controversial Fate of a Condemned Killer Who Believes his Cell is Possessed by Demons," *Daily Telegraph (London)* (January 7, 2004): 13.

19. Ibid.

20. Ibid.

21. "Final Words and Prepared Statement of Charles Singleton," Associated Press State and Local Wire (January 6, 2004): State and Regional.

22. Ibid.

23. "The full text of the statement: 'I am Charles Singleton, anointed by God, Victor Ra Hakim. The people that is, basically your footstool, do not want me to be someone glorified. But you have raised me even from a little child. The blind think I'm playing a game. They deny me, refusing me existence. But everybody takes the place of another. As it is written, I will come forth as you go. And in taking someone's place, you receive new instructions that you didn't know in your previous position. I too am going to take someone's place. You have taught me what you want done—and I will not let you down. God bless. Charles Singleton.'" Ibid.

24. Paul Greenberg, "Kill That Crazy Man," *Arkansas Democrat-Gazette* (February 19, 2003): 20. Greenberg also states in a second article: "talk about Catch 22: Until the prisoner relented, the government was in the position of protecting his privacy—even unto death. In the original Catch 22, poor Yossarian realizes that claiming he's crazy in order to escape the lunacy of war would be proof he's sane. This case, too, sounds fictional—like some kind of macabre joke. But by now some of America's most distinguished jurists have solemnly debated whether the state can medicate Charles Laverne Singleton in order to kill him." Paul Greenberg, "Time is Running Out and So is Sanity in the Curious Case of Charles Singleton," *Arkansas Democrat-Gazette* (January 4, 2004): 72.

25. Greenberg, "Time is Running Out."

26. "Invariably Cruel, Always Unusual," *Minneapolis Star Tribune* (February 17, 2003).

27. Warren Richey, "Forced Medication: When Does It Violate Rights," *Christian Science Monitor* (March 3, 2003): 1.

28. Richard Burr in Lynn Neary, Robert Siegel, and Libby Lewis, "Legal Dispute over Whether a State Can Force a Man Who is Psychotic to Take Medication to Make Him Legally Sane In Order to Execute Him," *All Things Considered*, National Public Radio (February 12, 2003).

29. I should emphasize here that I am describing the popular rhetorical role played by the names of the three writers—not any actual points or arguments they might actually have been making with their work.

30. In her critique of Deleuze and Guattari's discussion of desire and distributed subjectivity Hayles describes a similar model. Like Hayles, I am reading desire here as something far less directed than it might initially appear to be: "this conclusion exposes the gap that separates Deleuze and Guattari from the extended mind models with which they seem to have affinities. Constraints are not lessened by the interactions that make organism and environment into a self-organizing system; rather, it is the specific nature of the constraints that drive the configurations. One of Andy Clark's examples will serve to illustrate the point. Marine biologists have discovered that the bluefin tuna can swim significantly faster than the rate predicted by physiological considerations such as hydrodynamic efficiency and muscle strength. They account for this difference by noticing that the fish, before it leaps forward, swims around in tight circles, creating a circular hydraulic flow. By following this flow, the fish benefits from a slingshot effect as it shoots off on a tangent, gaining velocity from the way it has configured its local environment. The environment has physical properties that determine the fish's behavior, and the fish's behavior changes the environment in ways beneficial to its survival. By insisting that flows of intensities follow only the dictates of desire, Deleuze and Guattari erase the powerful role of constraints in creating complex feedback loops that make organism and environment into an integrated system. Within their text, desire manifests itself." Hayles, "Limiting Metaphors," 155.

31. Bushnell, *Women's Suffrage*, 32.

32. "Anthony and Rosewater," *New York Times* (October 16, 1882): 4, 4.

33. Ibid.

34. Ibid.

35. Edward Sandford Martin, *The Unrest of Women* (New York: D. Appleton, 1913): 71–72.

36. Quotation from the Southern California Association Opposed to Woman Suffrage in *Woman Suffrage: Hearings Before the Committee on the Judiciary: House of Representatives*, 62nd Congress, 2nd Session, March 13, 1912 (Washington, DC: Government Printing Office, 1912), 95. For the sort of jest that Chittendon was presumably criticizing, see: "The 'WOMAN-SUFFRAGE MOVEMENT' has an annual fit, and once every five or six years a sort of double-extra fit, when it thrashes around a good deal, contorts itself violently, and assumes various phases of hysteria; after which it subsides and is forgotten again until next time." "Cartoons and Comments," *Puck* (June 6, 1894): 242, 242.

37. Charles L. Dana, M.D., "Suffrage a Cult of Self and Sex," *New York Times* (June 27, 1915): 14, 14.

38. "Woman's Suffrage and Woman's Brain," *Scientific American* 70 (20) (1894): 315, 315.

39. Ibid.

40. "About 250 men and women were present, the latter being much in the majority. Things went smoothly until Mr. Harvey, in reply to a speech by Miss Ida Rauh, asserted that science and women were the two greatest foes to human liberty. . . . [S]cience, he went on, approved of the dissection of animals, and suffragists upheld the idea. Next it would be the cutting up of human beings. 'What term shall we apply to the women who are clamoring for the feminization of our American Institutions?' he asked." "Suffragists Hiss Attack on Women: A Reign of Terror Coming If They Vote, Opines Alexander Harvey at a Dinner," *New York Times* (February 3, 1910): 18, 18.

41. "Woman's Brain Not Inferior to Men's: Helen H. Gardener's, Tested at Cornell, to Which She Willed It, Meets Test," *New York Times* (September 29, 1927).

42. Ibid.

43. For a discussion of this phenomenon in the contemporary period, see among others, Ruth A. Miller, "On Freedom and Feeding Tubes: Reviving Terri Schiavo and Trying Saddam Hussein," *Law and Literature* 19 (2) (2007): 161–86.

44. Latour, for instance, describes the speech of scientific objects as akin to the speech extracted through torture. Bruno Latour, "Scientific Objects and Legal Objectivity," in Alain Pottage and Martha Mundy, eds., *Law, Anthropology, and the Constitution of the Social* (Cambridge: Cambridge University Press, 2004): 73–114, 81.

45. "But, as Miss Anthony and some of her abettors have learned by sad experience, instead of getting their votes into the ballot-box, they are only liable to incur fines and imprisonment by insisting on their imaginary right to vote, contrary to the provisions of municipal law." Cyrus Cort, "Woman Suffrage," *Reformed Quarterly Review* 30 (3) (1883): 343–64, 345.

46. "Antis Renew War on Suffragists," *New York Times* (March 24, 1918): 9, 9.

47. "Lays Evil to Suffrage: E.P. Wheeler Thinks Women Voters at Fault in Colorado," *New York Times* (October 11, 1915): 5, 5.

48. Edgar M. Cullen, "Man is for Justice, Woman for Mercy," *New York Times* (September 3, 1915): 8, 8.

49. "Under the pressure of this lobby, one of the two great parties has repudiated its historic policy; both parties have repudiated their national platforms; Mr. Hughes repudiated the national platform on which he was nominated; the President of the United States has repudiated the platform on which he was elected and his own utterances amounting to personal pledges during the Presidential campaign, and trusted delegates have ignored their constituents' mandates expressed at the polls. If the program for which the people vote is not carried out, if party platforms are not upheld and candidates' pledges are not fulfilled, then rule by the people no longer exists. Under present conditions the people's program is not carried out." "Antis Renew War on Suffragists," *New York Times* (March 24, 1918): 9, 9.

50. Kilbreth, "For a Suffrage Repeal," 10.

51. There is an echo here of the later philosophy of Carl Schmitt: "German romantics possess an odd trait: everlasting conversation. . . . [C]atholic political philosophers . . . would have considered everlasting conversation a product of a gruesomely comic fantasy, for what characterized their counterrevolutionary political philosophy was that their times needed a decision." Schmitt, *Political Theology*, 53. Or, "like every other order, the legal order rests on a decision and not on a norm" (10).

52. Henry Wilson, "The Great Necessity," *The Independent* (June 17, 1869): 1, 1.

53. Priscilla Leonard, "Woman Suffrage in Colorado," *Outlook* (March 20, 1897): 789–92, 790.

54. Carrie Chapman Catt, "Crisis in Suffrage Movement, Says Mrs. Catt," *New York Times* (September 3, 1916): SM5, SM5.

55. Justice Brandeis, concurring in *Whitney v. California* 274 U.S. 357 (Oct. 1925–May 1927): 375–77. The passage continues: "Only an emergency can justify repression. Such must be the rule if authority is to be reconciled with freedom. Such, in my opinion, is the command of the Constitution. It is therefore always open to Americans to challenge a law abridging free speech and assembly by showing that there was no emergency justifying it." An interesting question could be asked about the nature of the emergency envisioned by Brandeis, but since this is not my primary purpose in this essay, I just mention it briefly here.

56. "The remonstrants were to be allowed the first two hours, Mr. Brandeis having charge of their side of the case, and Henry B. Blackwell appearing for the women, who consider their rights a mockery if they cannot vote. . . . [M]r. Brandeis then read the following petition, written by Miss Dewey . . . 'we believe that the common good will be lessened by the voting of women on political questions. We believe in a wise division of labor, based on natural fitness . . .'" "Woman Suffrage: Arguments and Petitions Against the Extension," *Boston Daily Globe* (March 10, 1885): 5.

57. For a more nuanced take on Brandeis's opinions on such issues, see Philippa Strum, *Louis D. Brandeis, Justice for the People* (Cambridge: Harvard University Press, 1984): 54, 121–39.

58. This is an unlikely interpretation of this particular case, given that *Whitney* addresses specifically a woman's potentially harmful speech.

CHAPTER TEN

1. Prosuffrage writers also drew on "common sense" to support their cause. See, for instance, Mary Putnam-Jacobi, *"Common Sense" Applied to Woman Suffrage: A Statement of the Reasons Which Justify the Demand to Extend the Suffrage to Women, With Consideration of the Arguments Against Such Enfranchisement, and With Special Reference to the Issues Presented to the New York State Convention of 1894* (New York: G. P. Putnam's Sons, 1894). Unlike antisuffrage writers, however, prosuffrage writers frequently inverted or played with the "common sense" theme. See, for example, Mary Everts's discussion below.

2. This theme appears in a number of places (consider, for instance, the way in which attacks on Judith Butler's work for being "difficult" went viral on the Internet in the late 1990s). For just one mild example of this theme, though, see: "despite the transcendence of the issues, Ware does not allow her journey to catapult readers into the stratosphere of theory and jargon—the feminist outer limits of mumbo jumbo." Catherine Clinton, "White Mischief: *Beyond the Pale: White Women, Racism, and History* by Vron Ware," *Transition* 59 (1993): 130–36, 131.

3. "Shannon's equation for information calculated it in such a way as to have it depend both on how *probable* an element is and on how *improbable* it is. Having information depend on the probability of message elements makes sense from an engineer's point of view. Efficient coding reserves the shortest code for the most likely elements (for example, the letter *e* in English), leaving longer codes for the unlikely ones (for instance, x and z). Improbable elements will occupy the most room in the transmission channel because they carry the longest codes. Thus for a channel of given capacity, fewer improbable elements can be sent in a unit of time than probable ones. This explains why an engineer would think it desirable to have a direct correlation between probability and information. Why have information correlate with improbability? Partly compensating for the longer codes of improbable elements is the greater information they carry. To see why improbable elements carry more information, suppose that I ask you to guess the missing letter in "ax—." It is of course *e*, the most probable letter in an English text. . . . the letter *e* carries so little information that 'ax' is an alternate spelling." Hayles, *Chaos Bound*, 52.

4. Hayles, *How We Became Posthuman*, 4–5.

5. Hayles, *My Mother*, 144.

6. Ibid.

7. I should note that Hayles recognizes this problem, but reiterates that she has "not abandoned [her] commitment to the importance of embodiment." The reason for this stance, she continues, is that one can continue to focus on the importance of bodies by "repositioning materiality as distinct from physicality and re-envisioning the material basis for hybrid texts and subjectivities." I, however, have chosen to maintain the connection between physicality and materiality because doing so allows for a wider ranging discussion of text that need not be (although it *can* be) grounded in subjectivity. Ibid., 2.

8. Samuel T. Spear, "Bushnell on the Right of Suffrage," *The Independent* (July 15, 1869): 1, 1.

9. A. V. Dicey, "Woman Suffrage," *Living Age* (April 10, 1909): 67–84, 68.

10. Parkman, "Woman Question Again," (1880), 29–30. The *New York Times* article praising an earlier version of Parkman's essay likewise emphasizes the important role that common sense plays in demonstrating the absurdity of women engaging in political speech: "In his paper in the *North American Review*, he [Parkman] merely puts, in expressive and elegant language, the common sense and instinctive conviction of most men and women who are passive opponents of female suffrage, without knowing why clearly enough to have formulated their opinions and reasons for them. It is precisely because this common sense and instinctive conviction exist and have their foundation in human nature itself, that

the cause of woman suffrage makes scarcely any progress, at the same time that few feel the disposition to make any active opposition to it." "Wise Words About Women," *New York Times* (September 23, 1879): 4, 4.

11. Catherine Beecher, "Is Woman Suffrage Contrary to Common-Sense?" *Christian Union* (February 12, 1870): 98–99, 98–99.

12. Ibid.

13. "Woman's Suffrage—No. II," *Prairie Farmer* (March 12, 1870): 77, 77.

14. Buckley, "Wrongs and Perils," 620.

15. Mary K. Sedgwick, "Some Scientific Aspects of the Woman Suffrage Question," *Gunton's Magazine* (April 1901): 333–45, 334.

16. Ibid., 335.

17. "No Subject of Jest: Condition of Feminine Hysteria Should be Taken Seriously," *New York Times* (May 8, 1912): 10, 10.

18. "In the first place, the opinion in favour of the present system, which entirely subordinates the weaker sex to the stronger, rests upon theory only; for there never has been trial made of any other: so that experience, in the sense in which it is vulgarly opposed to theory, cannot be pretended to have pronounced any verdict. And in the second place, the adoption of this system of inequality never was the result of deliberation, or forethought, or any social ideas, or any notion whatever of what conduced to the benefit of humanity or the good order of society." J. S. Mill, *The Subjection of Women*, 4th ed. (London: Longmans, 1878): 8.

19. Mary E. Everts, "A Farmer's Wife to Catherine E. Beecher," *Christian Union* (March 12, 1870): 166, 166.

20. Ibid.

21. Ibid.

22. Pearl Tyer, "Idaho's Twenty Years of Woman Suffrage," *Outlook* (September 6, 1916): 35–39, 39.

23. Caroline H. Dall, "Mr. Parkman on Woman Suffrage in the 'North American Review,'" *Unitarian Review and Religious Magazine* 13 (30) (1880): 223–37, 236.

24. Mill, *The Subjection of Women*, 110–13.

25. Ibid.

26. Ibid.

27. Ibid.

28. "To see why improbable elements carry more information, suppose that I ask you to guess the missing letter in 'ax—.' It is of course *e*, the most probable letter in an English text. . . . the letter *e* carries so little information that 'ax' is an alternate spelling." Hayles, *Chaos Bound*, 52.

CHAPTER ELEVEN

1. Hayles, *My Mother*, 162.

2. S. R. F. Price, "The Future of Dreams: From Freud to Artemidorus," *Past and Present* 113 (November 1986): 3–37, 4.

3. Ibid., 13.

4. Dror Ze'evi, *Producing Desire: Changing Sexual Discourse in the Ottoman Middle East* (Berkeley: University of California Press, 2006): 123.

5. Katherine P. Ewing, "The Dream of Spiritual Initiation and the Organization of Self Representation among Pakistani Sufis," *American Ethnologist* 17 (1) (1990): 56–74, 57–58.

6. Sigmund Freud, *The Interpretation of Dreams*, trans. A. A. Brill (New York: Modern Library, 1994): 212–13.

7. For Foucault's take on this idea, see: "the subject of the dream, in Freud's sense, is always a lesser subjectivity, a delegate, so to speak, projected into an intermediate status, suspended somewhere in the play of the other, somewhere between the dreamer and what he dreams. The proof is that for Freud this dream play may actually represent someone else by an alienation, identification; or another personage may, by a sort of heutoscopy, represent the dreamer himself. . . . [For Binswanger] the dream-subject is not a later edition of a previous form, or an archaic stage of personality. It manifests itself as the coming-to-be and the totality of existence itself." Michel Foucault and Ludwig Binswanger, *Dream and Existence*, ed. Keith Hoeller (Atlantic Highlands, NJ: Humanities Press International, 1993): 57.

8. Freud, *The Interpretation of Dreams*, 196.

9. Ibid., 204.

10. Ibid., 207.

11. Ibid., 208.

12. Ibid., 207.

13. Ibid., 226.

14. Prefiguring others in this summary of Nietzsche's position, for instance: "the temptation to bring clarity to this obscurity is alleged to be misguided if not downright impossible. The urge to find in dreams 'coherent significations will clash fatally with the incoherence, the objective disorder, the unreason or in any case the ignorance of a limit to be attributed to human events invested into a more vast and profound disorder." Clayton Koelb, "Nietzsche, Malerba, and the Aesthetics of Superficiality," *boundary 2* 12 (1) (1983): 117–32, 124.

15. Consider, for instance, Hayles's discussion of strange attractors. It is in most ways contradictory to Freud's notion that all "quantities" within the dream, as it were, can be transformed or converted into quantities within analysis: "with strange attractors the reverse process takes place; information that was once inaccessible is created. Attractors operate irreversibly because their operation changes *what we can know about them*, not merely what we do know. [Robert] Shaw's analysis of an attractor's orbit as a flow of information creates a perspective fundamentally different from that of classical Newtonian dynamics. Unlike Newtonian paradigms, it does not assume that quantities are conserved. Information is not merely transformed, as matter and energy are. It really does come into being or disappear. Once an oscillator with a contracting information flow has made the transition to its steady state, the information contained in the initial conditions cannot be recovered. Conversely, knowing only the initial conditions and the relevant equations of motion will not allow one to predict where an oscillator with an expanding flow will be at some future time." Hayles, *Chaos Bound*, 159.

16. David S. Caudill, *Lacan and the Subject of Law: Toward a Psychoanalytic Critical Legal Theory* (Atlantic Highlands, NJ: Humanities Press, 1997): 8. For a negative example, see: "one might say that psychoanalysis gave the dream no status beyond that of speech, and failed to see it in its reality as language. . . . [T]he word, to say something, implies a world of expression which precedes it, sustains it, and allows it to give body to what it means. By failing to acknowledge this structure of language, which dreams experience, like every expressive fact, necessarily envelopes, Freudian psychoanalysis of dreaming never gets a comprehensive grasp of meaning. Meaning . . . must be extracted." Foucault, *Dream and Existence*, 35.

17. Paraphrasing Benvenuto. Caudill, *Lacan*, 55.

18. "In the dream of Irma's injection, it is just when the world of the dreamer is plunged into the greatest imaginary chaos that discourse enters into play, discourse as such, independently of its meaning, since it is a senseless discourse. It then seems that the subject decomposes and disappears. In this dream there's a recognition of the fundamentally acephalic character of the subject beyond a given point." Jacques Lacan, *The Ego in Freud's Theory and in the Technique of Psychoanalysis 1954–1955*, trans. Sylvana Tomaselli, ed. Jacques-Alain Miller. (New York: Norton, 1988): 170.

19. "And who would not have doubts about the transmission of the dream when, in effect, there is such an obvious gap between what was experienced and what is recounted? Now—and it is here that Freud lays all his stress—doubt is the support of certainty. He goes on to explain why—this is precisely the sign, he says, that there is something to preserve." Jacques Lacan, *The Four Fundamental Concepts of Psychoanalysis*, trans. Alan Sheridan, ed. Jacques-Alain Miller (New York: Norton, 1981): 35.

20. For instance, I make no reference to Foucault's writing on dreams in *History of Madness* or *Psychiatric Power*.

21. Or, as Koelb argues, "the dreamworld is the world of appearance—Nietzsche had made that equation from the first, in *The Birth of Tragedy*, and had never deviated from it. To be caught up in the dreamworld is to be enclosed entirely in appearance, but to be aware, at the same time that no other world exists. . . . [I]f the abuse of the dream had been the origin of metaphysics, its use by the 'knowing' dreamer destroys the basis for metaphysics. Dreaming is no longer seen as evidence of a 'second real world' but as the proper image of the only world there is. The recognition of the phenomenal world for what it is does not result in any denial of it or any attempt to escape from it into something more 'real.'" Koelb, "Nietzsche," 119.

22. Forrest Williams, "Translator's Preface," in Binswanger and Foucault, *Dream and Existence*, 20.

23. Ibid.

24. Ibid., 21.

25. Foucault, *Dream and Existence*, 44.

26. Ibid., 45.

27. Ibid., 35.

28. Ibid., 43.

29. Ibid., 44.

30. "Binswanger had recovered an earlier tradition of dream commentary within psychoanalysis, one that saw the meaning of dreams in what they did rather than what they said, in the representation of a world beyond the dreamer's ordinary reality." Jerrold Siegel, "Avoiding the Subject: A Foucaultian Itinerary," *Journal of the History of Ideas* 51 (2) (1990): 273–99, 282.

31. "Being completely alone means, psychologically speaking, dreaming—whether or not there is, at the time, a physiological state of sleep or awakeness." Binswanger, *Dream and Existence*, 97.

32. Ibid., 99 (quoting Hegel).

33. Ibid., 98.

34. Ibid., 99.

35. Ibid., 102.

36. Echoing in some ways Nietzsche's take on dreaming as it is discussed by Koelb: "the conclusion is that there is no more 'reality' for the realist any more than for the dreamer, that both are 'intoxicated,' but that the dreamer seeks to transcend, the realist to deny his intoxication. . . . [W]hat begins as an uncompromising desire to 'put aside . . . everything that would interpose a veil' is transformed into a love for veils, for coverings, for surfaces. Only a mystified truth-seeker wants to tear all the veils aside; the knowing sufferer knows that a perfectly successful unveiling would ultimately disclose the void." Koelb, "Nietzsche," 120–21.

37. "The subject of the dream, the first person of the dream, is the dream itself, the whole dream. In the dream, everything says 'I,' even the things and the animals, even the empty space, even objects distant and strange which populate the phantasmagoria. The dream is an existence carving itself in barren space, shattering chaotically, exploding noisily, netting itself, a scarcely breathing animal, in the webs of death. . . . [T]o dream is not another way of experiencing another world. It is for the dreaming subject the radical way of experiencing its own world." Foucault, *Dream and Existence*, 59.

38. Ibid.

39. As Williams notes, "in opposition to Freud's identification of the dream 'I' with a represented subject—either bearing the dreamer's own features or, by displacement, bearing another's features—Foucault proposed that the whole dream, and everything in it, may be regarded as its true 'I'." Williams, "Translator's Preface," 25.

40. Again, though, I am by no means arguing that Foucault's analyses of dreaming simply reproduces a sort of coherent, Cartesian subject. As Braidotti has argued, Foucault—in his work on dreaming, in this case, in *History of Madness*—is very much opposed to developing a theory of the unitary subject against the incoherence of the dreamscape: "unlike Derrida, we should not only view dreams as a universal factor that reveals itself everywhere, to everyone, the sign for all that all is doubtful: the sign of *difference* at the origin of *being*. Foucault refuses to take the example of dreams as a radicalization of madness: he views it as a quite different conceptual category. Foucault reaffirms his understanding of the *Meditations*, as a discursive event quite as much as discursive practice, making the Cartesian opposition between dreams and madness proof of the impossibility of formulating a really universal doubt; hence the implausibility of any stance

whereby the subject might 'constitute himself as a universally doubting subject.'" Rosi Braidotti, *Patterns of Dissonance: A Study of Women in Contemporary Philosophy*, trans. Elizabeth Guild (New York: Routledge, 1991): 58.

41. Williams, "Translator's Preface," 24.

42. Foucault, *Dream and Existence*, 50–51.

43. Ibid., 51.

44. Ibid., 52.

45. "The security that space provides, the solid support that it lends to my powers, rests on the articulation of near space and far space: the latter, by which one withdraws and eludes, or which one sets out to explore or conquer; the former, that of the rest, of familiarity, that which is right at hand. . . . [N]ow, far space may penetrate the immediate sphere of the subject like a meteor." Ibid., 61.

46. For example, "Muslim scholars, notably the tenth-century philosopher al-Farabi (d. 950), elaborated the ideas suggested by Alexandros, who maintained that intellect is an outer faculty in relation to the human soul, and therefore capable of reaching out of the physical body and actively seeking the divine source to obtain knowledge of the future. Other famous thinkers, among them al-Kindi (ca. 801–866) and later Ibn Rushd (1126–1198), chose to follow the arguments of Philoponus, who, using the same ancient categories of soul, intellect, and imitation, claimed that the intellect has no such powers. It cannot leave the body to seek divine enlightenment, and therefore a dream is merely a continuation of the thought process in waking, divorced from sensual perceptions." Ze'evi, *Producing Desire*, 101–2.

47. Hayles, *My Mother*, 162–63.

48. Ibid.

49. Or, alternatively, unlike Cartesian space, in which each point can be described with reference to a number of discrete, unambiguous coordinates, and in which points, lines, and planes are algebraically distinct from one another, in the non-Cartesian space of computer memory (or of the dreamscape), all data is arranged in a seemingly arbitrary manner throughout the space, with elements and data described not via distinct coordinates, but via their relationships with one another. A "point" can thus be simultaneously nonspace or infinite space in a non-Cartesian space.

50. "The theologian Caramuel, for instance, attacks St. Thomas's notion that reason is suspended in sleep. Once in a dream he carried on an academic dispute, using arguments that hold up very well by the light of day. From this experience, he concludes that reason, as well as perhaps the will, survive in sleep; hence dreams cannot be excused as a natural necessity, and the sleeper sins through a present free choice." Manfred Weidhorn, "Dreams and Guilt," *Harvard Theological Review* 58 (1) (1965): 69–90, 80.

51. Gareth B. Matthews, "On Being Immoral in a Dream," *Philosophy* 56 (215) (1981): 47–59, 48.

52. Lisa M. Bitel, "'In Visu Noctis': Dreams in European Hagiography and Histories, 450–900," *History of Religions* 31 (1) (1991): 39–51, 40–41.

53. Ibid., 45.

54. Ibid., 59.

55. Ibid., 45–46.

56. Ze'evi, *Producing Desire*, 102.

57. Bitel, "In Visu Noctis," 52.

58. Ibid., 59.

59. Carolyn M. Carty, "The Role of Gunzo's Dream in the Building of Cluny III," *Gesta* 21 (1–2) (1988): 113–23, 113.

60. Ibid., 119.

61. Statement of Ella Dorsey, House Committee on Woman Suffrage, 63rd Cong. 2d sess., December 1913, 95.

62. "Emotional Legislation," *Boston Daily Globe* (February 12, 1882): 4, 4.

63. "Suffragist Songs But No Talk in Park: Commissioner Ward Revokes Most Objectionable Features of Propaganda Permit," *New York Times* (September 23, 1916): 18, 18.

64. As far as the city is concerned, the potential harm that suffragists might cause derives not just from their presence in public space, not just their political activity, and not just from their insistence on being heard. It also derives from a familiar mode of linear speech activity, manifested in logical argument, productive of a sequential and chronologically meaningful temporal and spatial framework, the content of which might be construed by others as propaganda and thus destructive. As a result, instead of allowing suffragists to engage in this possibly damaging mode of human speech, the city requires them to reenact the role prescribed for them in the article a half century earlier on "Emotional Legislation"—this time executing their proto-code in song, however, rather than in poetry.

65. At least where "the environment" is understood (problematically) as "nature" rather than, or against, "politics."

CONCLUSION TO PART TWO

1. Wai Chee Dimock, *Empire for Liberty: Melville and the Poetics of Individualism* (Princeton: Princeton University Press, 1991): 117–19.

2. Stephen P. Knadler, "Francis Parkman's Brahmin Caste and the History of the Conspiracy of the Pontiac," *American Literature* 65 (2) (1993): 215–38, 216.

3. Wilbur R. Jacobs, "Parkman: Naturalist-Environmentalist Savant," *Pacific Historical Review* 61 (3) (1992): 341–56, 341.

4. Knadler, "Parkman's Brahmin Caste," 224.

5. Ibid., 223, Dimock, *Empire for Liberty*, 117.

6. Or, as Latour puts it, the scholarship of denunciation: "Luc Boltanski and Laurent Thévenot have done away with modern denunciation. . . . [Before] it was only a matter of choosing a cause of indignation and opposing false denunciation with as much passion as possible. To unmask: that was our sacred trust, the task of us moderns. . . . [W]ho is not still foaming slightly at the mouth with that particular rabies? . . . [Boltanski and Thévenot] do not denounce others. They do not unmask anyone. They show how we all go about accusing one another. . . . [I]nstead of practicing a critical sociology, the authors quietly begin a sociology of criticism." Latour, *Modern*, 44.

7. For a discussion of this issue in the realm of sexual and reproductive law, see Miller, *Limits of Bodily Integrity*.

INTRODUCTION TO PART THREE

1. In her essay "Freedom's Silences," for instance, Brown convincingly dismantles what she argues is a false dichotomy between silence and speech, and what she argues is likewise an unsustainable association between speech and truth or authenticity. In the process, she critiques the contemporary emphasis on speaking out—or, as she terms it, the contemporary "fetish of breaking silence"—and argues that it is time to question "the presumed authenticity of 'voice' in the implicit equation between speech and freedom entailed in contemporary affirmations of breaking silence." Brown, in other words, suggests that excessive talk—and especially excessive confessional talk, or talk absent response—is a damaging rather than empowering recent phenomenon. Brown, *Edgework*, 83–84.

2. An obvious recent example of this phenomenon is the media response to American vice presidential candidate Sarah Palin's admission in 2008 that she did not follow the news. That the theme is a long-standing one, though, can be seen from the following passage published in the *Boston Globe* nearly a century earlier: "[Hon. Mr. Bowdle's] conclusions, as reported, are that women buy one paper to 33 bought by men, and that in street cars one woman in 99 reads a newspaper as against one man out of every three. The press is not insensible to the delicately implied compliment that all who would share intelligently in the conduct of public affairs must be inveterate readers of newspapers. . . . [T]o deduce from observation of newspaper reading among the women of a single city, even facetiously, that the women of this Nation 'are not interested in affairs of state' is a reasoning process which, to women who are interested in statecraft, must be painfully edifying." "Women as Readers of Newspapers," *Boston Daily Globe* (January 14, 1915): 10, 10.

3. Computers of course existed long before the twentieth century—Pascal and Leibniz, among others, not only theorized computational machines, but actually built them. Machine code of the sort that serves as a model here, however, is ordinarily associated with twentieth-century interpretations of information theory. For a long-term history of computers and computational languages (unhindered by speculation about the past few decades of technological change), see Herman H. Goldstine, *The Computer from Pascal to Von Neumann* (Princeton: Princeton University Press, [1972] 1993): 3–10.

CHAPTER TWELVE

1. James Martel, *Textual Conspiracies: Walter Benjamin, Idolatry, and Political Theory* (Ann Arbor: University of Michigan Press, 2011): 2.

2. See, for instance, "by ['worlding' Spivak] means the ignored and imperial use of colonized people for the formation of the Western subject. This 'worlding' . . . was also an intrinsic part of the English movement for women's suffrage, which started around 1860." Also, "by retaining [class and race] hierarchies, and supporting the masculinist project of colonialism, the suffrage movement was able to evoke nationalist sentiment by making itself distinct from colonized women even while indicating their exploitation and thus similarity to them."

And, "thus both pro- and anti-suffragists saw the colonized nations as feminine, leaving unchallenged the notion of empire-building as a masculine endeavor or as a problematic project." Inderpal Grewal, *Home and Harem: Nation, Gender, Empire, and Cultures of Travel* (Durham: Duke University Press, 1996): 64, 67, 69.

3. For one example of such writing, see: "Feminist epistemologists have long been attentive to the relationship between knowing subjects' locations and their understandings of the world. Dissatisfaction with Enlightenment accounts of knowing subjects as faceless, disembodied spectators who hover over the Cartesian landscape has led feminist theorists to consider knowers as embodied subjects situated in politically identifiable social locations or contexts. Attention to knowers as socially situated creates a new angle of vision that allows us to consider the alternative epistemic resources these situated subjects offer, Patricia Hill Collins (1990) and Sandra Harding (1991), whose writings represent the variety of feminist standpoint theory I have in mind here, prefer this approach because it is attentive to the social and political structures, symbolic systems, and discourse that grant privilege to some groups at the expense of others. If the archetypal knower in Cartesian epistemic dramas is the disembodied spectator, then the starring role in feminist standpoint theory is played by the outsider within." Alison Bailey, "Locating Traitorous Identities: Toward a View of Privilege-Cognizant White Character," in Uma Narayan and Sandra Harding, eds., *Decentering the Center: Philosophy for a Multicultural, Postcolonial, and Feminist World* (Bloomington: Indiana University Press, 2000), 283–98, 284.

4. Gayatri Spivak, *In Other Worlds: Essays in Cultural Politics* (New York: Routledge, 1988): 81–82. She continues, "as long as American feminists understand 'history' as positivistic empiricism that scorns 'theory' and therefore remains ignorant of its own, the 'Third World' as its object of study will remain constituted by those hegemonic First World intellectual practices."

5. Ibid., 78.

6. For a further discussion of Derrida and woman as metaphysical crisis, see Braidotti, *Patterns of Dissonance*, 285.

7. For convincing and effective work in this vein, see, for instance, "imperial feminism efficiently helps to perpetuate the hierarchies that benefit elite women, but it certainly does not succeed in dismantling the category of woman, nor does it make good on its promise to establish unequivocal subjecthood for even those women most privileged by its discursive power. . . . [I]n other words, imperial feminism sows the seeds of the dismantling of its own subject position." Tracey Jean Boisseau, *White Queen: May French-Sheldon and the Imperial Origins of American Feminist Identity* (Bloomington: Indiana University Press, 2004): 211. Also, "thus, Kingsley's text, rather than being a 'feminine' text, or a 'colonial' text or for that matter a 'feminist' text, seems to be caught up in the contradictory clashes of these discourse one with another. No stable position can finally be given to the text." Sara Mills, *Discourses of Difference: An Analysis of Travel Writing and Colonialism* (New York: Routledge, 1991): 174. And, "thus I examine how English feminists use the image of what they saw as victimized 'sisters' in India, for instance, in order to position themselves as English citizens when the notion of 'citizen' was itself gendered. My emphasis is on examining specific formations in the period with a view to revealing that universalists fem-

inist discourses that have seen themselves only in relation to men have, in fact, been articulated in relation to other women. This use of other women, as Spivak and women of color feminists in the United States such as bell hooks have suggested, has been part of the discourse of western feminism in its utilization of the individual subject." Grewal, *Home and Harem*, 11.

8. Or, from a different direction, the critique that underlies "Can the Subaltern Speak"—that Foucault and Deleuze inappropriately conflate "representation as 'speaking for,' as in politics, and representation as 're-presentation,' as in art or philosophy"—becomes far less pressing than it was when human speech was the linguistic norm. By insisting on a distinction between these two types of representation, or on a distinction between "a proxy and a portrait" (276)—and by arguing furthermore that Foucault and Deleuze do *harm* by mingling the two—Spivak does convincingly demonstrate the violence at the heart of human speech. At the same time, however, she also inadvertently demonstrates the limitations of late twentieth-century theories of speech and politics that fail to consider nonhuman alternatives, and that fail to consider the possibility that speech might be associated far more effectively with *information* than with *knowledge*. She writes, for instance, "if this is, indeed, Deleuze's argument, his articulation of it is problematic. Two senses of representation are being run together: representation as 'speaking for,' as in politics, and representation as 're-presentation,' as in art or philosophy. Since theory is also only 'action,' the theoretician does not represent (speak for) the oppressed group. Indeed, the subject is not seen as a representative consciousness (one re-presenting reality adequately). These two senses of representation—within state formation and the law, on the one hand, and in subject-predication, on the other—are related but irreducibly discontinuous" (275). Latour similarly notes the humanistic impetus behind separating these two modes of representation by, once again, historicizing it. We have had to "see double," he argues, "and not establish direct relations between the representation of nonhumans and the representation of humans, between the artificiality of facts and the artificiality of the Body Politic. The word 'representation' is the same, but the controversy between Hobbes and Boyle renders any likeness between the two senses of the word unthinkable. . . . [S]oon the word 'representation' will take on two different meanings, according to whether elected agents or things are at stake. Epistemology and political science will go their separate ways." Latour, *Modern*, 27, 29.

9. The harm that Foucault and Deleuze do, in other words, might not be simply the political harm of discursively constructing Others as objects while denying their own subject positions. It might not be simply that in the process of these constructions and denials they "hide the relentless recognition of the Other by assimilation." In addition, and perhaps more so, they do *methodological* harm to approaches such as Spivak's—opening up a realm of nonhuman speech that effectively evades capture as coherent, identifiable "epistemic violence." Rather than being unaware of their gaffe in conflating these two forms of representation, that is to say, Foucault and Deleuze may also be deliberately associating them—and making a likewise deliberate, if implicit, point that proxies and portraits *can* be the same thing in a universe of nonhuman speech, where representation is largely beside the point. As Spivak writes, "to render thought or the

thinking subject transparent or invisible seems, by contrast, to hide the relentless recognition of the Other by assimilation." "Can the Subaltern Speak?" 294.

10. Ibid., 289. For another example of this critique, see: "Pasolini's startling analogy between the brutal physical violence of an executioner and the epistemic violence of writing could also characterize the potential for violence within feminist criticism's denial of the diverse experiences and genders of the global communities of women." And, "for Spivak, the articulation of feminist identity all too often repeats what she characterizes as the quintessential gesture of colonialism—blindness to the epistemic violence that effaces the colonial subject and requires her to occupy the space of the imperialists' self-consolidating Other." Also, "Only when the white woman's feminist movement recognizes its own voice as allegorical will it be able to repudiate its race and class—privileged—and therefore distorted—accounting for *all* women. Only then will it replace a univocal feminine voice with one that is plurivocal, for the allegorical mode connects women yet requires them to speak in many tongues." Laura E. Donaldson, *Decolonizing Feminisms: Race, Gender, and Empire Building* (Chapel Hill: University of North Carolina Press, 1992): 2, 15, 134.

CHAPTER THIRTEEN

1. Carl Schmitt, *Crisis of Parliamentary Democracy*, trans. Ellen Kennedy (Cambridge: MIT Press, 1992): 34, 49, 59.

2. Ibid., 13–14, 26.

3. Ibid., 26.

4. "In this series belong the identity of governed and governing, sovereign and subject, the identity of the subject and object of state authority, the identity of the people with their representatives in parliament, the identity of the state and the current voting population, the identity of the state and the law, and finally an identity of the quantitative (the numerical majority or unanimity) with the qualitative (the justice of the laws)." Ibid., 26–27.

5. Ibid.

CONCLUSION TO PART THREE

1. I use the term "behavior" here deliberately in Latour's sense of the word: "a thing," Latour states, "cannot be said to be an actor, in any case not a social actor, since it does not *act*, in the proper sense of the verb; it only behaves." Latour, *Politics of Nature*, 73.

2. Henry James, *In the Cage* (New York: Fox Duffield, 1906).

Bibliography

Note: A list of anonymous articles and editorials appears at the end of the bibliography.

Agamben, Giorgio. *Homo Sacer: Sovereign Power and Bare Life.* Trans. Daniel Heller-Roazen. Stanford: Stanford University Press, 1998.

Ahearn, Laura M. "Language and Agency." *Annual Review of Anthropology* 30 (2001): 109–37.

Allen, Danielle. "Burning *The Fable of the Bees:* The Incendiary Authority of Nature." In Lorraine Daston and Fernando Vidal, eds., *The Moral Authority of Nature.* Chicago: University of Chicago Press, 2004. 74–99.

Allen, Dennis W. "Viral Activism and the Meaning of 'Post-Identity,'" *Journal of the Midwest Modern Language Association* 36 (1) (2003): 6–24.

Aristotle. *The Politics.* Trans. Ernest Barker. Oxford: Oxford University Press, 1995.

Asad, Talal. *Formations of the Secular: Christianity, Islam, Modernity.* Stanford: Stanford University Press, 2003.

Asdal, Kristin. "The Problematic Nature of Nature: The Post-Constructivist Challenge to Environmental History." *History and Theory* 42 (4) (2003): 60–74.

Austin, J. L. *How to Do Things with Words.* Cambridge: Harvard University Press, 1975.

Bailey, Alison. "Locating Traitorous Identities: Toward a View of Privilege-Cognizant White Character." In Uma Narayan and Sandra Harding, eds., *Decentering the Center: Philosophy for a Multicultural, Postcolonial, and Feminist World.* Bloomington: Indiana University Press, 2000. 283–98.

Barad, Karen. "Getting Real: Technoscientific Practices and the Materialization of Reality." *differences* 10 (2) (1998): 87–128.

Baudrillard, Jean. *The System of Objects.* Trans. James Benedict. New York: Verso, 1996.

Beecher, Catherine. "Is Woman Suffrage Contrary to Common-Sense?" *Christian Union* (February 12, 1870): 98–99.

Bennett, Jane. *Vibrant Matter: A Political Ecology of Things.* Durham: Duke University Press, 2010.

Bitel, Lisa M. "'In Visu Noctis': Dreams in European Hagiography and Histories, 450–900." *History of Religions* 31 (1) (1991): 39–51.

Bodin, Jean. *On Sovereignty: Four Chapters from The Six Books of the Common-*

wealth. Trans. Julian H. Franklin. Cambridge: Cambridge University Press, 1992.

Boisseau, Tracey Jean. *White Queen: May French-Sheldon and the Imperial Origins of American Feminist Identity*. Bloomington: Indiana University Press, 2004.

Braidotti, Rosi. *Nomadic Subjects: Embodiment and Sexual Difference in Contemporary Feminist Theory*. New York: Columbia University Press, 1994.

Braidotti, Rosi. *Patterns of Dissonance: A Study of Women in Contemporary Philosophy*. Trans. Elizabeth Guild. New York: Routledge, 1991.

Braidotti, Rosi. *Transpositions: On Nomadic Ethics*. Cambridge: Polity Press, 2006.

Brown, Jennifer K. "The Nineteenth Amendment and Women's Equality." *Yale Law Journal* 102 (8) (1993): 2175–2204.

Brown, Wendy. "Freedom's Silences." In *Edgework: Critical Essays on Knowledge and Politics*. Princeton: Princeton University Press, 2005.

Buckley, J. M. "The Wrongs and Perils of Woman Suffrage." *Century Illustrated Magazine* 48 (4) (1894): 613–23.

Buechler, Steven M. *Women's Movements in the United States: Woman Suffrage, Equal Rights, and Beyond*. New Brunswick: Rutgers University Press, 1990.

Burfoot, Annette. "Human Remains: Identity Politics in the Face of Biotechnology." *Cultural Critique* 53 (Winter 2003): 47–71.

Burritt, Elihu. "Woman Suffrage and Its Liabilities." *The Independent* (October 5, 1871): 11.

Bushnell, Horace. *Women's Suffrage: The Reform Against Nature*. New York: Charles Scribner, 1869.

Butler, Judith. *Excitable Speech: A Politics of the Performative*. London: Routledge, 1997.

Butler, Judith. *The Psychic Life of Power: Theories in Subjection*. Stanford: Stanford University Press, 1997.

Cabell, Brian. "Arkansas Double Execution Nears." *CNN.com* (January 6, 2004).

Cairnes, J. E. "Woman Suffrage: A Reply to Goldwin Smith." *Every Saturday: A Journal of Choice Reading* (October 10, 1874): 395–440.

Cairnes, John Elliot. *Collected Works*. Ed. Thomas A. Boylan and Tadh Foley. Vol. 1. London: Routledge, 2004.

Caraway, Teri L. "Indonesia and Democratization: Class, Gender, Race, and the Extension of Suffrage." *Comparative Politics* 36 (4) (2004): 443–60.

Carty, Carolyn M. "The Role of Gunzo's Dream in the Building of Cluny III." *Gesta* 21 (1–2) (1988): 113–23.

Catt, Carrie Chapman. "Crisis in Suffrage Movement, Says Mrs. Catt." *New York Times* (September 3, 1916): SM5.

Caudill, David S. *Lacan and the Subject of Law: Toward a Psychoanalytic Critical Legal Theory*. Atlantic Highlands, NJ: Humanities Press, 1997.

Clinton, Catherine. "White Mischief: *Beyond the Pale: White Women, Racism, and History* by Vron Ware." *Transition* 59 (1993): 130–36.

Constable, Marianne. *Just Silences: The Limits and Possibilities of Modern Law*. Princeton: Princeton University Press, 2005.

Cook, Michael. *Commanding Right and Forbidding Wrong in Islamic Thought*. Cambridge: Cambridge University Press, 2000.

Cope, Edward D. "Relation of the Sexes to Government." In Edith M. Phelps, ed., *Debater's Handbook Series: Selected Articles on Woman Suffrage.* New York: H. W. Wilson, 1916. 128–29.

Cort, Cyrus. "Woman Suffrage." *Reformed Quarterly Review* 30 (3) (1883): 343–64.

Cott, Nancy F. "Marriage and Women's Citizenship in the United States, 1830–1934." *American Historical Review* 103 (5) (1998): 1440–74.

Croy, Terry, and Carrie Chapman Catt. "The Crisis: A Complete Critical Edition of Carrie Chapman Catt's 1916 Presidential Address to the National American Woman Suffrage Association." *Rhetoric Society Quarterly* 28 (3) (1998): 49–73.

Cullen, Edgar M. "Man is for Justice, Woman for Mercy." *New York Times* (September 3, 1915): 8.

Dall, Caroline H. "Mr. Parkman on Woman Suffrage in the 'North American Review.'" *Unitarian Review and Religious Magazine* 13 (30) (1880): 223–37.

Dana, Charles L. "Suffrage a Cult of Self and Sex." *New York Times* (June 27, 1915): 14.

Daston, Lorraine, and Fernando Vidal. "Introduction: Doing What Comes Naturally." In Lorraine Daston and Fernando Vidal, eds., *The Moral Authority of Nature.* Chicago: University of Chicago Press, 2004. 1–20.

Dicey, A. V. "Woman Suffrage." *Living Age* (April 10, 1909): 67–84.

Dimock, Wai Chee. *Empire For Liberty: Melville and the Poetics of Individualism.* Princeton: Princeton University Press, 1991.

Doane, William Croswell. "Some Later Aspects of Woman Suffrage." *North American Review* 163 (480) (1896): 537–48.

Donaldson, Laura E. *Decolonizing Feminisms: Race, Gender, and Empire Building.* Chapel Hill: University of North Carolina Press, 1992.

Drew, Kevin. "Arkansas Prepares to Execute Mentally Ill Inmate." *CNN.com* (January 6, 2004).

DuBois, Ellen Carol. *Feminism and Suffrage: The Emergence of an Independent Women's Movement in America.* Ithaca: Cornell University Press, 1978.

Dumm, Thomas. *Democracy and Punishment: The Disciplinary Origins of the United States.* Madison: University of Wisconsin Press, 1987.

Eichelberger, J. S. "Analysis of Woman Vote in 1916 Upsets Theories." *New York Times* (January 21, 1917): SM5.

Everts, Mary E. "A Farmer's Wife to Catherine E. Beecher." *Christian Union* (March 12, 1870): 166.

Ewing, Katherine P. "The Dream of Spiritual Initiation and the Organization of Self Representation among Pakistani Sufis." *American Ethnologist* 17 (1) (1990): 56–74.

Ford, Linda G. *Iron-Jawed Angels: The Suffrage Militancy of the National Women's Party, 1912–1920.* Lanham, MD: University Press of America, 1991.

Foucault, Michel. *Abnormal: Lectures at the Collège de France, 1974–1975.* Trans. Graham Burchell. New York: Picador, 2005.

Foucault, Michel. *Fearless Speech.* Ed. Joseph Pearson. Los Angeles: Semiotext(e), 2001.

Foucault, Michel. *The Government of Self and Others: Lectures at the Collège de France, 1982–1983.* Trans. Graham Burchell. New York: Palgrave-Macmillan, 2010.

Foucault, Michel. *History of Sexuality: An Introduction.* Trans. Robert Hurley. New York: Vintage, 1990.

Foucault, Michel. *Psychiatric Power: Lectures at the Collège de France, 1973–1974.* Trans. Graham Burchell. New York: Palgrave-Macmillan, 2006.

Foucault, Michel. *"Society Must be Defended": Lectures at the Collège de France, 1975–1976.* Trans. David Macey. New York: Picador, 2003.

Foucault, Michel, and Ludwig Binswanger. *Dream and Existence.* Atlantic Highlands, NJ: Humanities Press International, 1993.

Freud, Sigmund. *The Interpretation of Dreams.* Trans. A. A. Brill. New York: Modern Library, 1994.

Frost, Samantha. "Hobbes and the Matter of Self-Consciousness." *Political Theory* 33 (4) (2005): 495–517.

Gabrielson, Teena. "Woman-Thought, Social Capital, and the Generative State: Mary Austin and the Integrative Civic Ideal in Progressive Thought." *American Journal of Political Science* 50 (3) (2006): 650–63.

Goldstine, Herman H. *The Computer from Pascal to Von Neumann.* Princeton: Princeton University Press, 1993.

Gordon, Sarah Barringer. "The Liberty of Self-Degradation: Polygamy, Woman Suffrage, and Consent in the Nineteenth Century America." *Journal of American History* 83 (3) (1996): 815–47.

Gordon, Sarah Barringer. *The Mormon Question: Polygamy and Constitutional Conflict in Nineteenth-Century America.* Chapel Hill: University of North Carolina Press, 2002.

Graham, Elaine. *Representations of the Post/Human: Monsters, Aliens, and Others in Popular Culture.* Manchester: Manchester University Press, 2002.

Graham, Sara Hunter. *Woman Suffrage and the New Democracy.* New Haven: Yale University Press, 1996.

Green, Barbara. *Spectacular Confessions: Autobiography, Performative Activism, and the Sites of Suffrage, 1905–1938.* New York: St. Martin's Press, 1997.

Green, Elna. "From Antisuffragism to Anti-communism: The Conservative Career of Ida M. Derden." *Journal of Southern History* 65 (2) (1999): 287–316.

Greenberg, Paul. "Kill That Crazy Man." *Arkansas Democrat-Gazette* (February 19, 2003): 20.

Greenberg, Paul. "Time is Running Out and So is Sanity in the Curious Case of Charles Singleton." *Arkansas Democrat-Gazette* (January 4, 2004): 72.

Gregg, W. W. "The Third Sex." *New York Times* (September 15, 1918): X3.

Grewal, Inderpal. *Home and Harem: Nation, Gender, Empire, and Cultures of Travel.* Durham: Duke University Press, 1996.

Grossberg, Lawrence. "Cultural Studies and/in New Worlds." *Critical Studies in Mass Communication* 10 (1993): 1–21.

Hammer, David. "Mentally Ill Inmate Has Clemency Hearing." Associated Press State and Local Wire (December 12, 2003): State and Regional.

Haraway, Donna. *Simians, Cyborgs, and Women: The Reinvention of Nature.* London: Routledge, 1990.

Hayles, N. Katherine. "Afterword: The Human." *Cultural Critique* 53 (Winter 2003): 136.

Hayles, N. Katherine. "Limiting Metaphors and Enabling Constraints in Dawkins and Deleuze/Guattari." *SubStance* 30 (1–2) (2001): 144–59.

Hayles, N. Katherine. "Reconfiguring the Mindbody." In Robert Mitchell and Phillip Thurtle, eds., *Data Made Flesh: Embodying Information*. London: Routledge, 2004. 229–48.

Hayles, N. Katherine. *Chaos Bound: Orderly Disorder in Contemporary Literature and Science*. Ithaca: Cornell University Press, 1990.

Hayles, N. Katherine. *How We Became Posthuman: Virtual Bodies in Cybernetics, Literature, and Informatics*. Chicago: University of Chicago Press, 1999.

Hayles, N. Katherine. *My Mother Was a Computer: Digital Subjects and Literary Texts*. Chicago: University of Chicago Press, 2005.

Hobbes, Thomas. *Leviathan*. New York: Simon and Schuster, 1962.

Holmes, David. *Virtual Politics: Identity and Community in Cyberspace*. London: Sage, 1998.

Holton, Sandra Stanley. "'To Educate Women in the Rebellion': Elizabeth Cady Stanton and the Creation of a Transatlantic Network of Radical Suffragists." *American Historical Review* 99 (8) (1994): 1112–36.

Jacobs, Wilbur R. "Parkman: Naturalist-Environmentalist Savant." *Pacific Historical Review* 61 (3) (1992): 341–56.

James, Henry. *In the Cage*. New York: Fox Duffield, 1906.

Johnson, Helen Kendrick. *Woman and the Republic*. Rev. ed. New York: Guidon Club Opposed to Woman Suffrage, 1913.

Jones, Matthew L. "Descartes' Geometry as Spiritual Exercise." *Critical Inquiry* 28 (1) (2001): 40–71.

Kilbreth, M. G. "For a Suffrage Appeal: Position of the Women Who Demand Reconsideration of State Amendment." *New York Times* (January 14, 1918): 10.

Knadler, Stephen P. "Francis Parkman's Brahmin Caste and the History of the Conspiracy of the Pontiac." *American Literature* 65 (2) (1993): 215–38.

Koelb, Clayton. "Nietzsche, Malerba, and the Aesthetics of Superficiality." *boundary 2* 12 (1) (1983): 117–32.

Kovan, Seth, and Sonya Michel. "Womanly Duties: Maternalist Politics and the Origins of Welfare States in France, Germany, Great Britain, and the United States, 1880–1920." *American Historical Review* 95 (4) (1990): 1086–1108.

Kraditor, Aileen. *The Ideas of the Woman Suffrage Movement, 1870–1920*. New York: Columbia University Press, 1967.

Lacan, Jacques. *The Ego in Freud's Theory and in the Technique of Psychoanalysis 1954–1955*. Trans. Sylvana Tomaselli. Ed. Jacques-Alain Miller. New York: Norton, 1988.

Lacan, Jacques. *The Four Fundamental Concepts of Psychoanalysis*. Trans. Alan Sheridan. Ed. Jacques-Alain Miller. New York: Norton, 1981.

Ladino, Jennifer K. "Rewriting Nature Tourism in 'An Age of Violence': Tactical Collage in Marianne Moore's 'An Octopus.'" *Twentieth Century Literature* 51 (3) (2005): 285–315.

Latour, Bruno. *Politics of Nature: How to Bring the Sciences into Democracy*. Trans. Catherine Porter. Cambridge: Harvard University Press, 2004.

Latour, Bruno. "Scientific Objects and Legal Objectivity." In Alain Pottage and Martha Mundy, eds., *Law, Anthropology, and the Constitution of the Social*. Cambridge: Cambridge University Press, 2004. 73–114.

Latour, Bruno. *We Have Never Been Modern*. Trans. Catherine Porter. Cambridge: Harvard University Press, 1993.

Leonard, Priscilla. "Woman Suffrage in Colorado." *Outlook* (March 20, 1897): 789–92.

MacKinnon, Catharine A. *Feminism Unmodified: Discourses on Life and Law*. Cambridge: Harvard University Press, 1987.

Makowski, Lee J. *Horace Bushnell of Christian Character Development*. Boston: University Press of America, 1999.

Markell, Patchen. *Bound by Recognition*. Princeton: Princeton University Press, 2003.

Marshall, Susan E. "Ladies Against Women, Mobilization Dilemmas of Antifeminist Movements." *Social Problems* 32 (4) (1985): 348–62.

Martel, James. *Textual Conspiracies: Walter Benjamin, Idolatry, and Political Theory*. Ann Arbor: University of Michigan Press, 2011.

Martin, Edward Sandford. *The Unrest of Women*. New York: D. Appleton, 1913.

Matthews, Gareth B. "On Being Immoral in a Dream." *Philosophy* 56 (215) (1981): 47–59.

Maxse, Frederick A. (Vice-Admiral). *Reasons for Opposing Woman Suffrage*. London: W. Ridgway, 1884.

Mayhall, Laura E. Nym. "Defining Militancy: Radical Protest, the Constitutional Idiom, and Women's Suffrage in Britain, 1908–1909." *Journal of British Studies* 39 (3) (2000): 340–71.

Mayhall, Laura E. Nym. *The Militant Suffrage Movement: Citizenship and Resistance in Britain, 1860–1930*. New York: Oxford University Press, 2003.

MCA. "A Woman's Letters from Washington." *The Independent . . . Devoted to the Considerations of Politics, Social, and Economic . . .* (Feb. 4, 1869): 1.

McDonagh, Eileen. "Political Citizenship and Democratization: The Gender Paradox." *American Political Science Review* 96 (3) (2002): 535–52.

McNay, Lois. *Against Recognition*. Cambridge: Polity Press, 2008.

Milburn, Colin Nazhone. "Monsters in Eden: Darwin and Derrida." *MLN* 118 (3) (2003): 603–21.

Mill, J. S. *The Subjection of Women*. 4th ed. London: Longmans, 1878.

Miller, Joaquin. "Woman Suffrage Advocates at the Capitol." *Boston Daily Globe* (March 17, 1884): 6.

Miller, Ruth A. *The Limits of Bodily Integrity: Abortion, Adultery, and Rape Legislation in Comparative Perspective*. Aldershot: Ashgate Press, 2007.

Miller, Ruth A. "On Freedom and Feeding Tubes: Reviving Terri Schiavo and Trying Saddam Hussein." *Law and Literature* 19 (2) (2007): 161–86.

Mills, Sara. *Discourses of Difference: An Analysis of Travel Writing and Colonialism*. London: Routledge, 1991.

Mitchell, Robert, and Phillip Thurtle. "Data Made Flesh: The Material Poiesis of Informatics." In Robert Mitchell and Phillip Thurtle, eds., *Data Made Flesh: Embodying Information*. London: Routledge, 2004. 1–26.

Morita, Michiyo. *Horace Bushnell on Women in Nineteenth-Century America*. Lanham, MD: University Press of America, 2004.

Newman, Louise Michele. *White Women's Rights: The Racial Origins of Feminism in the United States*. New York: Oxford University Press, 1999.

O'Brien, Soledad, and Brian Cabell. "Execution of Mentally Ill Man Scheduled Today." *American Morning, CNN* (January 6, 2004).

Oransky, Ivan. "Who—and How—to Kill are Focus of US Death Penalty Cases." *The Lancet* 362 (October 18, 2003): 1287.

Parkman, Francis. "The Woman Question Again." *North American Review* 130 (278) (1879): 16–30.

Parry, John T. *Understanding Torture: Law, Violence, and Political Identity.* Ann Arbor: University of Michigan Press, 2010.

Pateman, Carole. *The Disorder of Women: Democracy, Feminism, and Political Theory.* Stanford: Stanford University Press, 1989.

Pratt, Mary Louise. *Imperial Eyes: Travel Writing and Transculturation.* London: Routledge, 1992.

Price, S. R. F. "The Future of Dreams: From Freud to Artemidorus." *Past and Present* 113 (November 1986): 3–37.

Pugh, Martin. *The March of the Women: A Revisionist Analysis of the Campaign for Women's Suffrage 1866–1914.* New York: Oxford University Press, 2000.

Putnam-Jacobi, Mary. *"Common Sense" Applied to Woman Suffrage: A Statement of the Reasons Which Justify the Demand to Extend the Suffrage to Women, With Consideration of the Arguments Against Such Enfranchisement, and With Special Reference to the Issues Presented to the New York State Convention of 1894.* New York: G. P. Putnam's Sons, 1894.

Ramée, Louise de la (Ouida). *Views and Opinions.* London: Methuen, 1896.

Rancière, Jacques. *Disagreement: Politics and Philosophy.* Trans. Julie Rose. Minneapolis: University of Minnesota Press, 1999.

Richey, Warren. "Forced Medication: When Does it Violate Rights." *Christian Science Monitor* (March 3, 2003): 1.

Ritter, Gretchen. "Jury Service and Women's Citizenship Before and After the Nineteenth Amendment." *Law and History Review* 20 (3) (2002): 479–515.

Rudelle, Odille. "Le vote des femmes et la fin de 'L'exception Française." *Vingtième Siècle Revue d'histoire* 42 (April–June 1994): 52–65.

Schmitt, Carl. *Concept of the Political.* Trans. George Schwab. Chicago: University of Chicago Press, 1996.

Schmitt, Carl. *Crisis of Parliamentary Democracy.* Trans. Ellen Kennedy. Cambridge: MIT Press, 1992.

Schmitt, Carl. *Political Theology: Four Chapters on the Concept of Sovereignty.* Trans. George Schwab. Chicago: University of Chicago Press, 2005.

Searle, John. *Speech Acts: An Essay in the Philosophy of Language.* Cambridge: Cambridge University Press, 1969.

Sedgwick, Mary K. "Some Scientific Aspects of the Woman Suffrage Question." *Gunton's Magazine* (April 1901): 333–45.

Siegel, Jerrold. "Avoiding the Subject: A Foucaultian Itinerary." *Journal of the History of Ideas* 51 (2) (1990): 273–99.

Simkins, M. E. "Suffrage and Anti-Suffrage." *Living Age* (February 6, 1909): 323–29.

Simon, Bart. "Toward a Critique of Posthuman Futures." *Cultural Critique* 53 (Winter 2003): 1–9.

Spear, Samuel T. "Bushnell on the Right of Suffrage." *The Independent* (July 15, 1869): 1.

Spivak, Gayatri. "Can the Subaltern Speak?" In Cary Nelson and Lawrence Grossberg, eds., *Marxism and the Interpretation of Culture*. Urbana: University of Illinois Press, 1988. 271–313.

Spivak, Gayatri. *In Other Worlds: Essays in Cultural Politics*. London: Routledge, 1988.

Strum, Philippa. *Louis D. Brandeis, Justice for the People*. Cambridge: Harvard University Press, 1984.

T. E. W. "All Illusion and Caprice." *New York Times* (February 21, 1915): XX2.

Terborg-Penn, Rosalyn. *African American Women in the Struggle for the Vote, 1850–1920*. Bloomington: Indiana University Press, 1998.

Thacker, Eugene. "Data Made Flesh: Biotechnology and the Discourse of the Posthuman." *Cultural Critique* 53 (Winter 2003): 72–97.

Thrift, Nigel, and Shaun French. "The Automatic Production of Space." *Transaction of the Institute of British Geographers* 27 (3) (2002): 309–35.

Tyer, Pearl. "Idaho's Twenty Years of Woman Suffrage." *Outlook* (September 6, 1916): 35–39.

U.S. Congress. House. Committee on Woman Suffrage. *Resolution Establishing a Committee on Woman Suffrage: Hearing before the Committee on Rules*. 63rd Cong., 2d sess., December 3–5, 1913. Washington, DC: Government Printing Office, 1914.

VanBurkleo, Sandra F. *"Belonging to the World": Women's Rights and American Constitutional Culture*. New York: Oxford University Press, 2001.

Ware, Vron. *Beyond the Pale: White Women, Racism, and History*. New York: Verso, 1992.

Warren, Marcus. "Arkansas to Execute a Schizophrenic. Marcus Warren in New York Reports on the Controversial Fate of a Condemned Killer Who Believes his Cell is Possessed by Demons." *Daily Telegraph (London)* (January 7, 2004): 13.

Watt, E. D. "Rousseau Réchaufée—Being Obliged, Consenting, Participating, and Obeying only Oneself." *Journal of Politics* 43 (4) (1981): 707–19.

Weaver, Warren. "Recent Contributions to The Mathematical Theory of Communication." September, 1949. http://grace.evergreen.edu/~arunc/texts/cybernetics/weaver.pdf.

Weidhorn, Manfred. "Dreams and Guilt." *Harvard Theological Review* 58 (1) (1965): 69–90.

Weiss, John. "Woman Suffrage." *The Radical* (June 1869): 1–18.

Wheeler, Everett P. "In Reply to Mrs. Harper: A Woman's Influence Is Better Than her Vote for the Lawmakers." *New York Times* (September 19, 1915): 14.

Wilson, Henry. "The Great Necessity." *The Independent* (June 17, 1869): 1.

Woman Suffrage: Hearings Before the Committee on the Judiciary: House of Representatives. 62nd Cong., 2d sess., March 13, 1912. Washington, DC: Government Printing Office, 1912.

Wood, Henry A. Wise. "Government a Man's Job: The War Teaches a Believer in Woman Suffrage to Oppose the Extension of the Right to Vote." *New York Times* (May 3, 1917): 14.

Ze'evi, Dror. *Producing Desire: Changing Sexual Discourse in the Ottoman Middle East*. Berkeley: University of California Press, 2006.

Žižek, Slavoj. *Enjoy Your Symptom! Jacques Lacan in Hollywood and Out*. London: Routledge, 1992.

ANONYMOUS ARTICLES AND EDITORIALS

"Anthony and Rosewater." *New York Times* (October 16, 1882): 4.

"Antis Renew War on Suffragists." *New York Times* (March 24, 1918): 9.

"Antis See Danger in Woman Autocracy." *New York Times* (January 12, 1918): 12.

"Bushnell on Woman Suffrage." *New York Observer and Chronicle* (June 17, 1869): 190.

"Cartoons and Comments." *Puck* (June 6, 1894): 242.

"Compulsory Voting." *The Independent* (March 3, 1881): 17.

"Current Literature." *Botanical Gazette* 51 (January–June 1911): 147.

"Emotional Legislation." *Boston Daily Globe* (February 12, 1882): 4.

"Excerpt from Gail Hamilton" in "Editors' Table." *Godey's Lady's Book* 77 (July 1868): 82.

"Final Words and Prepared Statement of Charles Singleton." Associated Press State and Local Wire (January 6, 2004): State and Regional.

"History of Woman Suffrage." *New York Evangelist* (June 23, 1884): 1.

"The Home: An Important Decision." *Outlook* (March 10, 1894): 451.

"Invariably Cruel, Always Unusual." *Minneapolis Star Tribune* (February 17, 2003).

"The Ladies Take Their Turn." *New York Times* (February 14, 1885): 3.

"Lays Evil to Suffrage: E.P. Wheeler Thinks Women Voters at Fault in Colorado." *New York Times* (October 11, 1915): 5.

"A New Insanity Defence." *The Economist* (March 1, 2003).

"New Woman a Freak, Says Bishop Doane: One Who Strives for Man's Work 'a Horrible, Misshapen Monster,' He Declares: Sees Suffragists' Doom." *New York Times* (June 9, 1909): 7.

"No Subject of Jest: Condition of Feminine Hysteria Should be Taken Seriously." *New York Times* (May 8, 1912): 10.

"One Man Who Had the Courage to Say 'No' to a Woman." *New York Times* (March 24, 1907): SM8.

"The Pacific Coast: Hot Weather—An Insane Advocate of Woman Suffrage." *New York Times* (June 22, 1872): 1.

"Right for Women to Vote: Suffrage Must be Theirs Declares Senator Palmer." *New York Times* (April 20, 1894): 2.

"Says Suffrage Idea is Only Sex Fad: Mrs. Arthur M. Dodge Insists Woman's Appeal for Ballot is Based on Sex Alone." *New York Times* (May 12, 1913): 2.

"Suffragist Songs But No Talk in Park: Commissioner Ward Revokes Most Objectionable Features of Propaganda Permit." *New York Times* (September 23, 1916): 18.

"Suffragists Hiss Attack on Women: A Reign of Terror Coming If They Vote, Opines Alexander Harvey at a Dinner." *New York Times* (February 3, 1910): 18.

"Suffragists Win [NY State] Senate Test Vote." *New York Times* (April 6, 1916): 1.

"Take Me Home to Mama: Placarded Boys Forced to Speak on Woman's Suffrage." *Boston Globe* (December 8, 1894): 12.

"Trouble When Women Voted." *New York Times* (May 6, 1894).

"Wise Words About Women." *New York Times* (September 23, 1879): 4.

"The Woman Question." *New York Times* (February 25, 1865): 2.

"Woman Suffrage: . . . Miss Anthony's Age Ascertained." *New York Times* (February 6, 1870): 8.

"Woman Suffrage: Arguments and Petitions Against the Extension." *Boston Daily Globe* (March 10, 1885): 5.

"Woman's Brain Not Inferior to Men's: Helen H. Gardener's, Tested at Cornell, to Which She Willed It, Meets Test." *New York Times* (September 29, 1927).

"Woman's Suffrage." *New York Evangelist* (June 24, 1869): 1.

"Woman's Suffrage and Woman's Brain." *Scientific American* 70 (20) (1894): 315.

"Woman's Suffrage—No. II." *Prairie Farmer* (March 12, 1870): 77.

"Women as Readers of Newspapers." *Boston Daily Globe* (January 14, 1915): 10.

A Man. "'A Man' Explains: He Didn't Ask for a 'Hysteria of Documents' on Suffrage." *New York Times* (February 21, 1910): 8.

Mother. "Two Letters on Woman Suffrage." *Putnam's Magazine. Original Papers on Literature, Science, Art* 2 (12) (1868): 701–12.

A Spinster and a Taxpayer. "The Demand for Votes: Woman Suffragists Should not Force Suffrage Where Not Wanted." *New York Times* (September 20, 1909): 6.

Index

Activism, 40, 44, 46–47, 49–51, 111, 168; viral activism, 39–40
Air, 17
Anachronism, 116, 118, 183–84, 190–91, 201, 211, 213–17
Androids. *See* Cyborgs
Animals, 60–62, 93, 133–34, 160, 189. *See also* Birds; Insects
Anthony, Susan B., 49, 104
Aristotle, 133–35, 139, 143, 157, 160
Artemidorus (of Daldis), 181. *See also* Dream interpretation
Asad, Talal, 66–67
Asdal, Kristin, 27, 30
Augustine, 192–93
Austin, J. L., 31–32, 37, 40, 78
Authoritarianism, 16, 32, 78, 91, 143, 155

Babble, 56, 99, 146, 151, 155, 209–10, 212, 220, 222. *See also* Cacophony
Beecher, Catherine, 167, 169–71
Belief, 12, 65, 70–72, 75, 80–81, 101–2, 124, 149, 178, 187. *See also* Faith; Grace
Bentham, Jeremy, 166
Binary, 37, 150–51, 157
Binswanger, Ludwig, 185–88
Birds, 61
Blood, 15
Bodies. *See* Embodiment
Boston University, 88
Botany, 93, 169–70
Boyle, Robert, 12–13

Brains, 146–48, 150–51, 157–58, 166
Brandeis, Louis, 158–60. See also *Whitney v. California*
Brown, Wendy, 16–18
Buckley, J. M., 77–78, 120–23, 167, 169
Bushnell, Horace, 69–74, 76–77, 87, 144, 147, 166, 171
Butler, Judith, 32–38, 40

Cacophony, 76, 212, 220. *See also* Noise
Catastrophe, 93, 95. *See also* Crisis
Catholicism, 65, 74
Catt, Carrie Chapman, 105–6, 109–10, 156, 207, 220
Central Park, 198–99
Chaos, 23, 109–10, 143; chaos theory, 27, 183
Charisma, 10
Children, 60, 89, 167
Chimeras, 87, 89, 93
Chinese Room, 135–36. *See also* Searle, John
Choice, 26, 37, 43, 78, 80, 114, 119, 140, 145, 184, 187–88, 191–92, 201, 212, 220, 224
Christianity, 68–72, 112, 192–94. *See also* Catholicism; Mormonism; Protestantism
Circe, 90, 94–96
Citizenship, 9, 24, 43–45, 48–50, 69, 72, 80, 106, 113, 117, 121–23, 126–27, 151, 155, 199–200, 205, 209–12, 216, 219

Printed and bound by CPI Group (UK) Ltd, Croydon, CR0 4YY

09/06/2025

14686141-0004